But What If I Don't Want to Go to College?

A GUIDE TO SUCCESS THROUGH ALTERNATIVE EDUCATION

But What If I Don't Want to Go to College?

A GUIDE TO SUCCESS THROUGH ALTERNATIVE EDUCATION

THIRD EDITION

Harlow G. Unger

☑Checkmark Books®
An imprint of Infobase Publishing

But What If I Don't Want to Go to College? Third Edition

Copyright © 2006 by Harlow G. Unger

Checkmark Books
An imprint of Infobase Publishing
132 West 31st Street
New York NY 10001

ISBN-10: 0-8160-6558-6
ISBN-13: 978-0-8160-6558-5

Library of Congress Cataloging-in-Publication Data

Unger, Harlow G.
  But what if I don't want to go to college? : a guide to success through alternative education / Harlow G. Unger.—3rd ed.
    p. cm.
  Includes index.
  ISBN 0-8160-6557-8 (alk. paper) — ISBN 0-8160-6558-6 (pbk. : alk. paper)
1. Occupational training—United States. 2. Vocational education—United States. 3. Alternative education—United States. 4. Vocational guidance—United States. I. Title.

HD5715.2.U53 2006
374'013—dc22   2005055521

Checkmark Books are available at special discounts when purchased in bulk quantities for businesses, associations, institutions, or sales promotions. Please call our Special Sales Department in New York at (212) 967-8800 or (800) 322-8755.

You can find Facts On File on the World Wide Web at http://www.factsonfile.com

Text design by James Scotto-Lavino
Cover design by Salvatore Luongo

Printed in the United States of America

MP FOF 10 9 8 7 6 5 4 3 2

This book is printed on acid-free paper.

CONTENTS

ABOUT THE AUTHOR

A former journalist, Harlow G. Unger has written eight books on education and five books on American history, including the award-winning biography *Lafayette* and the highly acclaimed *The Unexpected George Washington—His Private Life*. He is the author of the *Encyclopedia of American Education*, a three-volume reference work published by Facts On File and on the shelves of most major libraries. Mr. Unger is a graduate of Yale University and holds a master's degree from California State University.

ACKNOWLEDGMENTS

My deepest thanks to James Chambers, Facts On File editor in chief of humanities; to Amy L. Conver, copy editor; and to Vanessa Nittoli, associate editor, for their magnificent contributions to this book.

Part One

CAREER EDUCATION—ALTERNATIVE ROUTES TO SUCCESS

1

College Isn't for Everyone

Nurses, computer operators, chefs, air traffic controllers, actors, dancers, artists, musicians, television equipment operators, mechanics, police and security officers, firefighters, ambulance drivers, railroad engineers, telephone and electric company technicians, travel agents, carpenters, plumbers, glaziers, postal workers, dental technicians, real estate agents, medical technicians and EMT personnel, paralegals . . .

How could our towns, cities and nation—how could our world—get along without the talents and skills of the brilliant men and women who fill these and hundreds of other jobs? The answer is we couldn't, and all who are thinking of joining these important professions should be proud of the vital contributions they'll make to our world.

Aside from their essential nature, all of these jobs have something else in common: None requires a four-year college or university degree. Some don't require any schooling after high school—even at a two-year community college. That doesn't mean any of these jobs is easy. No important job ever is. All require hard work, dedication, knowledge, intelligence and on-the-job training. But, as in most occupations, success not only yields a sense of professional pride and accomplishment, it can yield considerable financial rewards—again, without ever going to college.

Almost anyone who wants to can go to college, but not everyone should. There are more than 1,800 two-year and more than 2,300 four-year colleges in the United States, and the vast majority admits almost everybody who applies. So, it's easy to get into college. But it's not easy to finish and graduate. In fact, more than 40 percent of students who enroll in American colleges and universities quit without graduating. In terms of real people, more than 6.6 million students drop out of college every year and end up in a career no-man's-land: They have no college degree to

3

get on the executive ladder, and they haven't learned any skills to earn a living—they can't fix a leaking pipe or sputtering car, save a drowning child or bandage wounds, protect a town from an onrushing forest fire, or help get an innocent person out of jail. So not everyone who goes to college belongs there.

The fact is, millions of students all over the world are not suited for and have no interest in traditional academic schooling—which is why alternative career education was developed: to teach students the skills they need to get a good job. Most European and Japanese schools automatically test all 14-year-olds to determine their aptitudes. Such tests let the academically skilled continue traditional schooling, while students with other talents move into alternative forms of education—career education that refines those talents and ensures their becoming successful, respected artisans and craftspeople.

Many U.S. schools offer the same choice, but a lot of students automatically reject alternative education because well-meaning, but often misguided, friends, teachers, counselors and parents pressure them to stick to traditional academics and go to four-year colleges to get a "good" job. The truth is that a four-year college is only one route to a good job. As you'll see later on in this chapter, there are many other routes to success and personal fulfillment.

WHERE THE NEW JOBS WILL AND WON'T BE

The U.S. Department of Labor estimates that the fastest growing industries in the United States will create about 13.5 million jobs between now and the year 2012—despite some job losses in a few shrinking industries. Here is a look at where you'll find the most new job opportunities in the next few years—and where you won't. It's important for you to know which industries are growing (and which are not) because of the broad scope of hiring in growth industries. As you can see in Table 1 on page 5, the retail trades are the fastest growing industry. That doesn't mean they will only be hiring retail salespeople. Think about it for a minute: A department store needs many other workers—carpenters, electricians, plumbers, maintenance workers, back-office clerks, computer operators, loading dock workers, buyers . . . and on and on! So, no matter what type of *job* or *occupation* interests you, you'll probably find the most opportunities in industries that are growing rather than those that are shrinking.

TABLE 1. Where the New Jobs Will and Won't Be			
A. Industries with the Largest Expected Number of New Jobs			
	Employed 2002	Estimated Employed 2012	Number of New Jobs
Retail trade	15,047,200	17,129,200	2,082,000
Employment services	3,248,800	5,012,300	1,763,500
State and local government education	9,876,000	11,606,000	1,730,000
Food services and drinking places	8,411,700	9,749,000	1,337,300
Health practitioners' offices	3,189,900	4,418,800	1,228,900
Construction	6,731,700	7,745,400	1,013,700
Educational services (nongovernmental)	2,650,600	3,409,800	759,200
Ambulatory health-care services (except offices of health practitioners)	1,443,600	2,113,400	669,800
State and local government (noneducation)	6,838,400	7,508,100	669,700
Wholesale trades	5,641,100	6,279,300	638,200
Computer systems design and related services	1,162,700	1,797,700	635,000
Hospitals	4,135,100	4,785,000	649,900
Individual, family, community and vocational rehabilitation services	1,269,300	1,866,600	597,300
Nursing care and residential mental health facilities	2,047,800	2,607,100	559,300
Truck transportation, couriers and messengers	1,897,100	2,404,300	507,200
Business support, investigation and security services	1,772,300	2,260,800	488,500

(continues)

TABLE 1. Where the New Jobs Will and Won't Be *(continued)*

	Employed 2002	Estimated Employed 2012	Number of New Jobs
Religious, charitable and social advocacy organizations	1,944,200	2,372,000	427,800
Amusement, gambling and recreation industries	1,307,600	1,717,300	409,700
Management, scientific and technical consulting	731,800	1,137,400	405,600
Community care and residential care facilities for elderly	695,300	1,077,600	382,300
Child day-care services	734,200	1,050,300	316,100
Internet services, data processing and other information services	528,800	773,100	244,300

B. Industries with the Largest Expected Drop in Available Jobs by the Year 2012

	Employed 2002	Estimated Employed 2012	Percent Drop
Sewing machine operation and garment work	281,000	77,100	−72.6
Leather manufacturing and finishing	28,500	15,300	−46.3
Textile industry manufacturing and production	612,600	382,900	−37.5
Metal ore mining	29,400	18,000	−38.8
Coal mining	74,900	52,300	−30.2
Chemical preparation and manufacturing	112,400	79,400	−29.4
Iron, steel and steel products manufacturing	107,100	76,000	−29.0
Oil and gas extraction	122,500	88,400	−27.8
Computer and peripheral equipment manufacturing	249,800	182,100	−27.1
Forestry, fishing, hunting and trapping	67,600	50,400	−25.4

Source: U.S. Bureau of Labor Statistics

Of the millions of new job opportunities in the industries listed above, the vast majority require only on-the-job training—as you can see in Table 2 below.

TABLE 2. Fastest-Growing Occupations and Required Training				
	Employed 2002	Estimated Employed 2012	Percent Growth	Training
Registered nurses	2,284,000	2,908,000	27	Associate's degree
College teachers	1,581,000	2,184,000	38	Doctoral degree
Retail salespersons	4,076,000	4,672,000	15	Short-term on-the-job
Customer service reps	1,894,000	2,354,000	24	Moderate on-the-job
Food prep, serving	1,990,000	2,444,000	23	Short-term on-the-job
Cashiers, except gaming	3,432,000	3,886,000	13	Short-term on-the-job
Janitors, cleaners, except maids and housekeepers	2,267,000	2,681,000	18	Short-term on-the-job
Managers	2,049,000	2,425,000	18	Bachelor's degree and experience
Waitpersons	2,097,000	2,464,000	18	Short-term on-the-job
Nursing aides, orderlies and attendants	1,375,000	1,718,000	25	Short-term on-the-job
Heavy truck and tractor-trailer drivers	1,767,000	2,104,000	19	Moderate on-the-job
Receptionists and info clerks	1,100,000	1,425,000	29	Short-term on-the-job

(continues)

TABLE 2. Fastest-Growing Occupations and Required Training *(continued)*

	Employed 2002	Estimated Employed 2012	Percent Growth	Training
Security guards	995,000	1,313,000	32	Short-term on-the-job
Office clerks	2,991,000	3,301,000	10	Short-term on-the-job
Teacher assistants	1,277,000	1,571,000	23	Short-term on-the-job
Sales reps, wholesale and manufacturing, except tech and scientific products	1,459,000	1,738,000	19	Moderate on-the-job
Home health aides	580,000	859,000	48	Short-term on-the-job
Personal and home-care aides	608,000	854,000	40	Short-term on-the-job
Light-truck drivers and delivery services	1,022,000	1,259,000	23	Short-term on-the-job
Landscape and grounds-keeping workers	1,074,000	1,311,000	22	Short-term on-the-job
Elementary school teachers	1,467,000	1,690,000	15	Bachelor's degree
Medical assistants	365,000	579,000	59	Moderate on-the-job
Maintenance and repairs	1,266,000	1,472,000	16	Moderate on-the-job
Accountants and auditors	1,055,000	1,261,000	19	Bachelor's degree
Computer systems analysts	468,000	653,000	39	Bachelor's degree
Secondary school teachers	988,000	1,167,000	18	Bachelor's degree
Computer software engineers	394,000	573,000	46	Bachelor's degree

Keep in mind that *new* jobs represent only a fraction of *all available jobs*. Millions of workers retire or quit each year and have to be replaced. Indeed, 56 million jobs will open up between now and 2012, of which 60 percent, or 33.6 million, will be *replacements* for retiring workers, while 40 percent, or 22 million, will be *new* jobs. Three-quarters of those job openings do *not* require a four-year college degree—only alternative career education or on-the-job training. Remember that only slightly more than one-third of Americans have four-year college or graduate degrees and that half the workers in America—more than 34 million—have only high school degrees or, in some cases, alternative career education. To know what level of education you'll need in your chosen career, take a look at Appendix D: It lists virtually every type of job in the nation, along with the Median income and necessary training. It also shows how many jobs will be available in each occupation between now and the year 2012 and whether there will be more or fewer opportunities.

BUT WHAT IF I CAN'T WORK FULL TIME?

There is an amazingly large number of opportunities for you. So don't fret! Whatever the reasons, you can find wonderful opportunities working part time. Nearly 16 percent of American workers in *all industries* work part time. Here is the percentage of part-time workers in the eight industries that hire the most part-timers:

Food-service and drinking places	37.9%
Grocery stores	30.1%
Clothing and department stores	29.2%
Child day-care services	29.1%
Arts, entertainment and recreation	28.1%
Movie and video industries	24.8%
Social services	21.8%
Educational services (see teaching assistants)	21.1%
Customer service representatives	14.0%

So that means you can tutor children; help families; star on stage, screen or television; or manage a restaurant or tavern—part time and without ever having gone to college!

The fact is there are only two good reasons for going to a four-year college or university: a deep desire to study traditional academic subjects (literature, history, philosophy, languages, science, and so on) or a deep commitment to career goals that can only be reached with a university education (law, medicine, engineering, and similar professions).

So if you're one of the millions of Americans who really don't want to or need to go to college or university, and your talents and career goals are in areas not requiring a college degree, consider alternative career education. Alternative education can open thousands of career opportunities in the arts, crafts, science and health care, sports, skilled trades, manufacturing, construction, travel, banking and finance and even in your own business—and there's no need to spend thousands of dollars and four precious years at a university if you don't really need to or want to.

What Is Alternative Education?

In simplest terms, alternative education is practical training that will convert your basic skills, talents and interests into a good job and a lasting, rewarding career. Alternative education will help you become a master craftsperson—an expert everyone wants and needs to hire.

Like traditional academics, alternative education is available through courses at almost every level of schooling—high school, community college, technical institutes and four-year colleges and universities. But it's also available in apprenticeship programs and on-the-job training programs provided by many companies and labor unions. In many cases, alternative education involves no formal classroom study. There are many career opportunities where alternative education simply involves getting an entry-level job in which you earn while you learn—and the more you learn, the more you earn. More than 60 percent of all factory workers, tradeworkers, craftspeople and office and clerical workers learn their skills on the job.

How much alternative education you'll need in an area will largely depend on the demands of your work and your employer—and your own interests. In some areas, you may want to continue learning new skills and improving old ones all your life. Some industries require skills that can be learned entirely in high school. Others require skills taught only at technical schools or community colleges, because high schools either don't teach them or don't teach advanced levels. Still other courses are available at four-year colleges and universities, where alternative education students may take them on a full-time or part-time basis during the day or evening, with or without studying for a degree. And you can even learn some job skills at home—by mail or over the Internet on your home computer—without ever leaving the comfort of your room or setting foot in a classroom. That's what this book is about: to show you exactly what type of alternative career education is available, where to get it and how much you'll need to get your first job in a wide variety of careers. The rest of this section will tell you all about alternative education—how to evaluate it and how to pick the right career track for you. Remember: Career education is worthless if it can't help you get a job. Part II lists hundreds of career and talent areas that do not require four-year college or university degrees for entry-level jobs and a clear track to success. Each career listing includes the education or training needed to get started, the pay range and some organizations that can help you learn those skills. Part III will show you how to get started in your new career area, with some easy-to-use tips for applying for, and getting, your first job: writing a good résumé, completing a successful job application and using the job interview to sell yourself and your talents.

One important thing to keep in mind as you read is that there are almost no limits to the personal *and* financial rewards available from the opportunities described in this book. Even jobs that pay only minimum wage to start can lead to opportunities in management and ownership after you've learned enough about your new craft or trade. Almost all owners and managers started out as ordinary workers in their trades and businesses. Many restaurant owners were once waiters, many store owners started as stock clerks and salespeople and many successful building contractors started as laborers or apprentices. The same is true for managers and owners in almost all of the trades and businesses in Part II, and they got to the top without spending four years at college. You can too. Let's find out how—and good luck!

GETTING STARTED

One exciting thing about alternative education is that it is basically open to all. There are no age limits, for example, and almost no background requirements. To sign up—and to succeed—all you really need is an interest in and a desire to learn a craft or trade. You can start at 16 or 60, whenever *you* are ready. Adults of any age, regardless of educational background, may enroll in virtually every type of program, whether it's on the job, at a two- or four-year college or at a local public high school or technical school. Indeed, more than one-third of all community college and junior college students are more than 30 years old. Most programs are available on weekends and at night as well as during the day, so as not to interfere with any job you may have. More than 60 percent of community college students are enrolled part-time.

Alternative education programs are also available to college students who want to switch from traditional academics or who wish to combine traditional academics with alternative education. High school students often have the same choices: They can switch from traditional academic programs to vocational education or combine the two. So, no matter how old you are or what your circumstances—whether you're in school or not—alternative education programs are open to you. It's only a question of finding the right one.

Even if you've already left high school without getting a diploma, or left so long ago you can't remember what you learned there, you can still take advantage of alternative education. Many alternative education programs don't require a high school diploma for admission. What you may want to consider, however, is enrolling in an equivalency diploma program to brush up on and master basic reading, writing and calculating skills while you take alternative education. Combining the two will give you a marketable skill *and* a high school diploma—a combination guaranteed to open the door to endless opportunities that await all bright, talented, hard-working men and women. Chapter 2 shows you how to get your equivalency diploma, and how to evaluate *yourself*, especially if you're convinced you have no skills. Everyone has skills and talents, and you do too! The problem is that not everyone knows how to determine what his or her talents are. One way is to identify your interests first. Whatever they are—sports, music or science—there are endless jobs to match those interests, even if you're not an athlete, musician or scientist. There are hundreds of vital jobs in every field, and, with alternative education, it's easy to learn how to do them. So keep reading!

COMBINING CAREER EDUCATION AND COLLEGE

Although none of the career opportunities in this book requires a four-year college degree, if you want to go to college or to a university, by all means do so. College can provide you with a useful and rewarding education, and it may, if you're not sure yet, help you determine how you want to spend the rest of your life. Most colleges are like enormous cafeterias of knowledge, offering endless choices of courses in traditional academics as well as preprofessional and alternative education. Many people, for one reason or another, often fail to recognize the value of traditional academics—the liberal arts. Often it's because they may have had some poor or boring teachers in high school, and they assume they won't enjoy or get anything out of further study in the liberal arts. But the liberal arts are designed to help students develop intellectual and creative abilities that will prove valuable in almost every occupation.

So, you can combine the best of many educational worlds at college and "taste" different areas of knowledge before you make any career decisions. What's more, hundreds of two- and four-year colleges across the United States now participate with local industries in the growing cooperative education movement to provide a mixture of liberal arts and practical arts education that will assure graduates of immediate jobs at cooperating companies. The exciting career opportunities available through cooperative education are described in the second half of this chapter.

Remember, too, that no matter what career you eventually choose, a degree from a two-year or four-year college will always be a big plus on your résumé. On average, workers with college degrees earn more, as you can see from these figures from the U.S. Department of Labor:

TABLE 3. Average Annual Earnings at Each Level of Education (2002)	
No high school diploma	$19,802
High school diploma	$27,526
Some post–high school study (includes alternative education)	$35,023
Associate (two-year) degree	$37,970
Bachelor's degree	$50,600
Master's degree	$60,830
Professional degree	$88,216
Doctorate	$76,147

But don't enroll in a full-time, four-year or even two-year college simply because others want or expect you to. For many, college can be the happiest years and worth every penny of tuition invested in it. For others, college can mean years of misery and a waste of a family's life savings. Remember, nearly one-fourth of U.S. college students drop out without getting a degree.

Only you can decide whether you will benefit more from college, alternative education or a combination of both. I hope this book will help you make that decision. One decision to avoid at all costs, however, is to pursue *no* education, either academic or vocational—in other words, to quit school. Fifty years ago, a decision to quit school and go to work at age 16 or 18 was perfectly sound for many people, because there were many jobs for unskilled workers. Elevators in almost every department store and office and apartment building had to be operated by hand. Streets were swept, roads were built and crops were harvested—all by hand. In offices and stores everywhere, all books were kept by hand. Most of this is no longer true. Elevators run automatically; machines sweep streets, pave roads and harvest crops. And scanners register sales at most supermarket and department store checkout counters—and automatically feed all data into computers that keep the books, do the accounting, control inventories and reorder out-of-stock merchandise. Stores won't—and many already do not—need as many bookkeepers, accountants, stocktakers and other behind-the-scenes workers. Self-service long ago eliminated many sales clerks, and scanning equipment is eliminating many cashiers and checkout personnel.

The same is true in almost every industry. ATM equipment is putting bank tellers out of work; e-mail is putting mail handlers out of work; voice mail is eliminating jobs for telephone operators; computers are eliminating the need for file clerks; automatic copying equipment is putting duplicating machine operators out of work. Even computer operators, who set controls and feed data into big mainframe computers, are losing their jobs as computers themselves become more sophisticated and do more things automatically. In fact, one Japanese robot manufacturing plant is using robots to make robots—to "reproduce themselves," in a sense. The list is endless. Table 4 below shows the types of jobs that automation—computers, robots, etc.—has reduced dramatically in the past 10 years.

As you can see, the job opportunities for unskilled and even semi-skilled workers are disappearing, because there are almost no more unskilled jobs. Indeed, the unemployment rate among the unskilled—those who dropped out of high school without getting their diplomas—is more than 20 percent, compared to just under 15 percent for high school graduates, less than 8 percent for people with some college but with no degree, 5.4 percent for those with an associate degree from a two-year college and 5.2 percent for those with bachelor's degrees or higher from four-year colleges and universities.

TABLE 4. Occupations with the Largest Declines in Available Jobs, 1995–2005	
Bookkeeping, accounting and auditing clerks	278,000
Farmers	272,000
Typists and word processors	212,000
Bank tellers	152,000
Sewing machine operators, garment workers	140,000
Household workers	108,000
Computer operators	98,000
Billing, posting and calculating machine operators	64,000

(continues)

TABLE 4. Occupations with the Largest Declines in Available Jobs, 1995–2005 *(continued)*	
Duplicating, mail and other office machine operators	56,000
Textile machine operators	47,000
File clerks	42,000
Freight, stock and material movers	41,000
Farm workers	36,000
Machine-tool cutting operators and tenders, metal and plastic	34,000
Central-office telephone operators	34,000
Central-office and PBX installers and repairers	33,000
Electronic and electronic assemblers	30,000
Telephone installers and repairers	26,000
Personnel clerks	26,000
Data-entry keyers	25,000

In other words, no one can afford to consider quitting school anymore. The only decisions for intelligent people today is what kind of school or training program to attend, what kind of education to get—academic, vocational or a combination of both—and how much education to get. Appendix D at the back of the book lists the kinds of training you'll need for hundreds of different occupations—including the ones you may be considering. Check *now* to see whether you qualify.

Keep in mind that the decision you make is not irreversible. It will naturally be less costly in time and money if you can decide what you'll do the rest of your life before you graduate from high school. But most people don't, and that's a fact. To prove it, just ask your parents or teachers whether they are now doing exactly what they planned to do when they were 16 or 17 years old. The chances are they're not, and, if you're still in high school, it's unfair to expect you to know what you're going to do 25 years from now.

For most people, the decision that seems right at one particular time is often not right at another time. So, if you make a decision now and find you're unhappy about it later on, there is absolutely no reason to feel bad about changing your mind and starting on a new course. It's important to remain flexible and be prepared to change with time and circumstances.

If you decide that vocational education is right for you at this time in your life and others disapprove of your decision, show them this book so they can see how alternative education can help you develop skills and talents to take advantage of rewarding career opportunities. There are many careers that don't require a college education but do provide millions all over the world with successful, rewarding lives. You must fulfill *your* ambitions, not those of your parents or friends or anyone else.

WHAT KIND OF ALTERNATIVE EDUCATION IS BEST?

Before exploring specific career opportunities, let's look at the various types of alternative education open to you and see how to evaluate them. Careful evaluation is the key to getting good alternative education. Just because your local high school or community college offers vocational courses does not mean you'll gain any useful knowledge if you take them. According to U.S. government studies, as many as half the students who take high school vocational courses graduate with obsolete, *useless* skills. So just because a high school or college counselor says a vocational course or program is good doesn't make it good. And just because a vocational school advertises on television doesn't make it good or even honest. Many private trade schools that advertise on television are operated by con artists—which is why careful evaluation of alternative education programs is so important. Even some of the largest private career schools and colleges make false claims to try to get you to enroll. One *national chain of trade schools* told prospective applicants they could expect starting salaries of $50,000 to $100,000 in their *first year* after graduation—more than enough to pay off a student loan for tuition. A subsequent investigation by the California Bureau for Private Postsecondary and Vocational Education found that the average income of the school's graduates was only $26,000, and all had complained that, contrary to the school's promises, it had provided no job placement help. Each of the students had accumulated $74,000 in debts to pay for tuition. So *please* be careful to evaluate alternative educations thoroughly. Too many students have wasted their time *and* life savings pursuing useless vocational education programs. Many have gone into debt without learning useful job skills. Let's make sure that doesn't happen to you.

Let's look at the various kinds of alternative education available, and then at ways to find out if they're any good. There are 12 basic types of vocational education. Although many are not available in all communities, it's important that you know them by name so you can recognize them. They are:

1. Comprehensive high schools
2. Specialized vocational/technical (vo-tech) high schools
3. Cooperative education programs
   a. High schools
   b. Colleges
4. "Two-plus-two" tech-prep programs
5. Community colleges
6. Technical institutes
7. Private, not-for-profit junior (two-year) colleges
8. Private, for-profit (proprietary) trade schools
9. Four-year colleges and universities
10. Distance learning
11. Employer/union apprenticeship programs
12. Employer-sponsored training programs

Let's take a closer look at each of them and at their advantages and disadvantages. Then let's try to work out the best possible program for you.

1. **Comprehensive high schools.** A comprehensive high school is an ordinary high school—the kind kids attend everywhere in the United States. It offers *everything* for *everyone*—academic education and vocational education. Less than 12 percent of all high school students are in vocational education, however. That's a huge drop from 10 years ago, when nearly 27 percent of all high school students enrolled in such programs. More than one-third of the students in high school vocational education courses are older than 30, and many schools offer evening as well as daytime courses to accommodate working adults.

ADVANTAGES: These programs can offer an early opportunity to learn a little about a trade or occupation without making a long-term commitment and without sacrificing academic education. Although fewer than 12 percent of all high school students are enrolled in vocational education *programs*, 97 percent take one or more vocational education courses that give them a taste of what each field is like and allow them to decide whether or not they might want to pursue that type of work. Comprehensive vocational education also has the advantage of allowing a student to switch easily from academic to vocational education without having to change schools and make new friends.

DISADVANTAGES: Unless tied to a high school cooperative education program (see Number 3 on page 20), the overwhelming majority of vocational education programs in comprehensive high schools are, by themselves, inadequate. In fact, they're terrible. Half the vocational training in comprehensive high schools centers about agriculture, home economics and industrial arts—all of them areas in which the number of job opportunities is shrinking. Moreover, most comprehensive high schools usually teach only one or two courses in each occupational area, and that's not enough education to get a good job. Most high school vocational courses lack adequate resources and equipment, and so many teachers lack up-to-date training in the fields they teach that many employers simply won't recognize diplomas in vocational education from comprehensive high schools as valid evidence of a young person's skills. And that's why there has been such a dramatic drop in student enrollment. As one U.S. government report put it, the typical high school vocational education program "neglects academic skill development, trains for occupations not in demand, teaches with outmoded equipment, and offers limited placement assistance." The report found that *less than half* of all students who take high school vocational education are able to use what they learned in full-time jobs following high school.

2. **Specialized vocational/technical (vo-tech) high schools.**   These are two- to four-year high schools where all students major in some form of vocational education, although all receive the same fundamental academic instruction of conventional high schools.

ADVANTAGES: Many are outstanding schools. They offer far more comprehensive, in-depth training by skilled craftspeople in each trade than ordinary high schools, thus making each graduate more skilled and employable. Employers generally respect the credentials of graduates from vo-tech schools, which usually have strong job placement services and close ties with employers. Vo-tech students emerge stronger in academics as well, because students learn English, math, science and other subjects in conjunction with their vocational education and, therefore, find these areas more interesting. In other words, they learn *applied* rather than theoretical mathematics. Student self-esteem is usually higher, because the entire administration and faculty are devoted to vocational education instead of traditional academics. In comprehensive high schools, vocational education is often held in low esteem by school administrators, who tend to assign less able teachers to vocational education students than to students in the academic, college-prep curriculum. Another advantage of specialized vo-tech schools is the time and opportunity allowed to sample many trades and occupations before deciding on a specialty. The best vo-tech schools offer prevocational courses that offer students an in-depth look at "career clusters" such as agriculture, manufacturing, health, public service and other broad categories, and then examine the hundreds of specific jobs within those clusters.

DISADVANTAGES: Usually there are none in terms of educational quality. Unfortunately, there are only about 325 vo-tech schools across the entire United States. Most communities have none. Only 16 states have more than two: Arkansas (nine), Connecticut (17), Delaware (five), Florida (25), Maryland (12), Massachusetts (43), Michigan (12), New Jersey (38), New York (25), Ohio (68), Pennsylvania (16), Rhode Island (four), Tennessee (three), Texas (25), Washington (10) and West Virginia (five). Alabama, Colorado and Kentucky have two each, and Alaska, Minnesota, Nevada, North Carolina and Wisconsin have one each. Twenty-six states have no vo-tech schools. If there's a vo-tech school in or near your community, by all means evaluate its program and look into the possibility of enrolling.

3.   **Cooperative education programs.**   There are two kinds of cooperative education programs: One is at the high school level, the other at the college level. Both offer excellent vocational education.

a. **High school cooperative education programs:** These programs allow students to take vocational courses at a comprehensive high school in the morning and immediately apply all new knowledge on the job in the afternoon at local companies that provide supervision and instruction and work closely with vocational education teachers.

ADVANTAGES: Skills taught are up-to-date and immediately applicable in the workplace. Close ties with local industry and employers can be a big help in getting students jobs after graduation. Involvement of local industry also assures schools of the most modern equipment and continuous training for teachers.

DISADVANTAGES: The quality of the academic education offered to vocational education students is often inadequate. That's because administrators of comprehensive high schools often hold vocational education in lower esteem than academic education. So they sometimes reserve their best teachers for college-prep programs and assign less-skilled faculty to students of vocational education. These students, however, need just as many skills in reading, mathematics, problem solving and science as academic track students. Unfortunately, voc-ed students usually do not get an adequate academic education in comprehensive high schools.

The lack of interest by school administrators in vocational education is evident in the small number of comprehensive high schools that have bothered establishing cooperative education programs. Only about 3 percent of high school students are enrolled in formal "co-op" programs. From your own personal point of view, another disadvantage of a high school cooperative education program is the possibility that a decision to specialize in a trade at age 16 or 17 may be premature. You may find that, after graduating and working at your new trade for a year, you dislike it intensely. A change then, however, may be economically impossible or, at best, difficult. It will mean going back to school either to learn another trade or to get an academic degree.

b. **College cooperative education programs.** Without question, these provide the finest vocational education for students who are certain about their career goals. Cooperative education programs are available at several hundred public and private two-year and four-year colleges and universities across the nation. The programs integrate your daily college classroom studies with a part-time paying job at a local company, which works closely with your school and your teachers to mesh everything you learn in the classroom with what you'll be doing at work. About 200,000 students now participate in co-op-ed programs at every level, from the associate to the doctoral degree. An estimated 50,000 employers in every industry are employing them, including the federal government, which employs 14,000 co-op students in 36 federal departments and agencies at almost 2,000 work sites. Although 85 of the 100 largest American corporations employ co-op students, the vast majority of co-op employers are small organizations employing one to three co-op students. There are two types of programs: alternating and parallel. Students in *alternating programs* rotate periods of full-time classroom studies with terms of full-time employment. Students in parallel programs work part-time and attend school part-time during the same term.

ADVANTAGES: This is just about the best vocational education you can get anywhere in the world! Students who do well are almost guaranteed good jobs on the "fast track" after graduation. And remember: You'll be choosing the type of work *you* really want to do—and that's a sure-fire formula for doing well! About 60 percent of co-op-ed students continue working for their co-op employer after graduation and 95 percent find jobs immediately after graduation. Fifteen percent continue their education by getting bachelor's degrees. Some go on to graduate school programs in law, medicine, dentistry or other professions. Another tremendous advantage of co-op-ed is that it allows high school students to concentrate on academics, knowing that they can enroll in excellent community college vocational studies that will almost guarantee them a good job. And still another tremendous advantage of co-op education is that you're getting paid while you learn. Students earned between $2,500 and $14,000 a year in wages last year from their co-op employers—and they were still eligible for the conventional financial aid available to all college students: scholarships from the colleges they attend and grants and student loans from state and federal government agencies. Some of America's largest companies are involved in co-op education: American Airlines, the American Hockey League, American Stock Exchange, Citibank, General Electric,

IBM, John Hancock Insurance, Johnson & Johnson, Gillette, Polaroid, Kidder Peabody, the New York Giants (that's right!), Off-Track Betting, Queens Symphony Orchestra, Sears Roebuck . . . the list is endless—and so are the opportunities in virtually every type of occupation you or I could ever think of. And the list of colleges is equally impressive: Boston University, Fairleigh Dickinson University, George Washington University, Michigan State University, Montclair State University, Northeastern University, Pennsylvania State University, Seton Hall University, Syracuse University, Temple University, University of Connecticut, University of Massachusetts, University of Michigan, U.S. Merchant Marine Academy. . . . Again, the list seems endless—as are the programs they offer: agriculture, natural resources, applied arts and crafts, business, computer science, health care, home economics, technologies and vocational arts, including construction, food service, repair and maintenance, trade and industry. Appendix F lists several hundred colleges with cooperative education programs and their web sites.

DISADVANTAGES: There are none, except for the lack of similar programs everywhere. Instead of only hundreds of colleges, every American college and university should be offering similar programs. If you know what career interests you most and you can find a college cooperative education program near you, by all means enroll.

4.   **"Two-plus-two" tech-prep programs.**   Two-plus-two programs are a form of vocational education that combines the last two years of high school with two years of community college education. In other words, it is a *four-year program* that begins in the junior year of high school and continues through community college and leads to an associate degree in a particular vocation.

ADVANTAGES: Four years of comprehensive, in-depth training and a college associate degree give students the highest qualifications for the workplace. Because the entire program is usually organized and supervised by the faculty at the community college, a two-plus-two program assures students of superior education at the high school level. Moreover, because it is a comprehensive four-year program, high school seniors must work seriously instead of goofing off and wasting time. Failure to perform well in 12th grade, the second year of the two-plus-two program, can mean failing the entire program. In addition to extensive vocational education, community college faculties see to it that two-plus-two students receive the same academic training and learn the same skills as students in the academic track—that is, reading speed and comprehension, analytical skills, problem-solving, decision-making, computation, computer literacy, human relations and communications skills. Still another advantage is that if, for one reason or another, a student decides against pursuing a particular trade, he or she can either remain in community college and study a new trade or transfer to a four-year college and work toward a bachelor's degree. Two-plus-two programs normally have extremely active and effective job placement services, and employers eagerly recruit graduates from these programs. More than 90 percent of the graduates find work in the fields in which they trained.

   DISADVANTAGES: There are none in terms of educational quality. Unfortunately, the two-plus-two concept is not available in most communities. If it is available in your area, sign up!

5.   **Community colleges.**   Community colleges were originally designed as two-year public academic institutions that would serve as a transition between high school and four-year colleges and universities. Most still offer a wide range of academic courses, but almost all have added vocational training programs, many of which are among the best in the United States. As previously mentioned, many offer excellent cooperative education programs that allow you to "earn while you learn." Others integrate vocational education with nearby high school programs (see "two-plus-two" tech-prep programs on page 23). Still others offer their own independent vocational education programs. Most community colleges try to specialize in only one or two areas of vocational training such as hotel and restaurant management, health care, the graphic arts or some other career cluster.

   ADVANTAGES: The cost is relatively low, because community colleges are part of state or city public-university systems. Average tuition for full-time students at American community colleges is about $1,500 a year, although costs vary widely from state to state, from as low as $350 to as high as $4,500. Community colleges also offer an opportunity to combine academic studies with vocational training. So, if you feel you need to brush up on academic skills—in math or English, for example—you can do so and still learn a craft or trade. Unlike high school, you can go to school part time and maintain a job while you're continuing your education. You can take as little or as much time as you need to complete your degree. You can take as many or as few courses as you want. You can just study one course to learn a trade without signing up for a degree program. Teachers at community colleges are usually part-time professionals. That's good, because they're up to date and knowledgeable about what's happening in their fields, and they're usually in close touch with job markets. Another point about community colleges: They are usually exceptionally caring institutions that provide far more individual attention than most four-year colleges. Their name, "community," says it all and defines their role: to serve the needs of the community and its students. Most try sincerely to do just that.

DISADVANTAGES: Not all community colleges offer worthwhile vocational education. Indeed, a U.S. Department of Education study found that only about 60 percent of community college students are able to use the college vocational training to get and keep a job. The low "course-utilization rate," however, could reflect a number of things. On the one hand, it might very well reflect poor educational quality. On the other hand, it might also reflect the failure of a lot of students to take enough courses. Students who only take 12 credits—about one-quarter the number needed for an associate degree—have almost three times the unemployment rate of students who take the full complement of credits and graduate from community college with an associate degree. Fewer than 6 percent of students who graduate remain unemployed after a year—almost as low an unemployment rate as those who graduate with a bachelor's degree from four-year colleges.

So, the more courses you take in a particular vocation, the more likely you will be to get a good job and use your training. But it's essential for you to evaluate community college (and all other) vocational programs before enrolling. I'll show you how to do that in the next chapter. Assuming you find a good community college, and many of them are great, it really will be up to you how much you get out of it.

6. **Technical institutes.**   Like community colleges, these are usually two-year schools, but they are highly specialized and seldom offer extensive academic programs. They expect incoming students to have a firm command of English, mathematics and basic science. Many offer cooperative education programs of the kind discussed earlier.

    ADVANTAGES: Technical institutes usually offer high quality, in-depth training by professionals who are up-to-date on technological advances and in touch with job markets. Technical institutes normally have close working ties with nearby industries and have extensive job placement facilities for their students.
    DISADVANTAGES: Again, there are very few of them across the United States, and most are usually costlier than community colleges and require more intensive study. That makes it difficult for some students to handle the work part time. Indeed, it's best to attend full time.

7. **Private, not-for-profit junior (two-year) colleges.**   These are the same as community colleges, except that they are privately operated (although not for profit).

    ADVANTAGES: On average, they offer much broader academic programs than community colleges and more athletic and other extra-curricular activities. Many have boarding facilities for full-time resident students. The main reason for considering private junior colleges is to see whether they offer superior programs or vocational courses and job placement services that may not be available at a local community college. Many offer cooperative education studies as discussed earlier.
    DISADVANTAGES: Although usually better than community colleges, they cost more: an average of $10,800 a year, compared to $1,500 for public community colleges.

8. **Private, for-profit (proprietary) trade schools.**   One of the fastest growing sectors in education, these are often specialized private schools offering intense training in one or more trades; for example, auto mechanics, hairstyling, cosmetology, keyboarding, computer operations, etc. Most schools obtain their students by advertising—

often making exaggerated claims. In the last decade, large corporations have moved into the trade-school sector, establishing national chains that give each member school the benefit of a brand name.

ADVANTAGES: Training is quick and concentrated. Students are ready for the job market in as few as two weeks, depending on the trade. In some communities, private trade schools are the only organizations that teach certain trades, such as bartending or barbering. So students may have no choice but to attend a private trade school if they want to learn such trades.

DISADVANTAGES: There are no opportunities for academic work, and all training is limited to one field. Training can be extremely poor, because teachers are paid far less than at community colleges and technical institutes. Runaway schools that open one day and close the next are only one danger of proprietary schools. Of far greater danger is the unethical operator, who preys on high school dropouts, immigrants (legal and illegal) and poor, semiliterate students, convincing them to enroll and obtain government-backed student loans to pay for tuition. If, as is likely, the student drops out before completing the course work, the school keeps the money, and the student is in debt to the government for every penny of the loan. The advent of big corporations into the trade-school industry has transformed it into a $7.5 billion-a-year cash machine. There are seven major chains: Apollo Group (34 states and Puerto Rico), Career Education Corporation (24 states), Corinthian Colleges (24 states), Education Management Corporation (24 states), ITT Educational Services (30 states) and Strayer Education (eight states). Each of the corporations pretends to set high, universal education standards in each of its schools, which uses the national brand name to its benefit in local advertising. But a member school in one of the biggest national chains reportedly lured students to enroll with promises that they could expect starting salaries of $50,000 to $150,000 in their first year after graduation—more than enough to pay off student loans to cover tuition. Not one graduate that year, according to California investigators, earned even $50,000; the average income of graduates turned out to be $26,000, while the average student debt was $74,000. So, beware of proprietary school advertisements. The promises they make may be lies! There are so many disadvantages to proprietary schools that if there's a good alternative, it's wise to use it. If there's no choice, however—let's say the trade you want to learn is only taught by a proprietary trade school—then be certain the school is *accredited* by the Accrediting Commission of Career Schools and Colleges of Technology, 2101 Wilson Boulevard, Arlington, VA 22201 (http://www. accsct.org). Chapter 2 will tell you more about the importance of accreditation in evaluating vocational schools. Meanwhile, keep in mind what a U.S. government study of proprietary schools had to say:

> Our study found patterns of misrepresentation to prospective students, lack of attention to . . . standards, low (student) completion rates, and faulty use of federal financial aid programs. Three-quarters of the students admitted without a high school degree and half the students with a high school degree dropped out . . . Certificates from many proprietary schools have little reliability.

9.   **Four-year colleges and universities.**   Many state and private four-year colleges and universities offer extensive vocational training programs, including excellent cooperative education programs discussed earlier and listed in the directory of the National Commission for Cooperative Education. Students can enroll full time or part time and take as few or as many courses as they want or need. Like two-year community and junior colleges, you don't have to enroll in a degree-granting program at many colleges or universities. You can just go and study the courses needed to learn a trade.

ADVANTAGES: Training can be more intensive and in greater depth than at two-year colleges, and there are far more opportunities to supplement vocational training with academic courses. You can even transfer from vocational to academic education, or vice versa. Some four-year colleges may offer training in areas not covered by two-year schools. Job placement facilities may also be more extensive. Four-year colleges usually have boarding facilities for resident students and larger recreation facilities.

DISADVANTAGES: Costs are usually much higher than at two-year schools.

10. **Distance learning.** For students unable to attend school for whatever reason (work schedule, child-care responsibilities, disabilities, geographic distance), the Internet now provides electronic delivery of formal courses and educational programs to your home computer. Distance learning is, in effect, the electronic equivalent of correspondence courses that come by mail. Now the fastest growing segment of education, distance learning allows you to take more than 5,000 different academic and vocational courses for full credit at more than 1,000 accredited two- and four-year colleges as well as proprietary for-profit schools, colleges, technical institutes and trade schools. You can earn an associate's degree, bachelor's or master's degree or learn a profitable trade, without ever setting foot in a classroom. You're eligible for the same financial aid and government grants as all students.

ADVANTAGES: Distance learning provides faster learning at lower costs than conventional institutions. It allows anyone with a computer to attend classes via the Internet 24 hours a day, without following a strict schedule or ever leaving your home. You study and complete your work or training at your own pace, whenever you have free time, day or night, 365 days a year. You can also get electronic help when you need it. (There are even professional e-tutoring services to which you can subscribe.) You take tests electronically when you're ready. All course materials arrive over the Internet, and you can order books electronically from the college or school bookstore and access the school library. Financial aid is available for distance learning, and most distance-learning colleges accept course credits from other distance-learning schools, which gives you enormous flexibility in planning your curriculum.

DISADVANTAGES: With no one to push you, distance learning requires self-discipline. You have to do all the work *on your own,* and that can be a long, lonely task. Making it even lonelier is the lack of other students, meaning no classroom discussions and no chatting with friends about homework assignments. A second disadvantage is the difficulty of hands-on training in such courses as automotive repairs. And a third—important—disadvantage is the lack of quality control over distance-learning courses. Your only way of gauging the quality of a course is by the reputation of the providing institution and the professor teaching the course. Some Web-based courses are useless rubbish. Before enrolling in a distance-learning program, consult the appropriate accrediting associations in Appendix A and *Barron's Guide to Distance Learning* or *Peterson's Guide to Distance Learning Programs*, both of which you can find in bookstores (see Appendix B for more details).

11.   **Employer/union apprenticeship programs.**   For students with a solid high school education, these programs usually offer the best vocational education in their specialties, especially in fields such as construction, where students earn while they learn. Most programs require about 2,000 hours of supervised, on-the-job training plus related instruction either in classrooms, by correspondence or self-study. There are more than 800 types of apprenticeship programs officially recognized by the U.S. government and the 50 states. As you saw in Table 2, nearly 80 percent of the fastest growing occupations between now and 2012 will be the result of on-the-job training. Appendix A lists the addresses of the U.S. Labor Department's Bureau of Apprenticeship and Training web site. Check with the office to make certain that any apprenticeship programs you're considering in your area are accredited.

   ADVANTAGES: The pay is usually good, and students begin their training with a job already in place. Apprenticeship programs are supervised by master craftspeople and usually represent applied education at its finest.
   DISADVANTAGES: There are too few programs, and all are extremely difficult to get into. Less than 1 percent of American high school graduates (usually sons and daughters of union members) get into such programs. Most trades don't even offer apprenticeships. Fewer than 200,000 people are enrolled in these programs in the United States today, and fewer than 20 percent are under the age of 23. The programs are mainly meant to train adults in their mid-twenties, and the competition to get in is fierce. That lets employers choose the most skilled and most

mature applicants. In other words, it's not the type of training most people can ever count on getting.

12.   **Employer-sponsored training programs.**   Unlike apprenticeship programs, these programs are usually not associated with any union. They are taught by master craftspeople and company executives and usually combine on-the-job training with limited classroom training.

ADVANTAGES: As in apprenticeship programs, trainees earn while they learn, and successful completion usually assures them permanent jobs. Instructors are usually the best the company has to offer. Once again, it is "applied" education at its best and, as mentioned earlier, nearly 80 percent of the fastest-growing occupations between now and 2012 will result from on-the-job training, either union- or employer-sponsored. Widespread availability makes these programs outstanding opportunities for millions of workers.

DISADVANTAGES: There are two possible disadvantages for applicants to be careful about. The first is that some companies may offer training that is so specific that the trainee never learns to do another job and cannot transfer the skills to another company or occupation. A car assembler who only learns to install door handles won't find many job opportunities if the car plant shuts down. So, it's important that the training program be broad-based and offer *career* training as well as *job* training.

The other major disadvantage to beware of is an employer's offer to train workers in labor-short markets. Be suspicious whenever you see an advertisement that says, "Carpenters wanted. No experience necessary. Will train. . . ." These ads usually appear when there's a housing boom, often in resort areas that attract young people with few nonrecreational skills. In their eagerness to profit from market conditions, some builders hire workers whose only experience may have been to help their parents complete do-it-yourself projects at home. The jobs offer no real training, only the opportunity to help and observe more experienced workers. The sad results are often shoddy workmanship for the builder's clients and few marketable skills for the young workers. Compared to professionals who trained as apprentices, such trainees are slow and incompetent—even those who have worked many years. Their work may be a quick means of earning money without alternative education, but it is only temporary, because every local construction boom eventually ends and workers are left without jobs or real skills. Few professional construction firms in stable labor markets hire workers who have not gone through accredited apprenticeship programs. So it's as important to evaluate employer-sponsored training programs as it is to evaluate all other forms of alternative education.

2

How to Pick the Right Career— And the Right Training for It

As you saw in Chapter 1, there are many types of vocational education, each with its own advantages and disadvantages. With so many choices, how can you decide which is the right program for you?

Well first of all, where you live may limit the number of your choices, because only a few large cities such as New York or Chicago offer all programs listed in Chapter 1. Most areas only offer two or three, and isolated rural areas may only offer one program at the local high school.

No matter how many or how few programs are available, however, it's important for you to evaluate each of them carefully so that you can choose the one that is indeed *the best for you* in your area—and there is almost always one that is better than all others. That's why evaluation is so important—to make certain you pick a program that will get you started properly in a successful and happy career. Remember: *The basic purpose of vocational education is to get a job*. If a school or training program can't teach you the skills you need to get and keep a job, it's a poor school or program, and you shouldn't waste your time with either.

Looking at it from another point of view, vocational education is an investment. You're going to invest a lot of time and perhaps a lot of money. So, as with any investment, it's important to find out *in advance* what the return on your investment will be.

There are two things to determine in evaluating any vocational education or training program: educational quality and educational results. The checklist opposite, for evaluating vocational education, outlines 10 factors that make up educational quality and five that measure educational results.

Use this checklist for evaluating a vocational education program. Most of the data should be available from the school's course catalog, the rest from school administrators. Here is how to use it:

CHECKLIST FOR EVALUATING VOCATIONAL EDUCATION

I. Educational Quality

1. Accreditation by appropriate organization in Appendix A   _____

2. Program depth
   (at least four courses in your field, two at advanced levels)*   _____

3. Link to local vo-tech or community college program*   _____

4. Links to on-the-job training programs in local industry
   (cooperative education)   _____

5. Up-to-date classroom equipment   _____

6. Strong, required academic program
   (minimum two years English, math and science)*   _____

7. One-semester course on "World of Work"
   (résumé preparation, interviews, and so on)*   _____

8. Skilled faculty (years on the job they teach)   _____

9. Active job placement office   _____

10. Readily available performance data   _____

II. Educational Results

1. Program completion rate (at least 75 percent)   _____

2. Test scores and/or state certification rates
   (at least 75 percent passing grades)   _____

3. Training-related job placement rate (at least 80 percent)   _____

4. Average starting wage (at least twice the minimum wage)   _____

5. Duration of employment (at least two years) and
   unemployment rate among graduates (no more than 15 percent)   _____

*Not appropriate for private trade schools

I.   EDUCATIONAL QUALITY

1.   **Accreditation.**   *Do not consider* a school or program that is not accredited by an appropriate independent accreditation agency. Accreditation assures you that a program or school has met minimum educational standards set by impartial authorities in the particular field. It also means, first and foremost, that the school clearly has stated educational goals and the methods for achieving those goals. In the case of any vocational high school or college, the goals should be to teach each student a skill and to make sure the student obtains a job practicing that skill. Without such clearly stated goals and effective methods for achieving them, no school can obtain accreditation. Every good high school and college seeks accreditation by one of the six regional accreditation associations for schools and colleges listed in Appendix A on pages 147–149. Lack of school accreditation almost always means substandard education. Don't even bother to continue your evaluation if a school is not accredited. Carefully check that any private trade school you're considering is accredited by the Accrediting Commission of Career Schools and Colleges of Technology, 2101 Wilson Boulevard, Arlington, VA 22201 (http://www.accsct.org) and that its owners are approved by the Better Business Bureau and Chamber of Commerce. Check also that the school has been in business for at least 20 years in the same general location. In some areas, some proprietary schools may be set up by con artists, eager to steal student funds. All legitimate trade schools should be accredited. Appendix A lists the names, addresses and telephone numbers of the various school accreditation agencies and associations. Part II on career opportunities gives the names of professional associations that also accredit specific occupational training programs. There is one possible exception to the accreditation rule: Some small companies that train their workers may not have formally accredited training programs. Nevertheless, it's important to evaluate the training they offer as best as you can. Check on the company's reputation in the community by calling the

Better Business Bureau and the Chamber of Commerce and by asking employees what they think of the training they received. If you're looking at vocational schools, be certain they are accredited by one of the agencies listed in Appendix A.

2. **Program depth.** With some exceptions such as bartending, which is taught in a single two-week course, a program that offers fewer than four courses in most occupational areas is probably only providing superficial training, which won't teach you how to be a master craftsperson. Check on the number of advanced *second-level* and *third-level* courses, which offer specific *job* and *career* training as well as *skill* training. A course in basic welding, for example, probably isn't enough to get you a job as a welder even though it teaches you a basic skill. For a welding program to have any market value, it must have courses that show you how to weld parts and materials for *specific jobs*. Vehicle-repair companies usually don't hire "welders"; they hire welders who know how to work on vehicles. So, make sure the program has advanced "occupationally specific" courses—and that usually means at least four courses (20 credit hours) in each area.

   In terms of the "return on your investment," the more courses you take in your major, the better chance you'll have of getting a job with higher wages. Indeed, every additional 30 credit hours in your major will increase your wages 12.2 percent, which is a better return on your investment than you usually can get on Wall Street. Don't consider any school that can't offer you enough credits to get a good job with good pay—or a school that has not been in business for 10 to 20 years at the same location.

3. **Ties to other vocational education institutions (for high schools only).** If you're looking at a program at a comprehensive high school, be certain it has ties to a nearby vo-tech high school or community college program in the same field (see cooperative education and "two-plus-two" programs in chapter 1) so that you can get enough credits to get a good, high paying job.

4. **Integration of theoretical and applied aspects of vocational instruction.** Top-quality high school and college programs link what they teach in classrooms to on-the-job training and application. It's not enough for a school to have a small "shop." It must tie its vocational instruction to a cooperative education program (see chapter 1) with local employers in the same field and thus link formal school training with work experience.

5. **Up-to-date equipment.** Although few schools or colleges can afford to replace equipment annually, good programs offer students the opportunity to work with "state of the art" equipment that they will encounter on the job. There's no point learning auto mechanics on a Model-T Ford! More than 45 percent—nearly half—of the vocational high school teachers in America say they have little or no access to computers in their classrooms, and more than one-quarter of those teachers say their curriculum materials and standards are more than two years old. Two years is a lifetime in today's fast-moving technology.

6. **Integration of academic skills with vocational skills (does not apply to proprietary trade schools).** Every job today requires a firm knowledge of oral and written language communication skills as well as skills in computation and problem solving and a knowledge of basic principles of science and technology.* A top-quality vocational school teaches these and other academic skills along with vocational skills, because there is a direct connection between academic disciplines such as science and laboratory experiments, economics, computer science, mathematics and communication and real-life work such as accounting, agriculture, clerical and secretarial work, construction, electrical

---

* Leading educators agree that a basic course in Principles of Technology should explain the concepts of force, work, rate, resistance, energy, power, force transformers, momentum, energy converters, optical systems, transducers, time constants, vibrations and radiation. In evaluating any vocational education program, be certain that a Principles of Technology course is included and that it covers those topics.

service, food service, graphic arts, health services, marketing, mechanics, metal fabrication, transportation and other occupations. Good vocational education programs have the same academic skill requirements as college prep programs. One irony of the American job market is that despite increasing shortages of technically trained workers, too many U.S. schools are graduating uneducated, unskilled young people who are unable to cope with the expanding technology of the workplace. Every job in modern society will require that you are able to read and write well, that you are computer "literate," and that you can make logical decisions and act on the basis of complex data. That's why it's so important for you to evaluate carefully any vocational education program you're considering. As the U.S. Department of Labor explains in its *Occupational Outlook Handbook,* "The connection between high unemployment rates and low levels of education shows the importance of education in a job market that increasingly requires more training." An astounding 23 percent of Americans can't read, write or calculate adequately to hold a permanent job. Make certain you do not join them.

7. **The World of Work.**   Good schools now teach both academic and vocational students two courses called "The World of Work." One is a standard prevocational education course that explores a dozen or more "job clusters"—agriculture, manufacturing, health care, and so on— then explains the function of individual jobs within each cluster. The second course in "The World of Work" curriculum shows you how to look for jobs, write résumés, fill out job applications, have job interviews and handle all other details of looking for, finding and keeping a job. It also teaches basic job skills such as promptness, proper behavior and relationships on the job with coworkers, employers and clients. More employees are fired because they can't get along with others than for any other reason. A school that doesn't have courses on "The World of Work" is not doing a good job for its students.

8. **Faculty quality.**   Teachers in vocational education should have worked in the trades they teach and should continually update their skills. Almost two-thirds of all high school vocational teachers have had no work experience in the fields they teach! You have a right

as a consumer to ask the principal of any school or the director of vocational education whether that is indeed the case. A good school gladly will give you a list of its faculty and their credentials. If not, look for another school or program.

9. **Job placement office.**   A hallmark of quality in all vocational education programs is an *active* job placement office with skilled *job counselors*. They're not the same as guidance counselors. Job counselors have in-depth knowledge of and *ties* to the job market. They'll study your qualifications, help you write a good résumé, then personally *contact* prospective employers for you.

10. **Performance information.**   Top-quality schools and colleges measure how well their students and graduates are doing, and they are proud to share this data with prospective students. Availability and display of performance results are thus two other educational quality hallmarks of any vocational school. Any hedging about such performance results—any failure *to be specific*—is a clear signal that the school is *inferior*. So walk away! The type of data every good vocational school proudly displays—completion rates, job placements, earnings of graduates, and so on—are discussed under "Educational Results." Any vocational school or college that says it doesn't have this data or that the information is confidential is either not truthful or incompetent. In either case, you'll be wasting your time and money by attending. Beware of exaggerated word-of-mouth claims. Recruiters for some vocational schools often claim their graduates earn $50,000 or even $150,000 the first year after graduation. Make them show such statistics in writing and provide references to back them up. If they hesitate or refuse, walk away!

II. EDUCATIONAL RESULTS

1. **Completion rate.**   In evaluating any vocational education program, it's important to know how many students complete the program. A high drop-out rate (more than 25 percent) may reflect a poor program, which is unable to sustain student interest.

2. **Test scores and certification rates.**   A key measure of program quality is the percentage of graduates that successfully earns state certification or licensing in a field of study. If the certification rate is less than 75 percent, the program may either be teaching obsolete skills or may be poorly taught. Where no state certification is required, many states nevertheless require schools to administer tests of knowledge and skills in the field studied. Unfortunately, most high schools don't know how their graduates do after graduating, and that indifference is a sign of a poor-quality school. A good school knows and will gladly tell you how its students have performed on certification tests or on tests that measure competency or employability—in writing.

3. **Job placements *and* the degree to which those placements are *training-related.*** The quality of job placement assistance is the third important element in evaluating performance results of a vocational education program. After all, if you can't get a job with the training you get, what good is it? Any school or college whose placement service can't find jobs for at least 80 percent of its students either has a poor placement service or is offering inferior training. Nor is it doing a good job if it places its graduates in jobs *unrelated* to their training. There's no point in learning auto mechanics at a school that can only get you a job as a dishwasher after you graduate. Again, these schools don't know how or what their graduates are doing. Good schools do.

4. **Average starting wage for graduates and average wage at regular intervals thereafter.** A school that does not follow up on the effectiveness of the training it gives its students may be inferior. So, if the program director doesn't know or won't reveal these figures, try to find a better program. The *average* starting wage for graduates of a good vocational or technical school should be at least twice the minimum hourly wage.

5. **Duration of employment and unemployment among graduates of the program.** Why bother to enroll in a program whose students end up on unemployment lines? You have a right to know whether

the program you sign up for is an effective one. If it isn't, don't sign up! There are many other routes to success.

Regardless of what school catalogs and school officials may say about the effectiveness of their program, it's important to protect your interests by double-checking their claims independently. Be especially careful to double-check the educational quality, educational results and accreditation of proprietary schools, that is, the private trade schools that frequently advertise in the media. The best way is to call or meet a few former students and local employers and ask them what they think of the vocational education program at the school you're considering. In the case of graduates, ask them how they're doing. Did the school get them their jobs? Has the training proved useful? Could they have succeeded without the training at school? In other words, did they get their money's worth from the school? In the case of employers, ask how well graduates from the program are doing, how far they've advanced at the company, what they're earning after one, two, five or ten years, and how long they usually last at the company. Don't put 100 percent faith in what the school tells you. Check out some of the school's claims yourself! If a school won't give you a list of graduates or employers, walk out. Cross them off your list. If local companies say they don't know anything about the program or if they're reluctant to discuss it or are unenthusiastic about it, there's probably something wrong. People seldom hesitate to compliment good programs, but they do hesitate to criticize bad ones for fear of lawsuits. If you run into this kind of reluctance after two calls to local companies, pick out a third one—one you'd really like to work for—and ask for an interview with a personnel representative. At the interview, simply ask what qualifications you'd need to get the job you want. Then ask where they think you could get the best training. If they fail to mention the vocational education program you were considering, you know it can't be very good and won't help you get a job at that particular company.

Preliminary Evaluations

Before going to the trouble of making an in-depth evaluation of a school or its program, you can probably save yourself a lot of time and effort by simply getting a course catalog and doing a preliminary evaluation that will allow you to eliminate the poorest schools and programs. Most school course catalogs will give you enough information to fill most of the checklist on page 34 and thus help you decide if the school is good enough to warrant an in-depth evaluation. If it is, arrange to visit the school and interview the program administrators and a few teachers who can give you the answers to all the questions on the checklist. Then, if you still feel the program is a good one, double-check by contacting some local employers as suggested earlier.

Cross off your list any school without a course catalog and complete descriptions for each course—and, except for one-course trades like bartending, cross off any program that doesn't offer at least four courses in your chosen vocational area, with at least two advanced level courses or two courses that tie into advanced education at a nearby community college (tech-prep).

SELECTING THE "RIGHT" PROGRAM—FOR YOU

In general, the "right" program for you is the one that will get you a good job after graduating and put you on the road to a happy and successful career. Employers simply don't hire and keep poorly trained employees. So, after deciding what type of career interests you most, go to the people you'll eventually work for and ask them about the type of education and training they either require or prefer. Then find out if it's available locally. It's also a good idea to contact trade associations and professional organizations in the fields that interest you. Where available, their names and addresses are listed with each occupation in Part II on career opportunities.

As pointed out earlier, many communities in the United States simply don't have outstanding vocational education facilities such as area vocational schools, two-plus-two programs, technical institutes or employee/union apprenticeship programs. That leaves most available opportunities for vocational education limited to comprehensive high schools, most of which have inadequate vocational training programs that will only give you a taste of knowledge without any of the in-depth training you'll need to get a good job in the field you want to enter. Indeed, signing up for vocational studies in many high schools could actually hurt your chances of getting a job in the field you like when you graduate. That's because most comprehensive high schools spend more money on academics than on vocational education, and, as mentioned earlier, they assign their best, highest paid teachers to students studying for academic diplomas in "the academic track." That means students studying for vocational diplomas or general diplomas might get the educational leftovers. That's tragic but true, and it's something you may have to face and respond to appropriately if you plan to succeed in your chosen field. By choosing the vocational track in many high schools, you may get poor vocational *and* poor academic training—and that's an educational combination almost guaranteed to lead to unemployment after you graduate.

PICKING THE RIGHT HIGH SCHOOL COURSES

If you have a choice of courses in any basic subject—English, math, computer science and so on—always pick the most demanding level you can handle. There is no way to emphasize enough the importance of staying out of low-level academic courses—the ones everybody calls "easy math" or "math for dumb kids." You know the ones I mean. *Avoid them at all costs!* Any guidance counselor, teacher, or fellow student who urges you to take such courses in high school is insulting your intelligence and threatening to condemn you to a life of unemployment and poverty. More than 30 percent of American high school students fail to graduate, and most of them come from these undemanding, boring "easy" courses. More than half of these dropouts are unemployed. Any friend who tries to convince you that the easiest high school courses are fun is no friend, and any guidance counselor who says you'll be "better off" in such courses is lying. You'll be worse off. You'll pass the course, but you'll be worse off. It may be a struggle, but take the most difficult courses you possibly can.

"But," you may be asking yourself, "why bother working hard at high school if I can graduate by taking the easiest courses and still go to college?"

It's true that almost all community colleges and most state colleges and universities admit students on a first-come, first-served "open enrollment" basis. Almost anyone can get into a community or state college or technical institute regardless of the courses they took in high school or their high school grades. But getting *into* college won't get you a good job. You'll have to get *out* of college to do that. You'll have to *graduate* from community or state college, and there simply is no way you'll succeed if you took the easy way out in high school with easy courses that demanded less than your best effort. That's why more than 40 percent of all college students never finish. They can't. They didn't get a quality high school education to do so—probably because they thought too much about college *entrance* requirements and too little about college *exit* requirements and the type of high school preparation needed to fulfill those requirements.

Most high school students have unrealistic expectations about college, largely because guidance counselors only tell them about entrance requirements and seldom discuss exit requirements. A few years ago, Pennsylvania State University surveyed 18,000 incoming freshmen and found few that had any realistic idea about the requirements for completing their college programs. About 98 percent expected to earn B averages or better at college and 61 percent thought they'd only have to study about 20 hours a week or less. In reality, only about 10 percent of students at colleges such as Penn State earn B averages or better, and most students have to study at least 30 hours or more each week.

Community colleges are seldom as academically demanding as schools such as Penn State, but the expectations of high school students headed for community colleges are no less unrealistic than the Penn State students surveyed about their expectations. The point is not to let the ease of entry into college convince you not to take demanding courses at high school. You'll need that firm academic grounding to fulfill the college's *exit* or graduation requirements. So again, don't let a friend or guidance counselor talk you into taking the easiest courses simply because they meet all the college entrance requirements. Over the long term, they will prove useless and the preceding statistics prove that.

Be just as careful about enrolling in vocational studies in any comprehensive high school. No matter how good the school administrators, guidance counselors and teachers say the vocational program is, make certain *you* carefully evaluate the program and the courses offered. *Most vocational education in comprehensive high schools is substandard.* I can't emphasize enough the importance of relying on your own evaluation and not that of a guidance counselor, teacher or school administrator. Let's be realistic: It's unlikely that any counselor, teacher or school administrator will tell you, "Our vocational courses are not adequate, our program is quite poor, and I don't think you'll learn enough to get a good job when you graduate." So, use the rules previously listed and the easy-to-use checklist on page 34 to do your own evaluation; talk to graduates of the program; and get the opinions of local employers. Trust nothing else.

WHAT IF THERE ISN'T ANY GOOD VOCATIONAL EDUCATION?

Let's say your evaluation of the high school vocational education program shows it to be mediocre or poor. What course can you take to achieve your career goals? The best answer may be to postpone your vocational education plans and take advantage of what your high school can offer—namely, a firm grounding in academics in the college prep program.

Most businesses and industries now are demanding that the men and women they hire *for all jobs* be skilled in written and verbal communication, that is, English and perhaps a foreign language such as Spanish. Employers also insist that applicants have a firm command of mathematics and basic principles of science, a good knowledge of history and social studies and a command of basic computer operations. That means that vocational education students must have just about the same high school academic background that students headed for four-year colleges have. The importance of academics is that they teach students how to learn, and employers rank the *ability to learn as the most important skill* they seek in employees, regardless of the jobs they perform.

Language, math, science and computers are the tools of understanding. With a broad knowledge of academics, you can read complex instructions and understand the mathematical and scientific principles of almost any trade. You can learn almost anything, and that's the type of person American industry needs today, because rapid technological advances are making many jobs obsolete. *Careers* aren't becoming obsolete but the *jobs* are. Let's say you trained to be a secretary by learning shorthand and typing.

Most of that training could prove worthless in a company that replaced most of its typewriters with word processors, computers and other high-tech equipment. Word processors and computers did not eliminate secretarial *careers,* but they did eliminate *jobs* as typists and stenographers. Today's secretaries must be administrative assistants with sophisticated skills in communications and business technology. They must be able to write and speak well. Secretaries must have the organizational and mathematical skills needed to maintain records, provide financial data and produce and read spreadsheets, graphs and other reports. And, again, they must be technologically versatile enough to adapt to and use computers and other new electronic equipment.

It's the same story in almost every occupation today. What used to be a relatively simple (although back-breaking) job as a building maintenance engineer (once called janitors or superintendents) now requires a keen knowledge of mathematics and electronics. That's because so many functions in new buildings—climate controls, waste disposal and so on—are electronically controlled from computer consoles. Today's maintenance engineer may have to operate controls for a 100-story skyscraper or a complex of 1,000 or more apartments. That takes a sound education in English, math, basic science and technology.

That's why business and industry are demanding more generalists these days—men and women who have learned how to learn and how to solve problems. Someone with a firm command of written and oral communication skills, mathematics, basic science, computer technology and keyboarding can easily convert his or her job skills from stenography or typing to computer operations or word processing. But if that person's education was limited to shorthand and typing, he or she faces an enormous period of retraining to keep up with fast-changing technology. Similarly, someone who knows only how to shovel coal into a furnace is ill-equipped to move into maintenance engineering and regulate electronic controls in a modern building complex.

So, if you're still in high school and you have no access to good vocational education in a cooperative education program, a two-plus-two tech-prep program or a regional vo-tech school, postpone your plans. Second-rate vocational courses and lower-level diploma courses will lead only to low-wage jobs, at best, and more likely to unemployment, no matter what your guidance counselor tells you. Pick the most rigorous academic courses you can handle, then plan on getting your vocational education in the best available post-high school program you can find at a community college, a technical institute, a four-year college or an apprenticeship or company training program. Almost every employer today prefers employees and craftspeople with strong academic backgrounds, whether the work is in construction, business, health care or building maintenance. Almost every area of work has gone high-tech, and workers without strong academic backgrounds will find it difficult and, in some cases, impossible to adapt.

In addition to knowing how to learn, employees list the following as some essential employability skills: reading, writing, mathematics, computer literacy, communications, inter-personal relations, problem-solving and reasoning, business economics, personal economics and manual and perceptual skills. In cooperation with employers, community leaders and educators, the Colorado Department of Education put together a master list of "Essential Employability Skills" (Appendix C), which gives a more complete picture of what most employers seek in "the perfect employee." Use it only as a guide, and don't worry if you don't fulfill all or even most of the expectations; it's only meant to give you a more realistic picture.

Just because your high school's vocational courses are mediocre doesn't mean you shouldn't take any. As you can see in Table 5 on page 48, even in states with the strictest graduation requirements, you'll have more than 25 percent of your class time available for electives. That means you can take at least 8 elective courses, and in states with even fewer academic requirements for graduation, you can take as many as 12. That will give you ample opportunity to sample vocational courses and at least get a taste of what work is like in those fields. But don't count on any *one* course to teach you enough to get you a job after high school unless it's part of a broader vo-tech, two-plus-two, tech-prep or cooperative education program.

What If I Don't Know What I Want to Do?

Most young people and many older ones don't know what they want to do. Millions make one or more false career starts, and that's all right. There are five easy ways, however, to pick the right career and keep those false starts to a minimum. The first is to broaden your perspective by examining the thousands of different job opportunities waiting for you after you've obtained the right kind of education and training. Take a look at the job listings in Appendix D to get an idea of how many jobs exist. The huge number is not meant to confuse you; it's only meant to prove that there has to be one or more jobs out there that are right for you. Part II of this book will give you some details of occupations, each of which employs at least a half million or more. To get even more complete details of those jobs and others, consult the 700-page *Occupational Outlook Handbook,* which is published every two years by the U.S. Labor Department Bureau of Labor Statistics. It is available in major public libraries and school guidance offices; or you may buy a copy from the U.S. Government Printing Office web site, http://bookstore.gpo.gov, or you can telephone toll-free (866) 512-1800. You can also access the text online at http://www.bls.gov/oco. Additional information on occupational categories and individual jobs within those categories is available from the various professional and trade associations listed under specific career opportunities in Part II and in Appendix D.

A second way to help yourself discover your own occupational interests is to use as many high school electives as possible to "taste" vocational courses in several different areas, even if your school's vocational program is a poor one. You'll at least get an idea of what type of work you'd be doing in a variety of careers. Some guidance counselors may try to discourage you from using occupationally oriented programs as a career exploration activity, but don't let that deter you. It's your life, not theirs, and you have a right to use your electives any way you wish.

If you have the opportunity, take the prevocational course called "The World of Work," described earlier in this chapter. That's the course that examines career clusters (agriculture, health care, and so on) and the variety of jobs within each. If you decide to go to a vo-tech school or postpone your vocational education until community college, take a few beginning courses in various trades to see which ones you enjoy, and then take advanced courses in those that appeal to you most.

A third way of exploring careers is to visit businesses and factories in your area when on vacation. Many companies gladly talk to visitors and prospective job applicants about their firms and their industries. Some conduct tours on a regular basis. Even if such tours don't produce any career

TABLE 5. A typical four-year academic curriculum in comprehensive high schools leaves a minimum of eight elective courses that students can select from vocational education offerings. Unless a high school offers at least four courses in a specific area or ties its courses to a cooperative education program with local companies, vo-tech school community college vocational education program, it's unlikely that such courses will teach you enough to get a job in the trade you studied after you graduate. But even a mediocre vocational education program can give you an opportunity to sample a number of different occupational areas and help you decide whether to pursue vocational education at more advanced levels.

Subject	1st Year	2nd Year	3rd Year	4th Year
English	Grammar and composition Literary analysis	Grammar and composition English literature	Composition Literary analysis English/Amer. literature	Advanced composition World literature
Social studies	Anthropology Ancient history	Ancient/medieval or modern European history	American history and American govt. The Constitution	Electives
Mathematics	Three years required from among the following courses: algebra I, plane & solid geometry, algebra II & trigonometry, statistics & probability (1 sem.), precalculus (1 sem.) and calculus			Electives
Science	Three years required from among the following courses: astronomy/geology, biology, chemistry and physics or principles of technology			Electives
Foreign language	Three years required in a single language from among offerings determined by local jurisdictions			Electives
Physical education/ Health	Physical education/ Health 9	Physical education/ Health 10	Electives	Electives
Fine arts	Art history or Music history	Art history or Music history	Electives	Electives

ambitions, you'll find them interesting and often exciting. To see tons of molten steel (or chocolate) pouring from huge vats and transformed into a thousand different shapes is a thrill for most people, regardless of whether or not they plan a career in that field.

A fourth effective way to pin down career ambitions is to start from a completely different direction and list your personal interests and hobbies instead of job preferences. Forget about jobs for a moment and think about the activities and interests you enjoy most: sports, music, television, science, medicine, stamp collecting—whatever they are and no matter how far they may seem from the world of work. Make a comprehensive list of those *interests*. Only then should you begin to look at the huge number of jobs from Part II that are available and see which ones would allow you to participate in the areas that interest you most. Let's look at a few examples.

Take the sports and recreation industry. You don't have to be an athlete to have an important job in the sports world. As in any other industry, the behind-the-scenes office administrators and personnel are the people who keep the sports world functioning smoothly: in team offices, stadium and arena management firms, public relations and advertising firms, catering firms and personal agents' offices. For every athlete on the field or in the arena, there are dozens of administrative and clerical workers in team offices handling promotion, travel arrangements, contracts, endorsements, guest appearances and many other behind-the-scenes activities that are as important to the sports world as the games and players themselves. And that's true for every sport. In addition, every sport needs huge staffs to operate stadiums and arenas and run the concessions; and they need aides in the locker rooms and training camps. They need tradespeople—carpenters, electricians, painters, plumbers, millwrights, groundskeepers—to prepare the stadiums and arenas for the different events.

The same holds true in every area of show business, whether it's the opera and classical concert stage, rock-and-roll music or a Broadway theater. An army of administrative and clerical personnel must prepare all the appearance and travel schedules and arrangements, and just as many carpenters, electricians and other craftspeople are needed to build and tear down sets, set up the complex electrical connections for cameras, microphones and loudspeakers and prepare arenas and stages for performers. Few are performers or have any musical or acting talent, but they're as much a part of show business and participate in it as actively as any performing star.

Every industry needs most of the skills listed under career opportunities in Part II, and the best way to assure yourself a happy and successful career is to apply your skills and training in an area you enjoy most. You don't have to limit yourself to traditional areas. Just because you're good at carpentry or electrical installations doesn't mean you have to work in construction or home renovations unless you want to. You can sell your skills anywhere—at the Metropolitan Opera House, on the Broadway stage, at NBC-TV, or in Hollywood, or you can travel with your favorite rock-and-roll band.

And just as every TV station, theater, concert hall and sports arena needs carpenters, electricians, secretaries and other behind-the-scenes professionals, so does every hospital and newspaper and every other organization you can think of, including Congress and the White House. Every doctor, lawyer, architect, governor, senator, vice president and president needs a secretary, often more than one, and clerical staffs. So when considering what you want to do, don't limit yourself to traditional jobs if they don't interest you. Define your interests first, then match your skills to those interests. For example, just because you're a clerical worker doesn't mean you have to work for an insurance company if insurance doesn't interest you. Filling out job applications at a Hollywood studio or New York City publishing company is no different from filling them out elsewhere. So pick the businesses you enjoy the most. In every area of work, there are more "stars" behind-the-scenes than there are on stage.

The same principle holds true in less visible fields. Let's say you love science or medicine but don't want to go through years of study needed to be a scientist or doctor. Again, there are thousands of administrative support opportunities in hospitals, laboratories, pharmaceutical firms and government agencies involved in science and medicine. If law interests you but you don't want to spend seven years studying to become a lawyer, the huge court systems at city, state and federal levels all need clerks, secretaries, paralegals, carpenters, plumbers, electricians, maintenance personnel, security guards and a host of other support personnel. Most of the people that keep the court house doors open are not judges and lawyers.

Remember that if you work in a field you love, you'll do a better job and be more successful at it. Don't forget that your hobbies can also provide job opportunities. There are many jobs in stores that sell stamps to stamp collectors, coins to coin collectors, books to book lovers and diamonds to diamond lovers.

Finally, a fifth way of helping you choose the right career is to pick the type of people you'd most like to be with perhaps as much as eight hours a day, five days a week, 50 weeks a year. You'd better be with people you like; otherwise you'll wind up miserable, no matter how interesting the job. Let's say you like children. Well, again, that same army of administrative support personnel and craftspeople is needed in schools, pediatric hospitals and children's institutions. If you prefer a more scholarly world, universities and colleges offer many jobs for secretaries, clerks, laboratory technicians, maintenance staffs, craftspeople, security personnel and others. So here again, the principle of picking the right career is to choose the world in which you want to work and adapt your skills to that world. Pick your own world—even if it's in the circus—rather than letting the world pick you.

WHAT IF I HAVE NO SKILLS?

That's what vocational education is all about—to teach you skills. First, get that command of academics discussed earlier. Next, pin down your interests. Then, look at the types of jobs available under each area of interest. Finally, visit a company involved in that area of interest for a first-hand look at available jobs. You'll almost certainly find one and probably more that you'd like to do and could be good at. Then, it's simply a question of learning the particular craft, either at the appropriate vocational school or perhaps at the job itself in a company training program.

WHAT IF I DROPPED OUT OF SCHOOL?

If you dropped out of school, it's easy to catch up. Every state offers a High School Equivalency Testing Program for adults who have not completed a formal high school program. Usually called GED tests (for General Educational Development), they are given over a two-day period. There are five tests, lasting 45 to 80 minutes. Test 1 measures spelling, punctuation and grammar skills and the ability to organize ideas in clear, correct sentences. Test 2 measures understanding of social studies, and asks for the interpretation of a series of passages dealing with social, political, economic and cultural problems. Test 3 on the natural sciences offers a series of passages about high school science and asks questions that test your ability to understand and interpret each passage. Test 4 deals with the understanding of literature and asks for an interpretation of a selection of poetry and prose. Test 5 tests abilities in mathematics and covers ratios, percents, decimals, fractions, measurement, graphs, plane geometry and algebra.

To pass and receive a high school diploma, you must get a minimum passing score of 35 (out of 100) on each test but earn a total score of 225 for all five, or an average score of 45 per test.

The most difficult tests for people who have been out of school for a while are tests 1 and 5, but it's easy to prepare for those and the other three in adult education classes which are offered (usually free) in many public schools and community colleges to prepare students for the GEDs. Call the principal of the local public high school for information about the courses in your area. Also helpful—and fun to use—are some of the various GED home study books available in major bookstores. Two of the best are Arco's *GED BASICS* (Internet orders: http://www.petersons.com) and Barron's *Passkey to the GED* (Internet orders: http://www.barronseduc.com). Much of the descriptive material is repetitive, but each offers different sets of sample tests, so it's worthwhile getting both books if you're seriously considering taking the GED high school equivalency exam.

After you've completed studying, contact the education department of your state for dates and locations of the tests. Once you've passed them, you can go to almost any college to study a trade, brush up on academics and even learn how to own and operate your own business.

Part Two

CAREER OPPORTUNITIES—AND HOW TO FIND THEM

3

Help Wanted: 22 Million Needed

This chapter gives brief descriptions of the many occupations open
to serious, motivated men and women who don't want to go to a
four-year college or university. Each listing includes the vocational
education and training required. Some jobs don't even require a high
school diploma; others demand an associate degree from community
or junior college or a technical institute. Most jobs fall somewhere in
between. If formal training is required, you'll find the appropriate agencies to contact to make sure you attend an accredited school or program
for that occupation. Where no specialized accreditation agency is listed,
use the accreditation organizations for schools and colleges and for trade
schools (see Appendix A). Contacting the appropriate organizations is
simple: call, send a postcard or send an e-mail. You can send the same
message to each organization. Just say, "Please send me all available information on careers and training in (fill in the career or careers that interest
you)." Then legibly write your name and address. There's no need to make
it complicated or write formal letters.

Under each occupation, you'll find the pay range for beginning and
experienced workers, but they represent national averages. Pay scales may
vary widely from region to region as you can see from Table 6 (on the following pages), which lists average annual salaries by state. Although actual salary averages may have changed slightly since then, their relationships to each other and to the national average have not. Use the factor
for your state to estimate earnings in your area in the occupations that interest you most. Simply multiply the salary figures for each occupation by
the factor for your state to get an approximate idea of what you'd be paid
for that work in your state. For example, you'll find in Appendix D that
average earnings for brickmasons in the United States are $41,840 a year.
If, however, you live in Alabama, where salaries are below the national

average, you'd have to multiply the national earnings by the factor for Alabama in Table 6—namely, .85. That means that brickmasons in Alabama can probably expect to earn only $35,564 a year (.85 × $41,840). Remember, too, that the salaries listed do not translate into cash take-home pay. In addition to deductions for federal and state income taxes and Social Security, there may be set-asides for pensions, health insurance, and other employee benefits, which can add up to 10, 20 or even 25 percent of your total paycheck.

TABLE 6. Here are recent average annual salaries in the United States and in each state, according to the U.S. Department of Labor Bureau of Labor Statistics. Next to each salary figure is a comparison to the national average. Use that figure to multiply the national average salary for the occupations that interest you most in Part II and in Appendix D to obtain the probable average salary for that occupation in your state. Even if average salaries have changed since these were calculated, the relationship of state averages to the national average has probably remained the same.

State	Average Annual Pay	Relation to National Average
UNITED STATES	$36,764	—
Alabama	31,163	.85
Alaska	37,134	1.01
Arizona	34,036	.93
Arkansas	28,074	.76
California	41,419	1.13
Colorado	38,005	1.03
Connecticut	46,852	1.27
Delaware	39,684	1.08
District of Columbia	57,914	1.58
Florida	32,426	.88
Georgia	35,734	.97
Hawaii	32,671	.89
Idaho	28,163	.77
Illinois	39,688	1.08
Indiana	32,603	.89

(continues)

(*continued*)

State	Average Annual Pay	Relation to National Average
Iowa	29,668	.81
Kansas	30,825	.84
Kentucky	30,904	.84
Louisiana	30,115	.82
Maine	29,736	.81
Maryland	39,382	1.07
Massachusetts	44,954	1.22
Michigan	38,135	1.04
Minnesota	37,458	1.02
Mississippi	26,665	.73
Missouri	33,118	.90
Montana	26,001	.71
Nebraska	29,448	.80
Nevada	33,993	.92
New Hampshire	36,176	.98
New Jersey	45,182	1.23
New Mexico	29,431	.80
New York	46,328	1.26
North Carolina	32,689	.89
North Dakota	26,550	.72
Ohio	34,214	.93
Oklahoma	28,654	.78
Oregon	33,684	.91
Pennsylvania	35,808	1.05
Rhode Island	34,810	.95
South Carolina	30,003	.82
South Dakota	26,360	.72
Tennessee	32,531	.88
Texas	36,248	.99
Utah	30,585	.83
Vermont	31,041	.84

(*continues*)

(continued)

State	Average Annual Pay	Relation to National Average
Virginia	37,222	1.01
Washington	38,242	1.04
West Virginia	28,612	.78
Wisconsin	32,464	.88
Wyoming	28,975	.79

As you explore each occupation, remember that most listed occupations also offer management and ownership opportunities once you've acquired enough experience. So don't interpret *salary ranges* as limits on potential *earnings* for each job. Beginning workers in animal care facilities may earn only minimum wage, but owners often earn $50,000 to $100,000 a year. A security guard may start at minimum wage but can earn many thousands of dollars more as an owner of a security agency guarding scores of homes and businesses.

Don't, however, consider becoming an owner or even a partner before you've acquired a thorough knowledge of the business. That usually means at least 10 years' experience. Remember, *nine out of 10 new businesses end up in bankruptcy!* Your odds for success as an individual entrepreneur, in other words, are not very high. Now that does not mean there is no potential for outstanding success as an individual business owner in every field discussed in this chapter. There is, but you have to know what you're doing; you have to know every aspect of every minute operation in the business you consider—and that, as any successful business owner will tell you, requires at least 10 years' experience.

It is not enough, for example, to be a good cook and be able to prepare tasty dishes to run a successful restaurant. To operate a restaurant—or any other business—successfully, you need complex business-management skills similar to those acquired in MBA programs—programs of study leading to a master's degree in business administration. You must know how to keep costs of materials at a minimum, without lowering quality of meals; how to control personnel costs without reducing quality of service; how to eliminate waste—either because of spoilage or excess give-aways to clients. You must be able to pay for and control costs of a thousand things—food ingredients, beverages, furnishings, maintenance, personnel, and a host of other items—and still manage to make a net profit that will be enough to give you and perhaps your family a decent living. Few restaurant owners can do it. Net profits usually amount to less than 1 percent—as they do in a host of other small, independent businesses, including most retail stores, and most owners work 70, 80 or more hours a week to collect their meager rewards. For most people, it's best to work for someone else. The hours are limited, and, if you're good, you'll make far more than you will trying to start your own business.

So, put the idea of starting your own business out of your mind until you've learned all about the business on the job—working for someone else.

The job descriptions below are brief and are only meant to give you an idea of what you'd be doing if you decide to follow a career in that particular line of work. Occupation listings are limited to those employing at least 500,000 people. Remember, though, not all industries listed are expanding, and, in planning your alternative education, you must be aware of which occupations and industries are shrinking in terms of job opportunities and take these statistics into account. Go back to Table 4, page 15, in chapter 1 for a list of occupations with the largest decline in available jobs from 1995 to 2005.

Appendix D lists the anticipated job growth or shrinkage by industry and occupation between now and the year 2012. These figures will give you a clear picture of the opportunities—or lack of opportunities—in every industry and every job within each industry—including the ones you may be considering. As you'll see, farm jobs listed in the section on agriculture will experience a net loss of 273,000 jobs over the next few years—hardly a hotbed of opportunity for someone starting out in life. For more complete details of work in these and thousands of other jobs, get the *Occupational Outlook Handbook* of the U.S. Department of Labor Bureau of Labor Statistics from the U.S. Government Printing Office. Telephone toll-free at (866) 512-1800 or use the Internet: http://www.bls.gov/oco. You can also get more details about each occupation by writing to the trade and professional associations listed under many of the career areas and to leading corporations in each field.

CAREER OPPORTUNITIES

AGRICULTURE

If you love the outdoors, agriculture offers a wide variety of jobs in animal care, farming, forestry, conservation, groundskeeping, nursery work and fishing and hunting.

Animal Care

Feed, water, groom, exercise and train animals of all kinds in a variety of settings—ranches, farms, wildlife refuges and fisheries operated by the U.S. Fish & Wildlife Service (Department of Interior), zoos, circuses, amusement and theme parks, pounds, laboratories, animal hospitals, aquariums, kennels, stables and so on. Clean and repair animal quarters, cages, pens and tanks. Work may include careful record keeping, transporting animals and treating sick animals. All training is on-the-job, although some experience with animals (4-H Clubs, for example) is preferred. Must demonstrate love for and ability to get along with animals. Pay ranges from minimum wage to $20 an hour. Management jobs paying more than $25,000 require a high school diploma with a solid background in math, biology and other sciences plus a community college associate degree or bachelor of science degree from a four-year college or university in animal sciences such as animal hospital technology, animal husbandry or veterinary medicine.

Farm Work

Planting, cultivating, harvesting and storing crops, operating and maintaining farm machinery, tending livestock and poultry, and hauling produce, livestock or poultry to market. No schooling is required. All training is on-the-job. Pay is minimum wage permitted by state and federal laws. Work is seasonal, but workers may be laid off or hired on a day-to-day basis. There is no job security or benefits, but farm work has value as training for eventual ownership of your own farm.

Farm Management

Supervise planting, harvesting, maintenance and other farm operations. A highly technical profession requiring extensive skills and at least a community college associate degree (preferably a four-year college bachelor's degree) in horticulture, crop and fruit science, soil science, dairy science, animal science, farm personnel management or agricultural economics, business and finance. Farm management is as complex as managing any company in any other industry and requires a strong background in high school mathematics and science. Pay at private or corporation farms and ranches ranges between $35,000 and $60,000 a year, with starting salaries dipping below $25,000 and the highest-paid managers earning more than $80,000 a year. But remember that almost 85 percent of America's farms and ranches are managed by their owners. For more career information, contact your local county Agricultural Extension Service. For information about certification as an accredited farm manager, contact the American Society of Farm Managers and Rural Appraisers, 950 South Cherry Street, Denver, CO 80222 (http://www.asfmra.org). For information on agricultural education, contact your state university, which has a "land grant college" that usually provides the best agricultural education in the state at the lowest cost.

Forestry Management and Conservation

Planning, development, maintenance and protection of forests and woodlands, planting and raising seedlings, pest and disease control and soil conservation (control of soil erosion and leaching) for lumber companies, pulp and paper companies and the U.S. National Forest Service (Department of Agriculture) and National Park Service (Department of Interior). Although a bachelor's degree from a four-year college or university is usually required, some companies will hire applicants with a community college associate degree in forestry, agronomy or soil sciences. Hourly pay ranges from $10 to $40.

Timber Cutting and Logging

There are almost two-dozen specialized tasks in timber cutting and logging, including site clearing and cutting, trimming, grading, and hauling trees for major lumber companies, pulp and paper companies and logging contractors who hire out to big corporations to fill seasonal demands. Work is seasonal. All training on the job is given by more experienced workers. No experience needed to start, but strength and physical fitness are essential along with maturity and the ability to work with others as a team in an extremely hazardous occupation. There are only about 80,000 jobs in the forestry and logging industry, with fewer than 15,000 employed as forest and conservation workers and the rest employed in logging camps by logging contractors. One in four logging workers is self-employed—one of the highest proportions of self-employment in American industry. More than half work for the government, usually at the state or local level, and about 20 percent work for private tree farms and other timber-growing companies. Average hourly earnings range from minimum wage to $30 an hour. For more information, contact the school of forestry at your state land-grant college or state forestry association or contact the Northeastern Loggers Association, P.O. Box 69, Old Forge, NY 13420 (http://www.loggertraining.com).

Groundskeeping and Gardening, Caretaking

Maintenance of public or private property with hand and power tools. Mowing, trimming, planting, watering, fertilizing, digging, raking, sweeping, landscaping, building maintenance, pool maintenance, animal care and snow removal. Both full-time and part-time jobs are available, but they are seasonal, except in warm weather climates. Pay averages $7 per hour. Supervisory jobs at public parks and gardens, major resorts and amusement parks and some large private estates usually require some high school or community college courses in horticulture and landscape architecture. Pay ranges from $8 to $15 an hour. Ownership of landscape maintenance firms can produce an annual net income of up to $75,000 or more.

Nursery Workers

Planting, cultivating, harvesting and transplanting trees, shrubs and plants; landscaping client properties. Seasonal, except in warm climates. Pay is minimum wage. Supervisors, with some background in horticulture, plant and insect science and landscape architecture, can earn up to $25,000, and nursery owners can earn far more.

Fishing and "Outfitting"

Catching fish with nets, seines and lines on board oceangoing fishing vessels; cleaning and repairing equipment. Most companies are small, privately owned firms alongside the wharfs at fishing ports. Outfitters, mostly based in western and New England cities, lead tourists on camping expeditions into the wilderness to fish, hunt or simply hike and camp. Work is seasonal. Pay is usually minimum wage, although earnings for fishers may depend on sharing profits from the catch, while outfitters depend heavily on tips. Ownership of a fishing boat or of an outfitting company can increase earnings substantially, although the seasonal nature of the work and economic conditions make this an insecure occupational area.

ARTS AND CRAFTS

Design

If you're creative, imaginative, have an eye for form and color and are a gifted artist, the opportunities in design are endless. Advancement is only limited by your talent, training, imagination and interest. About 40 percent of designers are self-employed. Most designers specialize in one of seven areas: industrial design, package design, textile design, apparel design, set and display design, interior design and floral design. Except for floral design, which you can learn on-the-job or by taking a one-semester course at a community college or trade school, almost all jobs in design require a minimum of two years' study at a technical institute or community college. Almost all designers now use computers to allow for easy changes at the touch of a few keys and to produce three-dimensional images of their designs. So, in addition to formal design training, computer literacy has become essential in all types and phases of design. The median annual earnings of full-time, salaried designers in all fields is more than $52,000, with the range extending from about $30,000 to just under $85,000, and the vast majority earning between $40,000 and $70,000. Self-employed "stars" in every field but floral design earn somewhere in the range of six figures, and the best Hollywood and Broadway set designers can earn more than $1 million. Write to the National Association of Schools of Art and Design, 11250 Roger Bacon Drive, Reston, VA 20190 (http://nasad. arts-accredit.org) for a list of accredited colleges and institutes in the art and design field. Don't consider a school that is not on their list. About one-third of all designers are self-employed. The career opportunities available in design follow.

Industrial designers.   Create and draw designs for every conceivable manufactured product, except apparel, textiles, packaging products, stage sets and buildings. Design cars, home appliances, computers, toys, machinery, medical instruments, office supplies, furniture, sporting goods and other products that must first be in blueprint form before they can be manufactured. Virtually every manufacturer needs industrial designers. It's simply a question of picking the product area that interests you most. Industrial design requires a high school diploma with a strong background in drafting and art and at least a certificate or associate degree in the field from a technical institute, art institute or community college. Many companies and industrial design firms require a four-year college degree. Some require a mechanical engineering degree as well, because industrial designers must have a knowledge of mechanical drawing and computerized design in order to produce all the manufacturing specifications for the products they create. They're not just artists; they often are drafters and engineers and many have graduate degrees. The average base salary of entry-level designers is nearly $30,000, while senior designers with eight years' experience earn an average of nearly $70,000. Industry "superstars," with their own design firms, can earn more than $100,000 a year.

Package designers.   Design boxes, cans, bottles, and plastic packages and their labels and wrappings. Must have in-depth knowledge of every type of paper, paperboard, metal, plastic and composite material and the structural strength of each, whether it can or should be extruded or molded and which shape is most appropriate for the product it must contain. Just look at the enormous variety of packaging in a drug store or supermarket to get an idea of how complex package design is and why many package designers are graduates of four-year colleges and engineering schools. As in industrial design, however, two years at an art or technical institute is sometimes enough to get started; but a knowledge of mechanical drawing and computer-aided design (CAD) is essential. Average income is about $40,000 a year—about $30,000 to start and $50,000 for experienced designers. Again, there's almost no limit to the earnings of design "superstars" and owners of their own design firms.

Textile designers.   Design fabrics for garments, upholstery, rugs, draperies and every other type of textile product. Must have thorough knowledge of textiles, fabric construction and fashion trends. Textile manufacturers are the major employers, and pay is about the same as for package designers. Although a bachelor of fine arts degree is a definite plus, there are ample opportunities for designers with an impressive portfolio and a two-year associate degree or certificate in textile or fashion design from a community college or technical institute.

Fashion designers.   Design coats, suits, dresses, hats, handbags, shoes, gloves, jewelry, underwear and other apparel for manufacturers and department and specialty stores. Strong portfolio of original designs required plus high school diploma (solid background in art and fashion design) and at least a certificate or associate degree in fashion design from a two-year technical institute or community college. Many fashion designers have four-year university degrees and even graduate degrees in art, although some are so gifted they were able to go right to work after high school with no college training at all. It's important to have studied garment construction, however, along with fashion design and sketching. Knowledge of computer-aided design (CAD) is essential. Salaries range from $25,000 to well over $100,000, although there's almost no limit to earnings of top high-fashion designers who work for the most exclusive couturiers or for their own clientele. Other high earners in the field are the costume designers who work for theater, opera, television and movie production companies.

Interior designers.   Plan and furnish the interiors of private homes, buildings and commercial establishments such as offices, restaurants, hotels and theaters. Draw designs for use of interior space; coordinate colors; select furniture, floor coverings and draperies; design lighting and architectural accents. Must have knowledge of architectural drawing. Although many interior designers work on salary ($20,000 to $70,000) for furniture, home furnishings and department stores, builders, hotel chains and major resorts, the majority are self-employed and have their own clients, who regularly redecorate their current homes as well as newly acquired residences. Earnings for independent interior designers are limited only by the number and wealth of clients and a willingness to work hard and to find and get along with new clients. Although training varies, the minimum acceptable is a certificate or associate degree in interior design from a technical institute or community college. For career information, contact the American Society of Interior Designers, 608 Massachusetts Avenue NE, Washington, DC 20002 (http://www. asid.org).

Set and display designers.   Design stage sets for movies, television and theater, store displays in windows and on selling floors and advertising sets. In addition to artistic skills, set and display design requires a thorough knowledge of architecture and structural materials and the ability to draw rooms, buildings or street scenes in a manner that would *appear* to be realistic from the spectator's point of view at a play, in a movie theater, through a television screen or from the sidewalk looking into store windows. Many TV and movie sets that appear true to life are actually miniatures only inches wide. The camera makes them look life-size, and the set designer must know how to create such special effects. That means taking courses in set design at art school. Opportunities in set design range from small theaters and local television stations to Broadway theaters, major networks, Hollywood film studios, independent film and TV producers and advertising agencies. Starting pay for design assistants is seldom more than $20,000, but there's no limit to the income of an experienced set designer, whose name is featured among the credits for major theater, film and TV productions. Display designers earn between $20,000 and $40,000 depending on the size of the department store or advertising agency and whether it is in a small town or major city. Minimum educational requirements are an associate degree or certificate in set or display design from a technical institute or community college. Most theaters and studios, however, prefer a four-year bachelor of arts degree in theater production and set design.

Floral designers.   Arrange flowers in retail flower shops or at hotels, restaurants, banquet halls and other institutional consumers. No high school diploma required, and most florists will train workers on the job. A certificate in floral design from a trade or technical school is a plus, and a degree in floriculture and floristry from a community college is preferred for entry into management or ownership where knowledge of flower marketing and shop management is needed. Salaries range from about $15,000 to start to $30,000 for experienced designers. For career information, contact the

Society of American Florists, 1601 Duke Street, Alexandria, VA 22314 (http://www.safnow.org).

Photography and Camera Work

Here are two exciting areas—with vast, expanding, high-paying job opportunities that don't require a high school diploma or college degree. Both, however, require a deep interest, a lot of imagination, creativity, sense of timing and in-depth technical knowledge acquired either in school or on your own. About 1,000 colleges and vo-tech schools offer courses in photography and camera work, but both are areas where on-the-job training is the primary source of education. The two areas are quite separate, each has its own specialties, and each is a highly competitive field, with far more potential workers than job openings.

Photography involves still shots in portrait, fashion, advertising, industrial, special events, scientific, news or fine arts photography. Photographers may be salaried or work on their own as freelancers; some subcontract their laboratory work, others do their own. Advertising and industrial photographers take pictures of every imaginable person, place or thing—buildings, landscapes, animals, manufactured products, machinery, company executives and personnel for posters, catalogs, shareholders' annual reports, newspapers, magazines, educational presentations and advertising. Job opportunities exist with private photo studios, major corporations, advertising and public relations firms, book publishers, educational institutions and government at every level. Scientific photographers work for educational institutions, corporations in the scientific products and pharmaceutical fields and federal government agencies dealing with scientific research and health. News photographers work for newspapers, magazines, public relations and advertising firms, major corporations and government agencies. Most photographers spend two to three years in on-the-job training as photographers' assistants. Starting pay is usually between $15,000 and $20,000 a year, but quickly moves into the $25,000-to-$35,000 range as you begin taking over routine photographic work yourself. After five to 10 years, top-notch photographers can earn upwards of $50,000 a year. Self-employed photographers can earn much more. Some portrait photographers for Hollywood stars and other famous people earn more than $200,000 a year. For more information, contact Professional Photographers of America, 229 Peachtree Street NE, Suite 2200, Atlanta, GA 30303 (http://www.ppa.com).

Camera operators need no formal schooling, but, as in photography, they must show a deep interest and acquire knowledge on their own. Training is on the job as a first and second assistant to a camera operator setting up equipment and electrical gear. Salaries are similar to those of photographers. Skilled camera operators, either freelance or salaried, earn more than $50,000 a year and are in constant demand. Remember: They are the "eyes" of every film producer and the only way producers and directors can convey what they see to the public. (Don't confuse camera operators with projectionists, who set up and operate projection and sound equipment in movie theaters and are only paid by the hour, usually not more than $8. Like theater lighting projectionists, however, pay varies according to geographic area and whether or not the trade is unionized in that area.)

Art Photography

This is a highly specialized field with few opportunities for any but the most artistically talented. Most art photographers are graduates of fine arts colleges or universities and have simply chosen photography as their medium instead of canvas and paints or stone and chisel. Most art photographers rely on some other form of photography for a living.

Fine Arts

The fine arts include drawing, painting, sculpture, ceramics and a wide variety of crafts ranging from weaving to model making and from wood carving to glass blowing. Although no diplomas or college degrees are required, anyone considering the fine arts must demonstrate talent and have a portfolio to prove it. Most fine artists study art at four-year art schools or liberal arts colleges and universities, and many have graduate degrees. Job opportunities are limitless, although most are in commercial or graphic art as illustrators for magazines, books, newspapers, greeting cards, album covers, posters and films. Advertising agencies and the entertainment industry need artists to draw story boards, which tell a story in a series of pictures before the scenes are acted out. Other opportunities exist in the cartoon and comic strip fields as well as in film animation. Salaries range from $15,000 to $50,000, although earnings reach far higher for self-employed "superstars" in the trade. Graphic designers of publications earn between $20,000 and $25,000. The Graphic Artists Guild (90 John Street, New York, NY 10038 [http://www.gag.org]) has more information about the graphic arts. If you're interested in being an illustrator, contact The Society of Illustrators, 128 East 63rd Street, New York, NY 10021 (http://www.societyillustrators. org). Outside the commercial and graphic arts fields, fine artists may create original works for sale to the public through galleries and other retail outlets. Other opportunities exist in the decorative arts field in major cities and in the souvenir art field in major resort areas where many tourists prefer paintings of the sights they've seen to ordinary snapshots. In the decorative arts, there are many decorative arts houses in major cities that hire artists to create or reproduce paintings to size, that is, to fit a particular client's wall space in various areas of an apartment or house.

There are fewer opportunities for sculptors than painters. Most opportunities for three-dimensional art are in architecture, the production of public monuments, religious sculptures and mortuary art and existing statuary restoration. Artists' earnings are unpredictable and vary widely, from "starvation" wages to millions.

BUSINESS ADMINISTRATION— ADMINISTRATIVE SUPPORT OCCUPATIONS

This broad category of clerical operations critical to virtually every business and organization includes adjusters (customer complaints), account and bill collectors, advertising clerks (taking orders), bank tellers, billing clerks, bookkeepers, brokerage clerks (Wall Street firms), cashiers, computer operators, court clerks (see Government Service), credit checkers and loan authorizers, customer service representatives (telephone companies, other utilities and businesses), data entry clerks, company dispatchers (scheduling, dispatching workers), emergency dispatchers (police, fire, ambulance—see Government Service), file clerks, general office clerks, hotel desk clerks and cashiers (see Hospitality), insurance claims and policy processing clerks, mail clerks, messengers, meter readers, order clerks, payroll clerks, production planning clerks, real estate clerks, reception and information clerks, reservation and travel clerks, statistical clerks, traffic clerks (shipping, receiving and inventory), travel ticket agents, secretarial positions, stenographers, telephone operators, typists and word processor operators and many others.

Clerical support is essential to every organization in this country—every school, every corporation and business and every government agency—even the White House. Clerks in every organization are responsible for handling the data that makes that organization function. They receive, classify, store (in computers or file cabinets), distribute and retrieve all essential information and paperwork flowing through the organization. The paper they handle may be cash in the case of bank tellers, insurance claims in that industry, purchase orders, invoices and incoming and outgoing checks in every organization and airline tickets and reservation confirmations in the travel business. In addition to handling data, clerks are often "the front line" in an organization's dealings with clients and the public, greeting them over the telephone or in the reception area and either handling client needs themselves or referring clients to the right people or departments. Clerks are the heart of almost every organization, and no organization can function without their skills.

Technological advances, however, have muddied the waters of business administration, and many jobs have been eliminated by new machines and electronic devices. The copier alone has put thousands of typists out of work. The personal computer has eliminated and will continue to eliminate thousands of other clerical jobs; and automatic, computerized telephone answering devices are putting operators out of work. But the elimination of a job does not necessarily mean the elimination of a career, especially in business administration. That is why those entering this career must now get a broader education than many high schools offer. That is why it's essential to evaluate business education courses very carefully. It's essential to check with local employers and graduates of any business education program to determine its value. At most high schools, it will prove far more worthwhile to take good academic courses in English composition and writing skills than to learn obsolete vocational skills that no employer can use.

The fastest growing sector in business administration is customer service, where service representatives play a critical role interfacing between the company that employs them and company customers. Customer service representatives have become essential frontline workers for a wide variety of companies—insurance and credit card companies, retailers, banks, etc. They're the people who have to reply to customer inquiries about products and services and resolve problems and complaints. Working conditions are usually outstanding, with a private cubicle for each representative, who works with telephones, fax, e-mail, and regular mail. Because so many customer service centers operate 24 hours a day, seven days a week, working hours are enormously flexible and offer great opportunities for part-time workers. Pay averages more than $26,000 a year but ranges from just under $20,000 to as high as $45,000. Training is on-the-job, but, because they will work constantly with the public, applicants need to display strong skills in verbal communication, listening, problem solving, keyboarding, writing, spelling, and grammar. They must also come to the job with a warm, patient manner.

Unless your high school has a strong program in business administration, the best way to a successful career in this field is to take a strong academic program in high school and a strong business administration program at a community college. Anyone planning a career in business administration needs a broad background in technology, and that means high school math, science and English and the study of computers and electronic office equipment either in high school or community college or both. An associate degree in business administration from a community college will help you get a better job and prepare you for a career in which you can shift easily from one job function to another as technology eliminates some jobs but creates others. Here are the salary ranges for a sampling of administrative support occupations:

Adjusters, investigators and collectors	$29,000–60,000
Bank tellers	$15,000–30,000
Cashiers	$6–12/hour
Clerical supervisors and managers	$25,000–60,000
Computer and peripheral equipment operators	$20,000–50,000
Customer service representatives	$20,000–45,000
General office clerks	$15,000–35,000
Information clerks (receptionists, new-account clerks, reservation and ticket agents, hotel and motel desk clerks, etc.)	$18,000–35,000

(continues)

Postal clerks and mail carriers	$35,000–47,500
Record clerks (bookkeeping, order, billing, filing, personnel, etc.)	$20,000–30,000
Teacher aides	$12,500–30,000
Telephone operators	$7–15/hour
Data entry and information processing clerks	$17,000–40,000

The U.S. government pays office clerks an average of $27,750 a year if they are high school graduates and have had six months' experience. Clerical supervisors earn up to $45,000 a year.

COMPUTER INDUSTRY

Computer and Peripheral Equipment Operators

Computer operators have opportunities in areas that range from small businesses, where the work may be simple word processing and bookkeeping, to huge corporate facilities, where the work will involve mainframes and far-reaching computer networks. Computer operators must load tapes, disks and paper, monitor the control console and respond to messages. Most training is on-the-job, but applicants must come with a basic knowledge of computer operations learned either at high school or a post–high school business school. Average starting salaries for computer operators range from just under $30,000, but once you've logged some experience, expect to see salaries reach $50,000 or more for jobs with heavy responsibilities at larger companies. The average salary for computer operators employed by the federal government is more than $41,000. For career information, contact the Association for Computer Operations Management (AFCOM), 722 East Chapman Avenue, Orange, CA 92860 (http://www.afcom.com).

Computer (Automated Teller and Office Machine) Repairers

Often called computer service technicians, computer repairers usually need a two-year associate degree in electronics, available in any of the thousands of community colleges, technical institutes and cooperative education programs. Whether you work with computers, ATMs or such office equipment as copying machines, you'll need a basic knowledge of electronics, and, if you work as a field technician repairing customer equipment, you'll need good "people" skills that allow you to calm and get along with irate customers. Entry-level employees can expect on-the-job training. Average pay is about $16 an hour but ranges from as low as $10 an hour to as much as $30 an hour. Certification is a plus. For information on careers and certification, contact ACES International, 5241 Princess Anne Road, Virginia Beach, VA 23462 (http://www.acesinternational.org); Computing Technology Industry Association, 1815 South Meyers Road, Oakbrook Terrace, IL 60181 (http://www.comptia.org); Electronics Technicians Association International, 5 Depot Street, Greencastle, IN 46135; and the International Society of Certified Electronics Technicians, 3608 Pershing Avenue, Fort Worth, TX 76107 (http://www.iscet.org).

Semiconductor Processors

You'll need a solid mastery of math and physics in this field, and, although a high school diploma is all you need to start, a one-year certificate program in semiconductor technology at a community college is a big plus for getting a job. The work consists of manufacturing thin silicon wafers, or disks, eight to 12 inches in diameter, on which automated equipment imprints microscopic circuitry patterns. When the circuitry is complete, the wafers are cut into dozens of individual microchips for installation in a wide range of machines. Work is conducted in dust-free "clean rooms" where workers wear special lightweight outerwear that prevents lint or other particles from street clothes from contaminating the air. Average pay is almost $15 an hour but ranges from $10 to more than $20 an hour. More information is available from the Semiconductor Industry Association, 181 Metro Drive, San Jose, CA 95110 (http://www.semichips.org) and from Maricopa Advanced Education Center, 2323 West 14th Street, Tempe, AZ 85281 (http://www.matec.org/ops/career.shtml).

CONSTRUCTION TRADES

As in most categories in this section, construction offers endless opportunities to work for oneself, for small or large contractors, for major corporations and organizations, and for municipal, county, state or federal government agencies. Even the White House needs carpenters and plumbers. The construction trades offer opportunities in the city or country building, renovating, repairing and maintaining small structures and large ones, including the world's tallest skyscrapers. Crafts include bricklaying, carpentry, carpet installation, drywall installation and finishing, electric installation, glazing (glass installation), insulation installation, painting and wallpaper hanging, plastering, plumbing and pipefitting, roofing, stone, cement and concrete masonry, structural and reinforcing metal work (erecting steel frameworks of bridges and buildings), tilesetting, paving, heavy equipment operations, road and bridge building, and excavation and loading machine operations. In all areas, a high school diploma is not required, but it is certainly a plus. Today's technology requires a solid background in reading, writing, mathematics and science. The ability to solve problems quickly also is essential. Training can be on the job, but the best training is in apprenticeship programs that last anywhere from two to five years depending on the trade, and include both on-the-job and classroom instruction in subjects such as blueprint reading, layout work, sketching, mathematics, tool and materials technology and safety. Weekly earnings can be quite high, but there's no guarantee of year-round work. Here nevertheless, are the median hourly earnings of workers in a variety of construction trades—when there's work:

Bricklayers	$20.11
Carpenters	$16.44
Carpet installers	$15.67
Concrete masons	$14.74
Construction and building inspectors	$20.01
Construction equipment operators	$16.94
Cost estimators	$47,500/year
Drywall workers and lathers	$16.21
Electricians	$19.90
Glaziers	$15.20
Insulation workers	$13.91
Laborers	$11.90

Painters and paperhangers	$13.98
Plasterers	$15.91
Roofers	$14.51
Sheet-metal workers	$16.62
Structural and reinforcing ironworkers	$19.55
Surveyors	$40,000/year
Terrazzo workers	$13.42
Tilesetters	$17.20

For general information about apprenticeship programs in the construction trades, contact Associated Contractors of America, 333 John Carlyle Street, Alexandria, VA 22314 (http://www.agc.org) and Home Builders Institute, Educational Division of National Association of Home Builders, 1201 15th Street NW, Washington, DC 20005 (http://www.hbi.org).

In addition, the U.S. Department of Labor National Apprenticeship System has a registry of apprenticeships for more than 500 occupations and information on state apprenticeship programs (available on the Internet at http://www.doleta.gov).

GOVERNMENT SERVICE

Village, city, township, county, state and federal government agencies offer secure job opportunities in virtually every category listed in this chapter. Clerical work (see Business Administration) offers the most opportunities, many in especially interesting and unusual areas. Court clerks, for example, must prepare court case dockets, do research and retrieve information for judges and contact witnesses, lawyers and litigants. There are thousands of other job opportunities in government for postal clerks, mail carriers, school crossing guards, teaching assistants, emergency dispatchers, firefighters, highway maintenance workers, police officers, correction officers and other positions. Almost all government jobs require a high school diploma, six months' experience and a passing score on the appropriate civil service examination. Salaries range from minimum wage to over $100,000 a year depending on the job and its responsibilities, the level of government and the region of the country. In general, civil service jobs do not pay as much as private industry, and promotions tend to be slower. But there are far more benefits (health insurance, guaranteed retirement pensions and so on), far greater job security, and pay increases are usually automatic and tied to the cost of living and length of time on the job. For more information, contact the Civil Service Commission or state employment office of your state, county or city and the personnel department of the particular branch of government that interests you most. Contact your local elementary, middle, or high school if you like working with and teaching children. The demand for teaching assistants is soaring, with some 300,000 new positions opening in public schools across the nation. Teaching assistants tutor and assist children in learning class material, from preschool through high school. Educational requirements vary by state and range from a high school diploma to an associate degree from community college—all of which can be obtained over the Internet from the comfort of your own home. Teaching assistants largely work part time, so the job is a wonderful opportunity for parents of preschoolers and school-age children. For federal jobs, contact the personnel department of the individual branch or the local U.S. Office of Personnel Management Job Information Center. The Office of Personnel Management (OPM) is what the federal government calls its civil service. OPM has branch offices and testing centers in most major cities. You can get the location and telephone number of the branch nearest you by calling the toll-free number of the Office of Personnel Management in Washington, DC: 1-800-877-8339; http://www.usajobs.opm.gov. They'll also give you all information about job vacancies, salaries and application procedures. For careers in the U.S. Postal Service, contact your local U.S. Post Office. For careers in protective services, contact your local government authorities and any of the following organizations:

> **Corrections.** For careers on the local level: The American Jail Association, 1135 Professional Court, Hagerstown, MD 21740 (http://www.corrections.com/aja). For careers at the federal level: Federal Bureau of Prisons, National Recruitment Office (http://www.bop.gov).

> **Firefighting and fire protection.** International Association of Fire-fighters, 1750 New York Avenue NW, Washington, DC

20006 (http://www.iaff.org); U.S. Fire Administration, 16825 South Seaton Avenue, Emittsburg, MD 21727 (http://usfa. fema.gov).

Police, detectives, special agents. Contact appropriate federal, state, and local law-enforcement agencies for career opportunities in all but the following federal agencies: FBI, contact nearest FBI office in your state; U.S. Marshals Service, Human Resources Division—Law Enforcement Recruiting, Washington, D.C. 20530-1000 (http://www.usdoj.gov/marshals).

Teacher aides. Contact local school principals. For information on training and certification, contact American Federation of Teachers, Paraprofessional and School Related Personnel Division, 555 New Jersey Avenue NW, Washington, DC 20001 (http://www.aft.org/psrp) and the National Education Association, Educational Support Personnel Division, 1201 16th Street NW, Washington, DC 20036 (http://www.nea. org). For career information, contact National Resource Center for Paraprofessionals, 6526 Old Main Hill, Utah State University, Logan, UT 84322 (http://www.nrcpara.org).

HEALTH CARE

A high school diploma—and an interest in science and helping people—are all you need to take advantage of some exciting and almost unlimited opportunities in the expanding field of health care. An associate degree from an accredited community college or technical institute opens up many more opportunities, of course, but you can get started in the field with a diploma and move on at your own pace by taking the necessary college courses part time. In addition to the specialized accreditation organizations for each occupation listed below, make certain that any health-care program at a community college or technical college is also *accredited* by the Accrediting Bureau of Health Education Schools, 777 Leeburg Pike, Suite 314, Falls Church, VA 22046 (http:// www.abhes.org).

Write to them both when exploring educational opportunities in the health care field. Otherwise you may waste your time and money and find yourself unqualified for state licensing—and a job.

Here are the opportunities in this rapidly expanding field grouped according to minimum educational requirements:

Health-Care Careers Requiring Only a High School Diploma

Dispensing opticians.   Most dispensing opticians learn their trade on the job. All that's required to enter the field is a pleasing personality to deal with patients and a high school diploma with a heavy concentration in math and science. High school physics, algebra, geometry and mechanical drawing are important, because training will include the study of optical mathematics, optical physics and use of precision measuring instruments for fitting patients with glasses. Apprenticeships lasting two to five years are required in 22 states to earn a license to practice. Formal training programs lasting from several weeks to two years are available at community colleges, technical institutes, trade schools and lens manufacturers. For a list of home-study programs, seminars, and review materials, contact the National Academy of Opticianry, 8401 Corporate Drive, Suite 605, Landover, MD 20785 (http://www.nao.org). Earnings for salaried dispensing opticians average about $27,000 a year and range from $16,000 to $45,000. Many experienced dispensing opticians go into business for themselves and earn far more—as much as $100,000 a year in some areas. For more information, contact the Opticians Association of America, 10341 Democracy Lane, Fairfax, VA 22030 (http://www.oaa.org).

Emergency medical technicians (paramedics).   The job requires a high school diploma plus a nine-month training program that includes the following three courses: a 110-hour Emergency Medical Technician's (EMT) course designed by the U.S. government and available in all 50 states and the District of Columbia at police, fire and health departments, hospitals and, as a nondegree course, at medical schools, colleges and universities; a two-day course on removing trapped victims; and a five-day course on driving emergency vehicles. Students must also take a 10-hour internship in the emergency room. For the EMT certificate, graduates of accredited EMT training programs must pass a written and practical exam administered by the National Registry of Emergency Medical Technicians. Earnings range from about $25,000 at the start to an average of about $32,000 a year for experienced paramedics. For further information write to your state's Emergency Medical Service Director at the state capital and to these two organizations: National Registry of Emergency Medical Technicians, P.O. Box 28223, Columbus, OH 43229 (http://www.nremt.org) and National Association of Emergency Medical Technicians, P.O. Box 1400, Clinton, MS 39060 (http://www.naemt.org).

Licensed practical nurses.   Rapid advances in medical technology may soon require a two-year associate degree from a community college. For now, however, most states only require a high school diploma and an LPN license available upon completion of a state-approved program given in high schools, community and junior colleges, hospitals and health agencies. Earnings range from $23,000 to $45,000 a year, depending on the area and the type of employer, and average about $26,500. A list of approved training programs is available from the National League for Nursing, 61 Broadway, New York, NY 10006 (http://www.nln.org). Additional information is available from the National Federation of Licensed Practical Nurses, Inc., 605 Poole Drive, Garner, NC 27529 (http://www.nflpn.org).

Nursing aides and home health-care aides.   Also known as nursing assistants, geriatric aides or hospital personnel, nursing aides are the principal caregivers in most hospitals. They answer patients' call lights, serve meals, make beds and help patients eat, dress and bathe. They provide patients with skin care, take temperatures, pulse and respiration rates and blood pressure and escort patients to various parts of the hospital. Working under the supervision of the nursing and medical staff, they need to complete 75 hours of on-the-job training and pass an evaluation test to receive a certificate and be listed on the state registry of nursing aides. Home health-care aides do similar work in the patient's home. Aides do not need high school diplomas. They represent one of the fastest-growing occupations, with an anticipated 345,000 more nursing aides and 280,000 more home health aides needed by 2012. Earnings of nursing aides average $10 an hour and range from $7 to $14 an hour; home health-care aides average $9 an hour but range from $7 to $12.50 an hour, with tips adding substantially to their earnings. Additional information is available from local hospitals and from the National Association for Home Care, 228 7th Street SE, Washington, DC 20003 (http://www.nahc.org).

Health-Care Careers Requiring an Associate Degree from Community or Junior College or Technical Institute

Cardiovascular technicians.   The job requires a high school diploma with a strong background in health, biology and typing and word processing. Training is on the job and usually lasts eight to sixteen weeks. Licensing by the National Board of Cardiovascular Testing is voluntary but extremely valuable in getting better jobs in this field. Salaries range from about $21,000 a year as a hospital trainee to $56,000 for experienced technicians. Lists of training programs are available from the Alliance of Cardiovascular Professionals, 4456 Thalia Landing Office, Building 2, 4356 Bonney Road, Suite 103, Virginia Beach, VA 23452 (http://www.acp-online.org).

Dental hygienists.   This is an exciting career that yields an average pay of more than $27 an hour, *part time*. That works out to about $45,000 a year for a 32-hour workweek. There is a wide range of opportunities— private dental practice, school systems, hospitals and public health agencies. Hygienists must be licensed by the state. That requires a two-year associate degree from one of several hundred schools of dental hygiene accredited by the Commission on Dental Accreditation of the American Dental Association (ADA) *and* passing a written and clinical examination administered by the ADA Joint Commission on National Dental Examinations. For a list of accredited programs, contact the Commission on Dental Accreditation, American Dental Association, 211 East Chicago Avenue, Suite 1814, Chicago, IL 60611 (http://www.ada.org/prof/ed/accred/commission). For information on careers in dental hygiene, contact the Division of Professional Development, American Dental Hygienists' Association, 444 North Michigan Avenue, Suite 3400, Chicago, IL 60611 (http://www.ada.org).

Medical assistants.   Medical assistants are the chief administrators in offices of physicians, chiropractors, osteopaths and other medical practitioners. They are not *physicians assistants*, who examine, diagnose and treat patients. They are office administrators, whose duties vary according to the size of the practice. They may include answering telephones, greeting patients, updating and filing patients' medical records, filling out insurance forms, handling correspondence, scheduling appointments, arranging for hospital admissions and laboratory services, billing and bookkeeping, etc. Training in medical assisting is available in one- and two-year programs at vo-tech high schools and in community colleges, which teach basic anatomy and physiology, medical terminology, recordkeeping, office practices, accounting and insurance processing. Students also learn laboratory techniques, pharmaceutical principles, first aid, patient relations, medical law and medical ethics. Earnings average about $25,000 a year and range from $18,000 to $35,000 a year. It is a fast-growing field that will add 200,000 new jobs in the coming years.

Medical laboratory technicians. These technicians perform a wide range of routine tests and laboratory procedures in hospitals, clinics, and medical and research laboratories. Training can be on the job, but most lab technicians have at least a two-year associate degree from a community college. Earnings range from $30,000 to $40,000 a year depending on the area of the country and the type of institution. Contact the Accrediting Bureau of Health Education Schools, 777 Leeburg Pike, Suite 314, Falls Church, VA 22046 (http://www.abhes.org) for a list of accredited training programs. Also contact the National Credentialing Agency for Laboratory Personnel, P.O. Box 15945-289, Lenexa, KS 66285 (http://www.nca-info.org).

Medical record and health information technicians. A key figure in hospital care, the medical record technician is in charge of patient medical histories and charts essential for proper treatment and care. Training is available in two-year associate degree programs accredited by the Accrediting Bureau of Health Education Schools, 777 Leeburg Pike, Suite 314, Falls Church, VA 22046 (http://www.abhes.org). Training includes courses in biological sciences, medical terminology, medical record science, business management, legal aspects of medical and hospital practices and computer data processing. After graduation, medical record technicians obtain professional credentials by passing a written exam of the American Health Information Management Association. Earnings range from

$15,000 to more than $25,000 a year. Contact the American Health Information Management Association, 233 North Michigan Avenue, Suite 2150, Chicago, IL 60601 (http://www.ahima.org).

Radiologic (X-ray, CT, MRI, etc.) technologists and sonographers. Technicians in physicians' offices who take routine X-rays are usually trained on the job and need only a high school diploma. The more complex work in hospitals and medical centers requires one to two years of formal training in radiography, radiation therapy technology and diagnostic medical sonography (ultrasound). There are more than 1,000 programs—mostly two year associate degree programs at community colleges and technical institutes—accredited by the Accrediting Bureau of Health Education Schools, 777 Leeburg Pike, Suite 314, Falls Church, VA 22046 (http://www.abhes.org). One of the fastest growing sectors of health care, radiology offers starting salaries of almost $40,000 a year, with experienced radiologic technologists earning more than $55,000 a year. Contact the following organizations: American Society of Radiologic Technologists, 15000 Central Avenue SE, Albuquerque, NM 87123 (http://www.asrt.org) and the Society of Diagnostic Medical Sonographers, 2745 Dallas Parkway, Suite 350, Plano, TX 75093 (http://www.sdms.org).

Registered nurses.   With more patient care responsibilities being handed over to registered nurses, there is growing pressure to make all R.N.s obtain a four-year bachelor's degree. For now, however, there are two other training programs available—a two-year associate degree from community and junior colleges and a three-year diploma program given in hospitals. Both of them, along with four-year R.N. programs at colleges and universities, qualify graduates for entry-level positions as hospital staff nurses. Earnings range from $35,000 to $75,000 and are likely to climb as the demand for nurses grows. Head nurses can earn $75,000 a year or more. Nursing homes pay an average of $45,000 a year, compared with $50,000 in hospitals. Nurses also earn extra pay for working evening and night shifts. Don't confuse a *registered nurse* with a practical nurse (LPN) or any other kind of nurse. To become a registered nurse requires attending an accredited program leading to a degree as an R.N. from one of the more than 1,400 accredited programs and a *license,* which is only available after passing a national examination administered by each state. For more information, contact the American Association of Nursing, 1 Dupont Circle, Washington, DC 20036 (http://www.aacn.nche.edu) and the American Nurses' Association, 600 Maryland Avenue SW, Washington, DC 20024 (http://www.nursingworld.org).

Surgical technicians.   A high school diploma is required for admission to these programs, which last at least nine to ten months when taken on the job in hospitals but extend to two years at community and junior colleges awarding associate degrees. The shorter, in-hospital programs are generally limited to licensed practical or registered nurses with experience in patient care. The work involves preparing patients for surgery, setting up the operating room and passing instruments and other materials to surgeons and surgeons' assistants during an operation. Starting salaries average about $22,000 a year and, depending on education, experienced technologists can earn nearly $40,000 a year. Contact the Association of Surgical Technologists, 7108-C South Alton Way, Englewood, CO 80112 (http://www.ast.org).

HOSPITALITY

Food and Beverage Preparation

Chefs, cooks and other kitchen workers need no formal education to start. They can learn all their skills on the job. But that's the hard way. An easier and better way is to get a high school diploma, a strong background in business mathematics and business administration courses and formal training in either an apprenticeship program or a two-year or four-year college. Apprenticeship programs last up to three years and are offered by professional culinary institutes, industry trade associations and trade unions. Two-year community colleges offer associate degrees and a few four-year colleges and universities offer bachelor degrees. Some high schools offer courses in food preparation, but these seldom have any value for obtaining any but the least-skilled jobs in the lowest-paying sectors of the industry, such as fast-food restaurants. Formal training at an accredited culinary institute or other advanced educational institution is the surest way to a good job. For a directory of two-year and four-year colleges with courses in the food service field, write to the Educational Foundation of the National Restaurant Association, 250 South Wacker Drive, Suite 1400, Chicago, IL 60606 (http://www.nraef.org). Also write for a directory of colleges and schools from the Council on Hotel, Restaurant and Institutional Education, 1200 17th Street NW, Washington, DC 20036-3097 (http://www.chrie.org). There's some duplication in the two catalogs, but it's worth having them both. And finally, write to the American Culinary Federation, P.O. Box 3466, St. Augustine, FL 32084 (http://www.acfchefs.org), which offers apprenticeship programs and certifies chefs at the levels of cook, chef, pastry chef, executive chef and master chef. Earnings in the food preparation field vary widely, from minimum wage for inexperienced beginners to more than $100,000 a year for world-renowned master chefs at elegant French restaurants in cities such as New York or San Francisco. On average, however, food preparation personnel earn between $7.50 and $30 an hour depending on years of experience, position in the kitchen hierarchy and type of restaurant. Fast-food restaurants pay the least—usually minimum wage, regardless of experience. Elegant "white-tablecloth" restaurants usually pay the most but demand the most experience. In many areas, especially in big cities, hotel and restaurant workers must join unions.

Food and Beverage Service Workers

This category includes dining room attendants (busboys and busgirls), bartender assistants, serving persons, hosts and hostesses and bartenders. Most bartenders go to private trade schools for a standard two-week course, but most other food and beverage service work is learned on the job. Most employers prefer applicants with high school diplomas, a solid grounding in mathematics (for accurate handling of meal charges) and pleasing personalities. Pay ranges from minimum wage to $10 an hour for an experienced host or hostess who has been on the job for many years at an elegant "white tablecloth" restaurant in a major city. Average earnings, however, are about $7 an hour, but tips, which run between 10 percent and 20 percent of guest checks for waiters and waitresses, can double the totals. Bartenders earn similar salaries and can also double their incomes with tips. More information on hospitality careers is available from the Council on Hotel, Restaurant, and Institutional Education, 1200 17th Street NW, Washington, DC 20036-3097 (http://www.chrie.org); the National Restaurant Association, 1200 17th Street NW, Washington, DC 20036 (http://restaurant. org); and the Accrediting Commission of Career Schools and Colleges and Technology, 2101 Wilson Boulevard, Arlington, VA 22201 (http://www.accsct.org).

Other Career Opportunities in Hospitality

• Amusement and recreation park attendants, fee collectors, carnival and amusement park ride and concession stand operators, facility preparers at indoor game parlors (billiards, pinball machines, video machines and so on), servers at sports clubs and spas.

• Hotel baggage porters and bellhops.

• Business administration: hotels, amusement and theme parks, restaurants, stadiums and sports arenas. Clerical functions (office clerks, secretaries, reservations clerks, desk clerks and cashiers) are as essential to the hospitality industry as they are to every other industry. Basic training for these jobs, along with cash and materials management, desk clerks, operators, cashiers and receptionists is discussed in the section on Business Administration. Additional training to adapt business administration skills to the hospitality industry should take place on-the-job, although some might want to consider courses in hotel and restaurant administration at a community or technical college. Some institutions, such as Hocking College in Nelsonville, Ohio, operate their own hotel, restaurants, travel agencies and support systems as part of their hospitality programs.

• Housekeeping. See "Janitors and cleaners" under Service Occupations.

• Sports and activities supervision. See Sports and Recreation.

• Maintenance. See "Grounds maintenance" under Agriculture or "Janitors and cleaners" under Service Occupations.

• Theater ushers, lobby attendants, ticket takers, cashiers.

MARKETING AND SALES

Retailing

Retailing offers many job opportunities as cashiers, wrappers, floor and counter sales clerks and stock clerks in all types of consumer outlets, specialty stores, supermarkets, department stores, theaters, laundries, dry cleaners, video rental stores and car rental agencies to name a few. Retail sales represents the nation's fastest growing occupation requiring no formal education. Retailers will need about 600,000 *additional* employees between now and 2012—*not including* the hundreds of thousands of new hires they'll need to replace current workers who quit or retire. All training is on-the-job and applicants don't need high school diplomas, although employers prefer a strong background in mathematics for handling cash accurately and a pleasing personality for dealing diplomatically with customers. To advance into management ranks or to go into business for yourself, however, a high school diploma and at least a community college associate degree in business administration are essential. Some high schools call their vocational programs for retailing "Distributive Education." Don't let the fancy name confuse you.

Here are recent median hourly earnings in five areas of retail sales:

Motor vehicles	$19
Building materials and supplies	$11
Department stores	$8.50
Other general merchandise stores	$8
Clothing stores	$8

If you're interested in training for a career in car sales, contact the National Automobile Dealership Association, 8400 Westpark Drive, McLean, VA 22102 (http://www.nada.org).

Real Estate Agents

Although real estate agents must be licensed in every state and be high school graduates, most states do not require a college degree. All that's necessary is to pass a 60-to-90-hour course that is offered by many large real estate firms and by more than 1,000 universities, colleges, and junior and community colleges. At some colleges, students can earn an associate degree or bachelor's degree in real estate. Average earnings are $30,000 a year, and range from $15,000 to more than $1 million. Earnings are almost all from commission and depend on general market conditions and property values. For career information and a list of colleges offering courses in real estate, contact the National Association of Realtors, 430 North Michigan Avenue, Chicago, IL 60611 (http://www.realtor.org).

Wholesale Sales

Wholesalers, who buy goods from manufacturers and resell them to retailers, have armies of salespeople who sell in two ways: "Inside" salespeople solicit sales by telephone, while "outside" salespeople sell by personal solicitation with visits to retail store owners and managers. The variety of products sold by wholesalers is as wide as the variety of products in any department or discount store. Wholesale trade salespeople usually need associate degrees from community colleges and are then trained on-the-job—first as stock clerks to become familiar with the merchandise the wholesaler may carry and the complex pricing of such goods. Initial training generally leads to "inside" sales jobs, first as an order taker on incoming reorders from steady customers, then eventually as a troubleshooter soliciting telephone orders from customers who have not reordered. After two years on the inside, top salespeople acquire outside sales routes. College courses in wholesale distribution, marketing and business administration can speed advancement into management. Wholesale trade salespeople earn from $30,000 to more than $150,000 a year. Other career opportunities in wholesaling include the range of business administration functions (see Business Administration) and inventory controls and handling stock as it moves on and off company shelves. Stock work is usually a minimum wage job, but salaries improve with increased responsibilities. Contact the Manufacturers' Agents National Association, P.O. Box 3467, Laguna Hills, CA 92654 (http://www.manaonline.org).

MECHANICAL TRADES

The mechanical trades—mechanics, installers and repairers—offer some of the widest opportunities for personal and financial success of any professional area. Mechanics keep America's machinery running. They are the men and women who make it safe for us to fly in airplanes and ride in cars, trucks, transit systems and building elevators; they make it safe to use home appliances and keep our heating and cooling equipment operating; they keep us in touch with the world by maintaining and repairing communications equipment such as telephones, radios, televisions and computers. American industry could not produce the goods and services we all need without mechanics to keep production machinery humming. Indeed, without mechanics, our nation would be unable to function.

Here are just a few of the opportunities in this enormously important field of installation, maintenance and repair: aircraft and aircraft engines, diesel engines, cars and trucks, car bodies, office equipment and cash registers, computers, commercial and industrial electronic equipment (everything from radar and missile installations to medical diagnostic equipment), telephones and communications equipment, television and stereos, elevators, farm equipment, heating, air-conditioning, refrigeration equipment, home appliances and power tools, industrial machinery, heavy equipment, vending machines, musical instruments, boats and motorcycles and small engines. Any piece of equipment you can think of needs an expert who knows how it works to keep it running smoothly and fix it when it breaks down. That person is a mechanic.

Years ago, it used to be easy for everyone with "good hands" to go into the mechanical trades, even without a high school diploma. But like the field of business administration, the mechanical trades have become an area of constant change due to rapid technological advances. As in business administration, automation and other devices are eliminating jobs. They're not eliminating careers—just jobs. The auto repair business, for example, still offers wonderful career opportunities, but the job of hand-tuning engines on most cars has disappeared. The same is true in all areas of the mechanical trades, and that's why today's mechanics must be so well educated.

A high school diploma is virtually a must in every area of mechanical trades along with a solid understanding of mathematics and basic scientific principles (especially physics), and the ability to read and understand complex materials relating to the functioning and repairing of complex machinery and equipment.

In addition to academic requirements, entry into most mechanical trades requires two to four years of solid vocational education either in high school, an accredited trade school, community college or a formal company training program. And finally, at least two to four years on-the-job are needed to reach the status of master craftsperson. The rewards for this investment in time and study can be great. There are specialized mechanics for virtually every industry, many earning $50,000 or more a year. Telecommunications equipment mechanics earn about $24 an hour, aircraft mechanics $21 an hour, farm equipment and heavy vehicle mechanics $18 an hour, diesel engine mechanics $17 an hour, and automotive mechanics $15 an hour. The salary range is wide, the demand is great—and so are the rewards.

As in every other professional area, it's important to get the proper training. What follows are organizations which will send you career information, certification requirements (if any) and lists of accredited schools and colleges for each mechanical trade:

Aircraft

Professional Aviation Maintenance Association, 717 Princess Street, Alexandria, VA 22314 (http://www.pama.org)

Automotive

Automotive Youth Educational Systems, 50 West Big Beaver, Suite 145, Troy, MI 48084 (http://www.ayes.org)

National Automobile Dealers Association, 8400 Drive, McLean, VA 22102 (http://www.nada.org)

National Automotive Technicians Education Foundation, 101 Blue Seal Drive SE, Suite 101, Leesburg, VA 20175 (http://www.natef.org)

SkillsUSA-VICA, P.O. Box 3000, Leesburg, VA 20177 (http://www.skillsusa.org)

Heating, Air-conditioning and Refrigeration

Air Conditioning and Refrigeration Institute, 4100 North Fairfax Drive, Arlington, VA 22203 (http://www.coolcareers.org; http://www.ari.org)

Associated Builders and Contractors, Workforce Development Department, 4250 North Fairfax Drive, Arlington, VA 22203 (http://www.abc.org)

Plumbing-Heating-Cooling Contractors, 180 South Washington Street, P.O. Box 6808, Falls Church, VA 22046 (http://www.phccweb.org)

Heavy Vehicle and Farm Equipment Mechanics (Includes Diesels)

National Automotive Technicians Education Foundation, 101 Blue Seal Drive SE, Suite 101, Leesburg, VA 20175 (http://www.natef.org)

SkillsUSA-VICA, P.O. Box 3000, Leesburg, VA 20177 (http://www.skillsusa.org)

Home Appliance Repairers

International Society of Certified Electronics Technicians, 3608 Pershing Avenue, Fort Worth, TX 76107 (http://www.iscet.org)

Professional Service Association, 71 Columbia Street, Cohoes, NY 12047 (http://www.psaworld.com)

Industrial Machinery

National Tooling and Machining Association, 9300 Livingston Road, Ft. Washington, MD 20744 (http://www.ntma.org)

Millwrights

(Note: Millwrights install and dismantle the machinery and heavy equipment used in virtually every factory in America. They're the mechanics who unpack, inspect and set into place all new production machinery with cranes or whatever other equipment is needed. Earnings can reach well above $30 an hour.)

Associated General Contractors of America, 333 John Carlyle Street, Alexandria, VA 22314 (http://www.agc.org)

National Tooling and Machining Association, 9300 Livingston Road, Ft. Washington, MD 20744 (http://www.ntma.org)

Small Engines (Motorcycles, Boats, etc.)

American Marine and Watercraft Institute, 3042 West International Speedway Boulevard, Daytona Beach, FL 32124 (http://www.amiwrench.com)

American Motorcycle Institute, 3042 West International Speedway Boulevard, Daytona Beach, FL 32124 (http://www.amiwrench.com)

Marine Mechanics Institute, 9751 Delegates Drive, Orlando, FL 32827 (http://www.MMI-Marine.com)

Motorcycle Mechanics Institute, 2844 West Deer Valley Road, Phoenix, AZ 85027 (http://www.MMItech.edu)

Precision Instrument and Equipment Repairers

American Watchmakers-Clockmakers Institute, 701 Enterprise Drive, Harrison, OH 45030-1696 (http://www.awi-net.org)

Association for the Advancement of Medical Instrumentation, 1110 North Glebe Road, Arlington, VA 22201-4795 (http://www.aami.org)

The Instrumentation, Systems, and Automation Society (ISA), 67 Alexander Drive, P.O. Box 12277, Research Triangle Park, NC 27709 (http://www.isa.org)

National Association of Professional Band Instrument Repair Technicians, P.O. Box 51, Normal, IL 61761 (http://www. napbirt.org)

Piano Technicians Guild, 3930 Washington Street, Kansas City, MO 64111-2963 (http://www.ptg.org)

Vending Machines

National Automatic Merchandising Association, 20 North Wacker Drive, Chicago, IL 60606 (http://www.vending.org)

Other Career Opportunities
(On-the-job or Private Trade-School Training Only)

Bicycle repairs, medical equipment repairs, instrument and tool repairs, rail car repairs, rigging, tire repairs, watch repairs.

Additional Information

Accrediting Commission of Career Schools and Colleges of Technology, 2101 Wilson Boulevard, Arlington, VA 22201 (http://www.accsct.org)

Your state labor department (in the state capital) for lists of apprenticeship programs in various trades

Your state employment service (job opportunities)

PERFORMING ARTS

Unlike other professions, there is no sure way to success in the performing arts. Many talented actors, singers and dancers have spent their lifetime waiting tables in restaurants only steps away from Broadway theaters—waiting for the "big break" that never came. And many performers with questionable talents have made millions because they did get a "big break," or perhaps they had the right "connections." In either case, there are factors beyond one's control that can affect careers in the performing arts far more than in many other professions where study and hard work are usually the surest means of success.

Unlike many other professions, too, the performing arts offer opportunities for men and women with widely varying levels of formal education. Many have university degrees; others dropped out of high school and never spent another minute studying their crafts. Obviously, careers in classical music, ballet or theater require years of formal study. That's not necessarily the case for careers in popular music, television or movies. What most successful artists have in common, however, is talent, and most have spent years practicing what they do—whether it's acting, singing, dancing, playing a musical instrument or announcing on radio and television. Those who stayed in school have worked on school and college productions of all kinds or in local theater groups and informal musical groups.

Formal training can be a big help, because it often puts students in touch with professionals and job opportunities. Formal study in most of the performing arts is available at all levels: high schools, community colleges, four-year colleges and universities and private trade schools. For high school students, the finest education in the performing arts is at so-called magnet schools such as LaGuardia High School (once known as the High School of Performing Arts) in New York City. There are similar magnet schools in other major cities, all part of the public school system of their states. But admission is competitive by audition and restricted to the most-talented applicants.

In some states such as North Carolina, magnet schools have boarding facilities for applicants who live too far away to commute. Many community colleges and four-year universities have outstanding departments in one or more of the performing arts. Check with the state superintendent of schools to see if there are any magnet high schools for the performing arts in your state. Use the various guides to vocational and technical schools, two- and four-year colleges to identify those with outstanding music, theater and dance departments. Most guides are available in major bookstores. Among the best for two-year colleges is *Peterson's Two-Year Colleges*, published by Thomson

Peterson's, Lawrenceville, NJ. Thomson Peterson's also publishes a fine directory of four-year colleges, as does Barron's Educational Series, of Hauppauge, NY. Thomson Arco (the same company as Thomson Peterson's) publishes the most complete guide to vocational and technical schools—a two-volume work, with more than 2,600 vocational schools listed by occupational category in a volume for the eastern United States and a second volume for the western United States.

The performing arts also includes behind-the-scenes opportunities discussed elsewhere. These include broadcast technicians (see Technical Trades), administrative and clerical work (see Business Administration), camera crews (see Arts and Crafts, Photography and Camera Work), instrument tuning and maintenance (see Mechanical Trades), set design (see Arts and Crafts, Design) and carpentry and electrical work (see Construction Trades).

PRODUCTION TRADES

Production workers make every product produced by American industry—apparel, fabrics and textiles, toys, furniture, home furnishings, shoes and leather goods, books and publications, tools and machinery, eyeglass rims, dental bridges, jewelry, cars, ladders and every other product you can think of. It's an endless list. Everything you see around you has to be made by hand or machine. The products that are mass-produced by machine are made by production workers who earn between $10,000 and $60,000 a year depending on the area of the country, the specific industry and the skills and training involved. Tool and die makers, who need four to five years of apprenticeship training, are in great demand. They earn about $20,000 to start and average nearly $35,000 after several years. The top 10 percent of their craft earn more than $60,000 a year. Most production workers earn between $12,000 and $15,000 to start. In 2005, earnings for production work averaged $28,000 a year for all industries and ranged from $20,000 to $35,000 a year for workers with five to 10 years' experience. Skilled workers able to deal effectively with people can work their way up to supervisory positions as inspectors, graders, testers and, of course, production line and plant floor supervisors. Those jobs usually pay between $25,000 and $60,000 a year. Almost all training for production work is on-the-job, either in a formal apprenticeship program or as an assistant to a skilled worker who serves as a mentor. Not all industries require workers to have high school diplomas, but in today's world of advanced technology, most manufacturers prefer applicants with high school diplomas and strong backgrounds in math, science (especially physics) and English (for reading complex instructions). Many high schools, vocational schools, community colleges, technical institutes and private trade schools offer formal training in specific production areas. Here is a sampling of the types of production trades and the organizations to contact for more information about career opportunities and training programs.

Metal Workers and Plastic Workers

National Tooling and Metalworking Association, 9300 Livingston Road, Brecksville, OH 44141 (http://www.ntma.org)

Machinists

National Tooling and Metalworking Association, 9300 Livingston Road, Brecksville, OH 44141 (http://www.ntma.org)

Precision Metalforming Association Educational Foundation, 6363 Oak Tree Boulevard, Independence, OH 44131 (http://www.pmaef.org)

Tool and Die Makers

National Tooling and Metalworking Association, 9300 Livingston Road, Brecksville, OH 44141 (http://www.ntma.org)

Precision Metalforming Association Educational Foundation, 6363 Oak Tree Boulevard, Independence, OH 44131 (http://www.pmaef.org)

Welding, Soldering and Brazing

American Welding Society, 550 Northwest Lejeune Road, Miami, FL 33126 (http://www.aws.org)

Precision Metalforming Association Educational Foundation, 6363 Oak Tree Boulevard, Independence, OH 44131 (http:// www.pmaef.org)

Other Career Opportunities in Production Trades

Other production jobs include: assemblers and fabricators, food-processing operations, chemical equipment controllers and operators, chemical plant and system operators, coil winders and tapers, crushing and mixing machine operators, cutting and slicing machine operators, electrical and electronic assemblers, electronic semiconductor processors, kiln and kettle operators, gas and petroleum plant and systems operators, hand grinders and polishers, laundry and dry-cleaning machine operators, machine assemblers, machine feeders and offbearers, miners, packagers, quarry workers, roustabouts (oil field workers), tunneling machine operators, packaging and filling machine operators, separating and still machine operators, shipfitters, tire-building machine operators, stationary engineers and boiler operators, textile and apparel fabrication, furnishing fabrication, woodworking.

The best references for on-the-job training in these occupations are the human resources departments of companies in your area. For nonfactory training programs, the best references are the Thomson-Arco directories of vocational and technical schools (two volumes—east and west) available in major bookstores. The Accrediting Commission of Career Schools and Colleges of Technology, 2101 Wilson Boulevard, Arlington, VA 22201 (http://www.accsct.org) is another basic source for training programs at proprietary schools.

SERVICE OCCUPATIONS

Barbers

No high school diploma is required, but all states require barbers to be licensed. That means attending a state-approved barber school (nine to 12 months), then taking an examination for an apprentice license, working as an apprentice for one to two years and, finally, taking another examination for a license as a registered barber. Barbers seldom earn salaries.

Instead, they earn 60 percent to 70 percent of the money they take in—and they get to keep all tips. Earnings averaged about $20,000 a year in 2005, but ranged up to $40,000 for experienced hairstylists—plus tips. Many barbers own their shops and earn more. A list of accredited barber schools is available from the Accrediting Commission of Career Schools and Colleges of Technology, 2101 Wilson Boulevard, Arlington, VA 22201 (http://www.accsct.org).

Child-Care Workers

Although no experience or formal training is required, most day-care centers and other employers expect workers to have at least a high school education and to have studied some psychology, sociology, home economics, nutrition, art, music, drama and physical education. Moreover, a growing number of employers now require formal training and certification in childcare at the community college level. Many high schools and community colleges offer a one-year training program leading to a Child Development Associate (CDA) certificate. The program is open to anyone at least 18 years old with some child-care experience or related classroom training. For details, contact the Council for Professional Recognition, 2460 16th Street NW, Washington, DC 20005 (http://www.cdacoucil.org). Earnings in child care are low, starting at minimum wage and seldom exceeding $10 an hour.

Cosmetologists (Beauticians and Hairstylists)

Some requirements vary, but all states require licensing, and that means being at least 16 years old, passing a physical examination and graduating from a state-licensed school of cosmetology. Some states require a high school diploma; others only require an eighth grade education. Unlike barbering, cosmetology instruction is offered in both public and private schools. Public high schools and vocational schools usually offer free training combined with useful academic education. Private trade schools, which charge fees, only teach the trade. Students in both public and private cosmetology schools must buy their own tools. Day courses usually take six months to a year to complete, while evening courses take longer. After graduation, cosmetologists must take a state licensing examination, part written and part practical demonstration. Earnings vary widely from area to area but usually average about $19,000 and reach $35,000 or more for experienced professionals. Tips are an important factor, and many cosmetologists in wealthy communities earn between $30,000 and $50,000 a year. Gifted cosmetologists can earn even more working with a private clientele or in the performing arts—television, movies and theater—preparing actors and actresses for performances. For additional information, contact the National Accrediting Commission of Cosmetology Arts and Sciences, 4401 Ford Avenue, Arlington, VA 22203 (http://www.naccas.org) and the National Cosmetology Association, 401 North Michigan Avenue, Chicago, IL 60611 (http://www.salonprofessionals.org).

Homemakers and Home Health Aides

Although a high school diploma is desirable, most agencies only require an ability to read, write and complete a one- to two-week training program as a homemaker/home health aide, which the agencies usually pay for. Some agencies and states require a nursing aide certificate. Earnings range from $6.00 to $12.00 an hour for a 20- to 36-hour workweek. For details on training and career opportunities, contact the National Association for Home Care, 228 7th Street SE, Washington, DC 20003 (http://www.nahc.org).

Building Custodians (Janitors) and Cleaners

Most training is on-the-job, although workers must know simple arithmetic, how to read and write and how to make simple repairs. Shop courses at school can be helpful. No other formal education is required. Earnings average about $15,000 a year and range up to nearly $30,000 a year depending on the area of the country, hours worked and type of employer. About one-third of the more than 2.5 million janitors and cleaners work part time, that is, less than 35 hours a week. The largest employers are schools (including colleges and universities) and private maintenance firms, which clean buildings under contract. These two sectors employ about 20 percent each of the custodial work force. Hospitals and hotels each employ 10 percent, and the rest of the custodial force works in restaurants, apartment buildings, office buildings, manufacturing plants, government buildings and churches and other religious buildings. The field offers out-standing opportunities for experienced custodians willing to study small business management to establish private-home and apartment cleaning services. More information is available from the International Executive Housekeepers Association, 1001 Eastwind Drive, Westerville, OH 43081 (http://www.ieha.org).

Pest Control

This is usually a minimum wage job, although opportunities for self-employment after learning the trade can raise the annual income to between $30,000 and $50,000.

Private Household Workers

Usually no training or formal education is required, although most em-ployers insist on an ability to clean well and/or cook and/or take care of children—skills generally learned while helping with housework at home. Courses in home economics, cooking, child care, child development, first aid and nursing can lead to broader opportunities and better-paying jobs. Two-thirds of the one million private household workers work part time. Earnings range from minimum wage to $10 an hour, depending on the area of the country. Live-in workers employed by wealthy families earn more, between $800 and $1,000 a week plus room, board, medical benefits, a car, vacation days and education benefits, but such jobs require special training at schools for butlers, chauffeurs, nannies, governesses, and cooks.

Security Guards and Gaming Surveillance Specialists

Although no formal education is required, most guards endure rigorous background and fingerprint checks and must be licensed by the state. Train-ing is on-the-job and may require proficiency with weapons. The threat of terrorism is expected to increase the number of jobs for security guards by more than 300,000 over the coming years, while the growth of the casino industry will require tens of thousands more gaming surveillance specialists. Earnings of security guards average about $20,000 a year and range from

$13,000 to $32,000. Earnings of gaming surveillance specialists average about $23,000 a year and range from $16,000 to $36,000. Local and state police authorities usually have the best information on the industry.

SPORTS, FITNESS AND RECREATION

Recreation workers are needed on a full-time or part-time basis at various establishments—commercial recreation areas, hotels, resorts, amusement parks, sports and entertainment centers, wilderness and survival excursion companies, tourist centers, vacation excursion firms, camps, health spas, athletic clubs, apartment and condominium complexes, ocean liners, civic and religious organizations, social service organizations (day-care and senior citizens centers), residential care facilities and institutions, industrial plants and city, state and federal parks. To work at most schools and colleges, recreation workers and coaches must have a bachelor's degree in physical education from a four-year college and a teaching certificate. For other areas mentioned, only a high school diploma may be required along with experience in one or more recreational areas (art, music, drama and so on) or sports. Some jobs, such as lifeguards, require special certification. Fitness trainers and aerobics instructors must be certified to work at most gyms and spas, and some employers require a four-year degree in physical education. For career-track jobs in recreation, most employers require an associate's degree in park and recreation programs (available at several hundred community colleges). Earnings for recreation workers average about $9 an hour but range up to $16 an hour, while fitness trainers and aerobics instructors average about $12 an hour but can reach $30 an hour—and that's without tips, which can be exceptionally generous at upscale fitness centers. For information, contact your local parks department; for a broader picture and a list of academic programs, contact the National Recreation and Park Association, Division of Professional Services, 22377 Belmont Ridge Road, Ashburn, VA 20148 (http://www.nrpa.org).

For information on careers and certification in fitness training, contact the American Council on Exercise, 4851 Paramount Drive, San Diego, CA 92123 (http://www.acefitness.org) and the National Strength and Conditioning Association, 4575 Galley Road, Colorado Springs, CO 80915 (http://www.nsca-lift.org).

TECHNICAL TRADES

Broadcast Technicians

An associate degree from a technical institute or community college is required for operating and maintaining the complex electronic equipment, which records and transmits radio and television programs. Also required is a radio-telephone operator license issued by the Federal Communications Commission after successful completion of a series of written exams. Those entering the field must have strong backgrounds in high school algebra, trigonometry, physics, electronics and other sciences. Starting jobs at small stations pay about $15,000. As a profession, technicians average between $25,000 and $30,000 but can earn $75,000 or more at network-owned radio and television stations. Supervisory jobs can pay well over $100,000 at such stations. For information on licensing procedures, contact the Federal Communications Commission, 1270 Fairfield Road, Gettysburg, PA 17325. For career information, contact the National Association of Broadcasters, 1771 N Street NW, Washington, DC 20036 (http://www.nab.org). For information on certification, contact the Society of Broadcast Engineers, 9247 North Meridian Street, Indianapolis, II 46260 (http://www.sbe.org).

Drafters

Drafting—the drawing of exact design dimensions and specifications of every product and part that is manufactured and every structure that is built—is a profession requiring a two-year associate's degree from a technical institute, community college or trade school. Training includes courses in mathematics, physics, mechanical drawing and, of course, drafting. Salaries range from $25,000 for beginners and climb to $60,000 for senior drafters. The average salary is about $37,500 a year. Use *Peterson's Two-Year Colleges* (published by Thomson Peterson's) and *Arco Vocational and Technical Schools* (two volumes covering eastern and western United States, published by Thomson Arco). Both the Peterson's and the Arco are available in major bookstores. See chapter 2 for more information on these and other guides to professional schools, colleges and institutes.

Engineering Technicians

This is an exciting profession for the mechanically gifted with aptitudes in math and science, and it requires only an associate degree from a technical institute or community college. Be extremely cautious about selecting the right education for this field, however. For more information, contact the Junior Engineering Technical Society, 1420 King Street, Alexandria, VA 22314 (http://www.jets.org). The work of engineering technicians pays between $25,000 and $60,000 a year and involves assisting engineers and scientists in government and industry research and development. Engineering technicians set up experiments, help develop new products and solve customer problems with equipment ranging from production machinery to NASA missiles, space shuttles and satellites. For information on accredited training programs and certification, contact the Accreditation Board for Engineering and Technology, 111 Market Place, Baltimore, MD 21202 (http://www.abet.org).

Legal Assistants (Paralegals)

Although many employers prefer training their own legal assistants, more than 800 formal training programs for paralegals are available to high school graduates at community and junior colleges, four-year colleges, law schools and legal assistant associations. Lists of approved legal assistant training programs, career information and job opportunities are available from these organizations:

American Association for Paralegal Education, 407 Wekiva Springs Road, Longwood, FL 32779 (http://www.aafpe.org)

National Association of Legal Assistants, 1516 South Boston Street, Tulsa, OK 74119 (http://www.nala.org)

National Federation of Paralegal Associations, P.O. Box 33108, Kansas City, MO 64114 (http://www.paralegals.org)

Depending on the area of the country and the size of the law firm or employer, legal assistants earn between $25,000 and $65,000 a year.

Library Technicians

Library technical assistants, as they're often called, perform all the support activities of a library. They help librarians prepare, organize and catalog materials; help the public; operate audio-visual equipment; organize exhibits and help clients with microfiche equipment and computers. Library technicians need a two-year community college associate degree in library technology. Salaries vary widely but average $25,000. It's important for you to know, however, that credits earned for an associate degree in library technology *do not* apply toward a degree in library science, which is a four-year professional degree from a college or university in preparation for a job as a librarian. For more information, contact the American Library Association, Office for Human Resource Development, 50 East Huron Street, Chicago, IL 60611 (http://www.ala.org).

Science Technicians

For those with an interest in science, this profession offers the opportunity to work in research and development in the chemical, petroleum and food processing industries as well as in college, university and government research laboratories and the labs of research and development firms. Most junior and community colleges offer two-year associate degrees in science, mathematics and specific technologies such as food technology. Earnings of science technicians range from $14,500 to $47,000 a year. For information about a career as a chemical technician in chemistry-related fields including food, contact the American Chemical Society, Education Division, Career Publications, 1155 16th Street NW, Washington, DC 20036 (http://www.acs.org).

TRANSPORTATION

Air Transport

With the exception of flight crews, most airline and ground service personnel (flight attendants, ground crews, and so on) and airport operations staffs need no college education, although flight attendants on international routes must know appropriate foreign languages. Most training is on-the-job in formal company training programs. Earnings average about $45,000 a year. Most airlines require pilots to have two years of college and many insist on a four-year college degree. Pilots must attend a certified pilot school or pass a Federal Aviation Administration military competency exam if they learn to fly in the military. Pilot salaries average $50,000 and reach $100,000 for senior pilots on major airlines. For more information about career opportunities in air transport, write to the airlines themselves and to air transport companies such as United Parcel Service or Federal Express.

Ground Transport

Bus drivers.   Must be 18 to 24 years old, preferably high school graduates, and, depending on state regulations, have a commercial driver's license or special schoolbus license. In addition, intercity bus drivers must meet state or U.S. Department of Transportation qualifications. Training is on-the-job in formal company or transit system training programs lasting two to eight weeks. Drivers in local transit systems earn between $10 and $20 an hour. Experienced intercity bus drivers can earn up to $25 an hour. Information on school bus driving is available from the National School Transportation Association, 625 Slaters Lane, Alexandria, VA 22314 (http://www.yellowbuses.org). You can get information on local transit bus driving from the American Public Transportation Association, 1666 K Suite 1100, NW, Washington, DC 20006 (http://www.apta.com).

Truck drivers.   Qualifications vary widely depending on the types of trucks and where goods will be carried. In general, truck drivers need to be in good physical condition and at least 21 years old to engage in interstate commerce. They must have a commercial motor vehicle operator license and take written examinations on the Motor Carrier Safety Regulations of the U.S. Department of Transportation. Many firms won't hire new drivers under 25 years old because of insurance costs. Local drivers are paid by the hour, but wages vary from community to community and whether drivers are unionized. Average income ranges from $8 an hour for driving light trucks to about $15 an hour for driving medium trucks. Long-distance tractor-trailer drivers, many of whom belong to the International Brotherhood of Teamsters union earn from $12.50 to $25 an hour. For more information, contact American Trucking Associations, Inc., 2200 Mill Road, Alexandria, VA 22314 (http://www.trucking.org). For a list of certified tractor-trailer driver-training programs, contact the Professional Truck Driver Institute of America, 2200 Mill Road, Alexandria, VA 22314 (http://www.ptdi.org).

Other Transportation Industry Opportunities

- Shipping. Seamen on oceangoing vessels; mates aboard coastal and inland ships, boats and barges.

- Railroads. Locomotive engineers; brake, signal and switch operators; conductors; yard masters; yard equipment operators.

- Surface transport. Taxi drivers and chauffeurs; limousine drivers; hearse drivers; car-delivery drivers for new-car dealers; service station attendants; parking lot operators; car wash operators.

ARMED SERVICES
(FOR NONMILITARY JOBS, SEE GOVERNMENT SERVICE)

The U.S. Armed Services—the army, navy, marines and coast guard— offer millions of American men and women endless opportunities to learn a trade and serve their country at the same time. All branches require a high school diploma, and applicants must pass written examinations. Applicants must be at least 18 years old (or 17 with parental consent) and must agree contractually to serve at least two and usually three to four years. Together, the four services are the largest employers in the U.S. and offer the most job training and benefits. They offer training and work experience in nearly 2000 occupations, most of which are valuable in civilian life. Here are the jobs, in 12 broad categories, which are open to enlisted personnel (nonofficers) with no college education or previous experience. All training is on-the-job at full pay and at government expense.

1. Human services: recreation
2. Media and public affairs: musicians, photographers, camera operators, graphic designers and illustrators and foreign language interpreters and translators
3. Health care: medical laboratory technologists and technicians, radiologic technologists, emergency medical technicians, dental

assistants, pharmaceutical assistants, sanitation specialists and veterinary assistants. Military training as a health-care specialist automatically entitles a person to civilian certification

4. Engineering, scientific and technical occupations: mapping technicians, computer programmers, air traffic controllers and radio and radar operators

5. Administrative, clerical and functional support jobs: accounting clerks, payroll clerks, personnel clerks, computer programmers, computer operators, accounting machine operators, chaplain assistants, counseling aides, typists, word processor operators, stenographers, storekeepers and other clerical jobs

6. Service occupations: military police, correction specialists, detectives, firefighters, food preparation and service

7. Vehicle and machinery mechanics: maintenance and repair of aircraft, missiles, conventional and nuclear-powered ships, boats and landing craft, trucks, earth-moving equipment, armored vehicles and cars

8. Electronic and electric repair: repairs of radio, navigation and flight control equipment, telephones and data-processing equipment

9. Construction trades: carpenters, construction and earth-moving equipment operators, metalworkers, machinists, plumbers, electricians, heating and air-conditioning specialists and every other building trades occupation related to construction and maintenance of buildings, roads, bridges and airstrips

10. Machine operating and precision work: laboratory technicians, opticians, machinists, welders and shipfitters

11. Transportation and materials handling: truck drivers, aircrews, seamen, warehousing and equipment handling specialists and all jobs associated with the operation of transportation equipment— including trucks, ships, boats, airplanes and helicopters—and maintaining inventories of all spare parts

12. Infantry, gun crews and seamen specialists: the one area with few applications to civilian life, although some munitions experts find work in law enforcement and demolition, while seamen specialists often find jobs on merchant and passenger vessels

Enlistment is a contract—usually about eight years—in which, before you sign, *you* specify the occupational areas that interest you most and in which you want to be trained. You can also apply for Officer Candidate School, and if accepted, become an officer trained in managerial and administrative skills. Service in the military entitles you to scholarship funds to attend college while you're in the military or after discharge. Although the military can be a stepping stone to a rewarding civilian career, it is also a rewarding career in itself and should be considered seriously as such. Aside from pride of service, the military offers the most benefits and job security of any U.S. employer. Enlisted personnel earn take-home pay ranging from $12,775 to more than $40,000 a year, depending on grade and length of service. In addition, they receive free room and board (or a housing and subsistence allowance), free medical and dental care, a military clothing allowance, free on-base recreational facilities and 30 days paid vacation a year. Warrant officer earnings range from $25,600 to $62,000 a year, and commissioned officers earn between $26,200 and $142,000 but average about $55,000 a year. Military personnel are eligible for retirement benefits after only 20 years of service, including a pension worth 40 percent of base (cash) pay. Any veteran with two or more years of service is eligible for free medical care at any veterans administration hospital. For information on military careers, stop in at any military recruiting station or state employment service office. Most high schools, colleges and public libraries have similar materials. In addition, the U.S. Defense Department's Defense Manpower Data Center publishes *Military Career Guide Online*, which is available to everyone on the Internet at http://www.todaysmilitary.com.

4

Getting Started in Your New Career

Once you've selected the industry and career that interest you most and you've completed your alternative education for that career, you'll have to get a job. If you attended a cooperative education program, it's likely that the employer that helped train you will offer you a permanent job. In that case, you're all set. Good luck in your new job.

If you did not participate in such a program, but carefully evaluated the one you did attend and picked a good one, that program's job placement service will put you in touch with employers looking for your skills. You'll also want to contact employers on your own.

WHERE TO LOOK FOR JOBS

If you have no personal or school contacts to put you in touch with employers, you'll have to find job openings on your own, and there are many ways to do that. The most difficult is to cold-call—to pick a company you'd like to work for and speak to human resources or a department head and try to "sell" your way into an interview. That's tough unless you're an extremely gifted salesperson. An easier way is to use the classified ads of your local or regional newspaper. That allows you to pinpoint employers *in your area* who are specifically seeking your skills and talents. The problem with classified ads, however, is that they are usually vague and have to be brief because of space limitations. So that means that you might answer a dozen ads for a "retail salesperson" before you find the one that is exactly what you want and is located in an area that pleases you.

A third, more efficient method is to contact employment agencies or, if appropriate, executive search firms in your area. Such firms always interview you first to find out exactly what you're looking for and what you can bring to the job. Only then do they try to match you with the right employers and send you out on job interviews. Remember that employment agencies collect their fees from *you*, the employee, once you get the job, whereas executive search firms collect their fees from the employer. Either way, they don't make any commissions until you actually get the job. So it's always in their interest to prepare you as much as possible for job interviews and to match you up with an employer most likely to hire you.

The fourth, almost limitless resource for job openings is the Internet, which lists jobs electronically worldwide. The wonderful thing about the Internet is that it allows you to *broaden* and *narrow* your search at the same time. The Internet allows you to type in your job qualifications and requirements, and the magic of electronics does the rest, combing through all available jobs for the ones that fit you. Looking for jobs on the Internet may seem confusing at first, but it's really not. What you'll need to get started is a directory of employment sites, which are nothing more than electronic employment agencies. Like storefront agencies, there are hundreds of them, with the most famous and largest being Monster.com, which pioneered electronic job searching. But, like many other Internet employment sites, Monster.com is a generalist site, with more than 40 million recruiters in its database. Now that doesn't mean a generalist site can't help you; it probably can, and it's certainly worthwhile posting your résumé with a site such as Monster.com. But the advantage of having a directory of sites is that it cross-references all sites by occupational category and geographic reach. Without such a directory, you simply can't know whether a site is the right one for you. The name usually doesn't tell you anything, and many sites that seem to accept employment ads in all fields are actually quite specialized, niche sites. AAA Career Services, for example, sounds like it might have openings in every imaginable field, but it's actually the employment site of the American Anthropology Association.

Many site names are more helpful. Absolutely Health Care and Accountant Jobs Chicago are two examples of sites that tell you their area of specialization and, in the second example, the geographic area. And that's why you need a good directory of electronic employment sites. *Weddle's*

Guide to Employment Sites on the Internet, for example, lists more than 300 sites and breaks them down by industry (construction, health care, security, etc.) and region (state and cities). (Incidentally, neither I nor my publisher Facts On File have any association with the guides mentioned in this book.)

Regardless of the method you use to look for jobs, you'll have to use the same techniques in applying for jobs that interest you, whether you find them on the Internet, in newspaper ads, at employment agencies, or through personal contacts. The techniques will require time and patience, but they are relatively simple if you follow the instructions outlined below. Don't complicate the process, and *don't let others complicate it or discourage you.* Many friends and relatives will tell you "you're doing it all wrong" and flood you with endless articles and books about "How to Get a Good Job" and "How to Write a Good Résumé." Chances are all those articles and books contain good pointers, but you may find yourself spending more time reading about how to get a job instead of going out and getting one.

The principles in all those books and articles are the same. Identify your skills and positive traits, get them down on paper in summary or *résumé* form and get that résumé into the hands of one employer in ten or one hundred or one thousand who is looking for your combination of skills and personality.

WRITING RÉSUMÉS

A résumé is not an autobiography. It is a *sales pitch*—a written advertisement of skills and services for sale. It's the reverse of a help wanted ad. A help wanted ad never tells you any negatives about a job, only the positives. Like all ads, it's a teaser, which lures readers into contacting the employer to get more details. Which of these ads would tease you into making a call to get more details?

> *Administrative Assistant:* Top salary, flexible hours, interesting, congenial atmosphere on TV talk show team. Must be able to handle contacts with guest personalities. Call 555-0000.

Secretary: Take dictation (80 words/min), process letters, file documents, answer telephones, carry messages, run errands for busy executive. Hours 9 to 5, five days a week, but must be ready to work evenings and some weekends. Salary: $18,000. Call XYZ Productions. . . .

The two jobs are identical, but the top ad makes it more attractive by keeping details to a minimum and only listing positive aspects of the job. And that's what you've got to do with your résumé. Every job has negative characteristics, but the ad that features them will get few takers. The same is true for résumés. We all have our weaknesses, but they don't go in our résumés. Similarly, too many details can destroy the value of an ad by discouraging a response from an applicant who doesn't fit the job perfectly—the otherwise perfect candidate who can only take dictation at 60 words a minute, for example. That candidate might respond to the first ad but not the second, and the company would be the loser by not even getting a chance to interview the perfect candidate.

These same rules apply to résumés. Once again, a résumé is not your life history. It is an ad, a sales promotion piece. Keep it short (no more than one page); keep it simple; keep it positive; and, as in all ads, show readers how your skills and services can so benefit them that they'll invite you for an interview. And that's what your résumé is for—to get you an invitation for an interview. Don't misunderstand its purpose: A résumé will never get you a job, only a job *interview*.

A résumé has two elements: form and content. There are simple rules for both. Break these rules and your prospective employer will assume you cannot follow any rules. Your résumé will end up in a special file for rejected applications—the waste basket. The important thing to keep in mind in writing a résumé is that it is one of the few aspects in the job application process that is totally under your control. You cannot control job market conditions or the quality of other applicants competing with you. But you can control what goes into your résumé.

Here are the rules for résumé form:

1. **Brevity.** *No more than one page long*. An inability to reduce a résumé to one page shows either a lack of command of the English language, an inability to follow directions or an inflated

sense of self-importance—none of which are characteristics that employers admire.

2. **Neatness.** Absolute perfection is the rule. There is no excuse for not being able to produce a perfect résumé in the quiet and privacy of one's home away from all pressures. If you can't produce an absolutely neat one-page paper, potential employers will assume you can't do anything neatly.

3. **Factual accuracy.** Potential employers will check the facts in your résumé. Be certain they are accurate. If they're not, a potential employer will conclude that you are either dishonest or unable to do accurate work.

4. **Honesty.** Don't exaggerate by calling your summer job as a file clerk an "administrative assistant." And if you cut lawns as a summer job or picked vegetables, say so. Don't call yourself a landscape or agricultural technician.

5. **Writing accuracy.** Your résumé must be free of spelling, grammatical and typographical errors. Again, if you can't produce a one-page paper free of errors, employers will conclude you can't do any error-free work.

6. **Personal data.** You should not include a photograph of yourself or personal information such as height, weight, sex, race or religion. It is against state and federal law to mention any characteristics associated with discrimination based on race, religion, gender or age.

7. **Standard presentation.** Don't use off-sized or off-color paper. You are writing for businesspeople. Be businesslike. Use standard, high-quality eight- × 11-inch white paper. Unless you *are* an artist and your résumé is an opportunity to display your talents, artistic attention-getting devices that parents and teachers called cute and imaginative in school will be tossed away as unbusinesslike by potential employers. Use standard typography, and don't get cute with punctuation. Never use exclamation marks, for example. A simple period will do.

8. **Well organized.** The résumé should be organized into four or five basic categories, each headed by a capitalized or underlined heading. There are three basic methods of organization: chronological (in order of occurrence), functional (in order of

importance) and combined chronological and functional. The last format is usually the most effective and the one used in the following sample. It orders the broad categories by importance for the job you're applying for, but orders the information within each category chronologically, either backwards or forwards, depending on which is more effective.

9. **Typography.**   Word processing is by far the most preferable, because it allows you to use a basic format, which you can adapt slightly or "custom design" for each prospective employer. Someone interested in a secretarial career might want to modify the objective to read "Secretarial work in health care field" for one prospective employer and "Secretarial work, scientific research" for another. In other words, you can show a specific interest in a particular company. That's almost impossible with a printed résumé, whose tone must be general enough to send to a wide variety of prospective employers. It says the same thing to every company and shows no particular interest in any.

Here are the rules for content, followed by a sample résumé, which you can use by substituting your own data for the fictitious information:

Name, Address, Telephone Number and E-mail, Centered at the Top of the Page

If you don't have a personal e-mail address, it's essential that you get one now. Some search firms offer them at no cost, but whatever the cost, you'll find it worthwhile in your job hunt. Be certain to devise a business-like address, with your name as a primary component. If yours is a common name such as Jim Smith or John Jones, add a number or the initials of your town and state or your high school or college to distinguish it—jsmithusc, for example. Under no circumstances should you select a cute or, worse, a provocative name. If you already have an e-mail address with such a name, change it!

Career Objective

Notice that I've used the word *career* rather than occupational or job objective. That's because by stating a broad career goal, you give a potential employer who likes your résumé more flexibility than you would by stating the specific job you're seeking. If you list bartending as a job objective, for example, and there are better, more experienced applicants, you'll be rejected. But if you list restaurant and hotel service, the same employer who might reject you for the bartender's job may be eager to give you some other opportunity as a waiter or assistant host if your training warrants it. Similarly, the modest applicant who specifies "entry-level position in public relations" may get no job at all (because there is no entry-level job) or he might win that entry-level job and miss getting a better job for which his résumé kept him from being considered. If you specify an entry-level job, that's all you'll probably be considered for. So, again, don't close doors of opportunity on yourself by narrowing your goals or being unnecessarily modest.

Job Qualifications

The next category of data should tell the employer that you know how to do the job he or she has. If you've just graduated from school and learned those skills in a vocational education program, you should put "Education" as the next category in your résumé. If, on the other hand, you learned most of the skills you need through previous work experience, then "Work Experience" should be next. Within the category of job qualifications, list each experience chronologically, with the most recent one first. With each experience, indicate *briefly* what skill you learned or used that will be of value to your prospective employer. Also mention any special award or accomplishment associated with each experience. Whether you're submitting your résumé to a giant corporation or a local grocery store, prospective employers want to know the same thing: that you can do the job they're trying to fill. You can demonstrate that to them by showing that you either learned how at a good vocational school or that you've actually done it on-the-job.

References

List the names, addresses, telephone numbers and e-mail addresses of former employers or teachers who had key roles in teaching you the skills needed for the job you're applying for. There's no point listing a ninth-grade teacher who likes you a lot. The only teachers you should consider are those who taught you your trade and, perhaps, the director of the program in which you learned that trade.

Optional Categories

Special skills.   If you're fluent in a foreign language or have some other special skill or knowledge not mentioned under "Experience"—it could be a hobby or travel experience—that might prove *useful* to your employer, mention it under this listing. Remember: It must prove useful, not just interesting.

Awards and affiliations.   If you've won an award or have some position in a club or organization where you display other talents your employer could use, then add this category to your résumé. An example might be, "Treasurer, Smithville Boys Club. Managed membership dues collections, club solicitations, investments and disbursements and maintained accounts ledgers." Such an example shows your familiarity with handling and managing organization funds and with accounting and bookkeeping. It also reflects a community's faith in your honesty and trustworthiness. It displays another positive element of your character in just a few words, without any bragging or exaggeration.

Writing Style

Keep each statement short. Do not use complete sentences such as, "I worked as a salesperson behind the greeting card counter." Instead, the description of such a previous job should read, "Salesperson, greeting cards. Actively managed customer sales, cash flow, inventory controls, reorders of 16 product lines from five vendors." And, if your work was particularly notable, you would add to the description, "Salesperson of the Month Award, December 2005," or "Reorganized inventory controls to reduce perennial shrinkage from 3.24 percent of purchasing costs to 0.14 percent with annual savings of $46,542 to the department."

There are two other important elements in a good résumé writing style. One is the use of active, meaningful verbs to describe what you did on the job or learned in the classroom—for example, "reorganized" rather than "changed" or "managed" rather than "responsible for." Be careful not to write a job description, only what you did on the job and only those accomplishments that might be of use to your new employer. Follow each job title with an action verb: "introduced," "inspected," "maintained," "prepared," "organized," "controlled," "planned," "initiated," "executed," "analyzed," "documented," "designed," "monitored," "modified," "systematized," "streamlined," "converted," "promoted" and so on. In describing classroom training experiences, use the phrase "hands-on operation" or "hands-on production" to indicate you actually operated some equipment or produced some product.

The other important element in a good writing style is the avoidance of jargon, which is a wordy, meaningless phrase for which a single word can be substituted. Our daily speech is filled with jargon: "at this point in time" instead of "now," "at some future point in time" instead of "soon," "in order to" or "for the purpose of" or "with a view toward" instead of "to," "with respect to" instead of "about." In other words, keep your sentences short and to the point.

Figure 1 on page 120 is a sample résumé in which the job applicant is seeking a career in merchandising, or retailing. He has learned his skills both in college and working at summer jobs. Had he majored in English instead of marketing, his work experience would have been listed first. But the broad nature of his business education warrants its appearance before his work experience, which, after all, was only summer work and probably did not give him the in-depth understanding of retail operations that he studied in college. Had this been a résumé of a young man who had graduated two years earlier and then worked for two years in a department store, his work experience would have been listed before his education.

The résumé is purposely "average"—no awards, no super achievements—because most of us are average. The trick to résumé writing is to display the solidity, dependability and skills that someone with an average background and education can develop. Notice, too, how the résumé can be used to match individual employer needs with as little as a single word change. As it stands, it is a valid résumé for any department store. But, if he changed his career goal from "Merchandising" to "Fashion Merchandising" or "Merchandising, Menswear," it would be a particularly effective résumé for any menswear retailer. By leaving his career objective as it is, however, and by expanding his experience in the student book store, he could send his résumé to any store that sells student supplies in or near a college or university.

Eugene Everett Richards
687 Saybrook Court
Yalesville, NJ 10101
(203) 555-4839
eerichards@fergpubco.com

CAREER OBJECTIVE:	Merchandising
EDUCATION:	Rockdale Community College, Associate Degree, Marketing, June 2005. Courses: Accounting, Retail, Computer Applications, Marketing, Merchandising, Store Management.
	Rockdale High School. Graduated, June 2003 with honors. Academic Program with marketing and accounting electives.
WORK EXPERIENCE:	September 2004–May 2005. Hands-on management (as part of "Store Management" course). RCC Student Bookstore: purchasing, pricing, inventory controls, reorder of books and student supplies, including stationery, toiletries and college souvenir clothing; employee relations.
	Summer 2004. Salesman, men's furnishings (shirts, socks, underwear, handkerchiefs), Binghamton Department Store.
	Active selling: Guided customer selection with emphasis on sales of latest, high mark-up designer brands and fashionwear; processed all aspects of sales transactions.
	Summer 2005. Stock clerk, men's apparel, Binghamton Department Store. Managed restocking of floor racks and shelves with suits, sport shirts, dress shirts, socks, underwear and other furnishings; processed automatic reorders via computer terminals.
	Binghamton Department Store, summers, 2001, 2002.
SPECIAL SKILLS:	Fluent in conversational and commercial Spanish.
REFERENCES:	Mr. Donald Director President Binghamton Department Store 321 Downtown Mall Binghamton, NJ 07698
	Dr. Emma Educator President Rockwell Community College 876 Wisdom Road Rockwell, NY 10893

FIGURE 1. Sample résumé of a graduating community college student

THE COVER LETTER

In some cases, you hand-deliver your résumé to a prospective employer. Every résumé that's sent by conventional mail, however, should have a cover letter regardless of how you made initial contact with a prospective employer. Just as the résumé is designed to get you an interview, the cover letter is designed to get the recipient to read your résumé. The cover letter, therefore, is not a rehash of your résumé. It must be different. Like the résumé, it must be a teaser and intrigue its reader to look at the enclosed résumé.

The principles of résumé writing apply to the cover letter. It must be short (one page only), neat, accurate, free of spelling, grammatical and typographical errors and prepared on a word processor on standard paper or stationery in standard business-letter format, as in the following sample. If you have business-type stationery with your own letterhead, use it. Otherwise, type your letterhead in the upper right hand corner. Do not use small or decoratively printed personal stationery. Again, avoid cuteness such as "Hi!" or a pompous attitude, such as "Here's the letter you've been waiting for!" As in the case of the résumé, the cover letter is another aspect of keeping the job application process completely under your control. Produce a letter that will make you a desirable candidate.

You are writing to conservative business people who have one goal—to improve company operations. Your letter must be conservative and businesslike and indicate that you can make a contribution to the company. You can use the sample letter in Figure 2 on page 122 as a guide, substituting the facts of your own background for those of the fictitious job applicant. Use the sample in *this book* to guide you. It is *not* unethical for you to substitute names or jobs of your own choosing in the types of simple phrases seen here. However, *be warned!* It is *unethical* for you to copy more complex, sample cover letters and résumés available on the Internet and various web sites, and *it will certainly hurt and probably ruin your chances of getting a job.* The reason should be obvious: Tens of thousands of other people are doing the same thing—and employers know it! They and their human resources staff know Internet cover letters and résumés by heart, and whenever they see one, they assume the applicant who sent it is stupid (to think

Eugene Everett Richards
687 Saybrook Court
Yalesville, NJ 10101
eerichards@fergpubco.com

May 1, 2006

Ms. Cherie Lorraine
Director
Executive Training Program
Smith's Department Store
Barclay Square
New York, NY 10893

Dear Ms. Lorraine:

Mr. Donald Director, president of Binghamton Department Store, suggested I write to you to apply to Smith's Executive Training Program. As you can see in my enclosed résumé, I will be graduating from Rockdale Community College this June with an Associate Degree in Marketing. As part of my course in store management, I had the opportunity to participate in hands-on management of the Rockdale Community College bookstore. Together with my two summers as a stock clerk and a third summer as a salesperson in men's furnishings at Binghamton Department Store, my work in merchandising—especially with goods designed for younger men and women—has proved the most exciting experience in my life. I want to make it my career, and I would love to work at Smith's.

I would be most grateful for the opportunity of an interview with you to see if you think I might qualify for Smith's Executive Training Program.

With many thanks for your consideration.

Sincerely,

Eugene Everett Richards

FIGURE 2. Sample cover letter

the employer won't know), lazy (by not trying to be original) and un-ethical (anyone who steals someone else's written work might steal office supplies or worse on the job). So, again, use the sample cover letter here as a guide. It is simple and straight forward—just as your own cover letter should be simple and straight forward. And, don't forget to sign it!

In general, a cover letter should be no longer than three paragraphs, preferably two. You must make three points:

1. **Why you are writing.** Although the saying, "It's not what you know, it's who you know" doesn't always apply, contacts often can be important factors in getting a job. If you get the job, of course, you'll have to prove yourself, and contacts won't help you much. But for getting that first chance, the person with contacts and good references will usually win out over the applicant without them, all other things being equal. So, your opening sentence in any cover letter should mention your contact, if you have one, and his or her connection to either the company or to you. The contact may be a friend of the person you're writing, an official in the company, the job placement counselor at your school or college, a teacher or official at your college or school, an employment agent or a parent or relative. Whoever the contact, if you have one, use it—and use it to begin your opening sentence. Don't waste time: play your strong cards immediately.

"Ms. Doris Manning, vice president of marketing, suggested I write to you . . ." or "My father, Samuel Richards, an attorney at . . ." or "Dr. Frederick Walker, president of Rockdale Community College . . ." or "Mrs. Patricia Lane of the Rockdale Community College Job Placement Office, suggested I write you . . .".

If you do not have a contact, explain what motivated the letter: "I saw your advertisement . . ." or, if you contacted the company "cold" by telephone, "I enjoyed talking with you today about the possibility of my working at . . .".

Once you've explained who or what put you in touch with the company, finish the opening by explaining the reason for writing: ". . . about the opening for a salesperson in the Smith's Menswear Department" or "about an opening in the Smith's Executive Training Program" or "about the possibility of a job in merchandising at Smith's."

2. **Who you are.**   Again, keep this short. You're either a graduate of or will soon graduate from a school or college where you studied some courses or trade important in the job for which you're applying. In one sentence say why you want to make that trade your career and why you want to work at the company you're writing to. Those two short sentences are probably the most difficult sentences any job applicant ever has to write. They sound simple enough, but they're not. They require considerable soul searching and research—but you must do it. Anyone who eventually hires you will want to know why you want to go into your chosen field and why you want to work for that particular company. So, you might just as well pinpoint the reasons now. And if you can't figure out the reasons, perhaps you're going into the wrong trade or applying for a job at the wrong company. The way to get started is to list all the characteristics you like about the trade you've chosen. Then reword those characteristics to have more meaning for others who may be unfamiliar with that industry. Take the fictitious job applicant in the preceding letter who obviously likes working in stores. Why would anyone want to spend eight to 10 hours a day on his or her feet five or six days a week listening to complaining customers? Well, those who make a career out of and love merchandising don't see those as negative aspects. They see the positives—the excitement of facilitating the huge flow of goods from manufacturer to consumer. They enjoy the satisfaction of filling consumer needs, of discovering new products, of setting new fashion trends. They see themselves, to paraphrase an old General Electric Co. advertising slogan, bringing good things to their community and its people.

In the interview, which follows, you'll have to explain in detail why you like the trade you've chosen. For the second sentence of your cover letter, however, you must summarize it in one line, as the fictitious applicant has done: ". . . merchandising . . . goods designed for younger men and women has proved the most exciting experience in my life." And in the next line, explain why you want to work for that company. Your reasons may have to do with the company's standing in the community, in the industry or in the nation or your own experience with its products or services. They cannot be trivial or selfish. Just because you can walk to work is not a good primary reason. It's a good secondary reason, which you can bring up in the interview. After all, proximity to your work is valuable to your employer as well as to you, because it reduces employee lateness and absenteeism. But proximity cannot be a reason to put in your cover letter. It's essential to research the reasons for wanting to work for a company. Get an annual report to shareholders; study company brochures about its operations and its products and services; and speak to current and former employees and to customers. You may find you don't want to work for that company. But if you do, tell them why in one short sentence of your cover letter.

3. **What you want the reader to do.**   Obviously, you want the reader of your letter to read your résumé and interview you for a job. Say so quickly and politely at the end of your cover letter, as the applicant has done in the sample. You may use any acceptable sign-off: "Sincerely," "Sincerely yours" or "Yours truly."

Do not enclose any other material—only your résumé and a cover letter. If you have any supporting materials, such as letters of recommendation or charts or spreadsheets that show the kind and quality of work you did, bring those with you to the interview. Never send them by mail unless you are specifically requested to do so, and then include a self-addressed, stamped envelope for their return.

E-MAIL OR INTERNET

Do *not* e-mail your cover letter and résumé to prospective employers *unless* they specifically tell you to do so. An employer might, for example, contact you by telephone and ask you to e-mail your résumé, in which case you would preface it with a shorter cover letter that only touches on key points you want to make:

Dear Ms. Lorraine:

Thank you for calling me today. As I mentioned, I will be graduating from Rockdale Community College this June with an Associate Degree in Marketing. Two summers as a stock clerk and a third summer as a salesperson in men's furnishings at Binghamton Department Store proved such exciting job experiences that I want to make my career in merchandising. I would be most grateful for an interview with you and the opportunity to apply to Smith's Executive Training Program.

With many thanks for your consideration.

Sincerely,

Eugene Everett Richards

Or, an employer might specify e-mail responses to an advertisement or a posting on the company's web site, in which case you might begin your letter this way:

Dear Ms. Lorraine:

As you can see from the attached résumé, I will be graduating from Rockdale Community College . . .

and you'd continue as in the letter just above.

Make certain that both your e-mail cover letter and e-mail résumé have your name, address, telephone number and e-mail address. Don't ever put that information in the body of your cover letter—as in, "You may call me at . . ." Remember you are writing to intelligent people who are perfectly capable of reading your address at the top of your e-mail and the top of your résumé. To repeat that information in the body of your letter insults their intelligence. Similarly, don't insult their intelligence by telling them you're responding to their advertisement or web site posting. They know why you're writing! Get to the point and tell them who you are and what you want.

THE PERSONAL INTERVIEW

As in the case of the résumé and cover letter, the personal interview is another aspect of the job application package under your control. It is an opportunity for you to display a depth of knowledge and aspects of your personality that dry facts and statistics on an application or résumé cannot exhibit. The interview—sometimes there may be a series of two or three for the job you're seeking—is the final stage of your quest for employment. Do well in it, and you'll probably be hired.

The Interview Guidelines on pages 128–129 list the range of questions interviewers at one large U.S. corporation ask job applicants. The forms they use show you exactly how they handle the entire interview process. As you can see, the first thing interviewers look for is the applicant's appearance. So do enough advance research to determine the proper dress for the job you're trying to get. If people who hold similar jobs normally wear dresses or ties and jackets, then you must do so also. A company is not like school, where the person who stands out in the crowd because of unusual conduct or dress will win some admiration. The interview is the moment to prove you can be part of the company's team and play by the company's rules. In addition to dress, posture and grooming are important elements of everyone's appearance. Slouching in one's seat can cost an applicant a job. Failure to look the interviewer in the eye, nervous habits and any other unusual behavior can all go down as negatives in an application folder.

Here is the full range of questions most good interviewers will ask job applicants. Can you answer the ones appropriate for your background and the type of job you're seeking? If not, start practicing. There are three sections to the interview package. The first section lists a range of questions for the interviewer to ask you. The second section tells the interviewer what to listen and look for—especially appearance, manner, self-expression and responsiveness on the part of the applicant. And the third section asks the interviewer to rate the applicant on appearance, work experience, education and present activities and interests—and then recommend for or against hiring. Use this material to help you prepare for your interviews.

INTERVIEW GUIDELINES

Outlined below are the four major areas of the applicant you should investigate: Work Experience, Education and Training, Goals and Ambitions and Self-Assessment. The questions within each area are suggested topics for you to explore. Ask these questions in your own words and style, and add any questions you feel necessary within each category. Be sure to cover each area thoroughly. Remember, the following are only sample questions and are, by no means, an exhaustive list.

Work Experience

1. Please describe your present responsibilities and duties.
2. What were some of the things that you particularly enjoyed when you were working for the ABC Corporation?
3. Tell me about the personal progress that you made during your association with the ABC Corporation.
4. Looking back at the time spent with the ABC Corporation, what do you feel you have gained from your association?
5. What were your reasons for leaving the ABC Corporation?
6. In the past, for what things have your superiors complimented you? For what have they criticized you?
7. What were some of the problems that you encountered on your job, and how did you solve these problems?
8. As you see it, what would be some advantages to you were you to join our company? What disadvantages or drawbacks might there be?
9. Describe a typical day on your last job.

Education

1. How did you select the college or type of school you attended?
2. What did you hope to do with your education?
3. How do you think college or alternative education contributed to your development?
4. How would you describe your academic achievement?

5. Have you had any additional training or education since graduating?
6. Looking back at your education, how do you feel it has prepared you for a position as a _____ ?
7. How did you select your major course of study?

Goals and Ambitions

1. What are you looking for in a job?
2. Why does this job sound appealing to you?
3. What would you like to be doing in three years? five years?
4. What would you want in your next job that you are not getting now?
5. What are some of the things in a job that are important to you?
6. In considering joining a company, what are some of the factors that you take into account?
7. What are your present salary expectations?

Self-Assessment

1. In general, how would you describe yourself?
2. What do you regard to be your outstanding qualities?
3. Why have you progressed to where you are?
4. What kinds of situations or circumstances make you feel tense or nervous?
5. In which areas do you feel you would like to develop yourself?
6. What do you feel you have to offer us?
7. We all have our strengths and weaknesses. What do you feel are your greatest strengths, and what are those areas that you would like to improve upon?

Interviewers will note both the manners and language of applicants. The repetitive use of the word *like* and the phrase "ya know," as in "Like . . . ya know . . ." will certainly produce negative reactions from interviewers. So will responses such as "Cool!" and immature speech patterns such as, "Well, ya know, I kinda like computers, ya know, and, uh, like, ya know, man, electronic equipment and, ya know . . ." Clear, effective communication is important in every job involving other people. Everyone on the team has to be able to understand what other team members say and write. An applicant who has not yet learned how to communicate effectively will find it difficult to get a good job, because most employers seek applicants who have the ability to articulate well.

One-word answers also leave interviewers unimpressed and hurt any chances of getting a job—as it did this applicant, whose interview began this way:

> Interviewer: Did you find your way here all right?
> Applicant: Yeah.
> Interviewer: No trouble at all, eh?
> Applicant: Nah.
> Interviewer: Well, have a seat.
>
> Applicant sits without replying.
>
> Interviewer: Let's see . . . you're applying for the sales job in menswear, right?
> Applicant: Yeah.

Although such answers may be the result of shyness, they usually appear to others as unfriendly and rude. The ability to engage in conversation is always seen as a sign of good manners and friendliness.

Another error that can earn a job rejection is poor grammar, especially for office jobs. A lot of poor grammar such as "Things are going good" instead of "well" or "Me and my friends went to the movies" instead of "My friends and I . . ." may be the result of bad habits, not lack of knowledge. If that's the case for you, begin changing those habits in your everyday speech now before you begin the round of job interviews. Poor grammar can hurt your chances of getting a good job, and it can affect your entire career.

In addition to proper conduct, dress and speech, it's important to go into an interview knowing as much about a particular company as possible. Almost every interviewer will ask why you want to work for his or her company, and it's important that you know why, specifically, on the basis of your in-depth reading of its annual report, sales brochures, product catalogs and any other printed materials. Most major libraries carry directories of corporations that contain much data about all major companies. The most widely available are *Dun & Bradstreet's Million Dollar Directory, Standard & Poor's Register of Corporations, Moody's Industrial Manual, Thomas Register of American Manufacturers,* and *Wards Business Directory.* When an interviewer asks what you know about the company, you should know more than "just what I read in the newspapers." Your answer should demonstrate initiative and interest. You should know its history, the products and services it offers and something about its top officials. You should know what makes the company unique and exactly why you want to work for it. An applicant who doesn't know why he or she wants a job at a particular company should not be there in the first place. Even if the real reason is because you need a job and are willing to take anything you can get, don't say so. You'll probably never get work that way. Nor are you likely to get a job by saying that your friends work there, and they say, "It's a nice place."

Remember that most interviewers are probably quite proud of their companies. They see their firms as unique, and they see the job you're applying for as a unique opportunity. Do enough research to find out what makes each firm unique and why the job you're after is indeed a great opportunity for you. If you don't see it as such, perhaps you should consider waiting for a better opportunity.

In addition to knowing as much as possible about the company and the job, it's important to know all about yourself. Remember that the interview represents a common measuring stick for all applicants—no matter what schools or colleges they attended; no matter what contacts they have; no matter what previous jobs they've held and no matter what their social backgrounds. Everybody walks into the interview facing the same test. Whether you're shy or outgoing, the interview is something you'll have to face all your life. It's a chance to sell yourself. Use it to good advantage. If you're not skilled at having interviews, practice with friends or family. Have them ask you questions. Pages 134–135 list typical questions asked by professional job interviewers. Rehearse your entrance into the interviewer's office. Walk into the room with quiet self-confidence, smiling and looking him or her straight in the eye and firmly shaking hands. Rehearse your exit: shaking hands again, saying thanks for the interview, then turning and walking out, again with quiet self-confidence. Rehearse often. Move the furniture around in a room at home to make a stage set of an interviewer's office with a desk or table in the middle, you on one side and a friend or relative on the other.

Interview techniques vary widely from company to company and interviewer to interviewer. Some interviewers may be as new at it—and as nervous—as you. You might even be the first person they have ever interviewed. Most personnel executives, however, are quite skilled. Some will purposely make the situation more stressful for you than others to see how you respond to pressures. Typical *stress* interviews begin with such questions such as, "What can I do for you?" or "Tell me about yourself"; "What kind of job are you looking for?"; "Why do you think you're the right person for this job?"; "What do you know about the job (or company or 'me,' if the interviewer is your prospective boss)?"; "Where else are you looking?"; "Why did you leave your last job?"; "What did you like least about your last job?"; "Can you work under extreme pressure?" These are all tough questions, and you should be prepared for them in advance by thinking them through carefully and having a specific, direct answer— nothing vague.

Remember that you are there to describe your qualifications for the job. Don't let yourself get side-tracked. Answer the stressful questions, but immediately steer the conversation back to your skills. *Don't* focus on the stresses of the situation but on the reason for being there: to display the elements of your background, character, education, skills and personality that make you uniquely qualified for the job you're applying for.

Most interviewers will begin with a series of random questions to try to put you at ease. They'll find some topic that will get you talking comfortably so that you'll relax enough to talk openly and honestly about yourself. Good interviewers want applicants to do most of the talking during the 30 to 45 minutes of the interview so that they can get an idea of the applicant's personality and the way they think. *But be careful!* Don't get sidetracked by a friendly question about sports or music or some other interest aimed only at putting you at your ease. If an interviewer opens by asking whether you saw a specific concert or sports event, whether you answer "yes" or "no" is unimportant. You are there to get a job; you've only got 20 minutes or so to sell yourself, so switch back quickly to your qualifications and the reasons you want the job. There are all sorts of "tricks" for switching the conversation: "Yes, and I saw that your company was one of the sponsors. That's one of the reasons I'd love to work here"; or "No, it was on a midweek night, and I had to study for my exams and work on my résumé for this job." Think of your own ways to switch the conversation, but do so—and do so quickly, even if you have to be blunt: "I wonder if I could ask you some questions about the job opening?"

Before going into an interview, it's important to make a careful assessment of all those characteristics that qualify you for the job. Write them on a list in order of importance, and learn them so well that you can discuss your life and talents in any order—either in piecemeal answers to many questions or in an interesting discourse in answer to a single, general question such as, "Tell me about yourself." And don't be afraid to take notes with you. It's perfectly acceptable to refer to them during the interview. Try to know them by heart, of course, but don't be afraid to pause and look at them and say, "I just want to make sure I've covered everything." Be sure that you talk about your qualifications for the job. Describe specific, concrete examples of what you've done either in the classroom, school laboratory or on some other job that demonstrate your ability to do the job you're applying for and to fulfill the company's needs.

Take a notepad and pencil. It's important to listen to what your interviewer has to say and to demonstrate that you are a good listener and interested enough to take notes on what you consider essential information.

Notes are also helpful for questioning your interviewer. "Do you have any questions?" is a question almost every interviewer will ask—and you'd better have some or risk a poor score on your interview. One important one is to get an outline of the responsibilities of the job you're seeking. Some other obvious questions are, "What kind of person are you looking for?" "Why did the last person leave this job?" or "Where might this job lead, if I do very well?" Some better ones would be, "How would you like to see the work done on this job? Has it been done that way? How would you like to see it improved? What's a typical day on the job like? What's the best thing about the job? The worst thing? What are some of the problems I'll face on the job?" On a broader level, your reading about the company might produce these questions: "I read in the papers that sales are (slipping) (growing). Does this mean the company might (cut back) (expand) operations? Would this job (be in jeopardy) (have more responsibilities)?"

KEEP QUESTIONS OPEN-ENDED

Introduction		
Cover:		**Look for:**
Greeting Small talk Opening question Lead question		Appearance Manner Self-expression Responsiveness
Work Experience		
Cover:	**Ask:**	**Look for:**

Earliest jobs,
  part-time, temporary
Military assignments
Full-time positions
	Things done best? Done
	  less well?
	Things liked best? Liked
	  less well?
	Major accomplishments?
	Most difficult problems
	  faced? How handled?
	Ways most effective
	  with people? Ways
	  less effective?
	Level of earnings?
	Reasons for changing jobs?
	What learned from work
	experience?
	What looking for in job?
	  In career?
		Relevance of work
		Sufficiency of work
		Skill and competence
		Adaptability
		Productivity
		Motivation
		Interpersonal relations
		Leadership
		Growth and
		  development

Education		
Cover:	**Ask:**	**Look for:**

Elementary school
High school
College
Specialized training
Recent courses
	Best subjects? Subjects
	  done less well?
	Subject liked most?
	  Liked least?
	Reactions to teachers?
	Level of grades? Effort
	  required?
	Reasons for choosing
	  school? Major field?
	Special achievements?
	  Toughest problems
	Role in extracurricular
	  activities?
	How financed education?
	Relation of education to
	  career?
	Considering further schooling?
		Relevance of schooling
		Sufficiency of schooling
		Intellectual abilities
		Versatility
		Breadth and depth
		  of knowledge
		Level of
		  accomplishment
		Motivation, interests
		Reaction to authority
		Leadership
		Teamwork

Summary		
Cover:	**Ask:**	**Look for:**

Strengths
Weaknesses
	What bring to job?
	What are assets?
	What are best talents?
	What qualities seen by
	  self or others?
	What makes you good
	  investment for employer?
	What are shortcomings?
	What areas need
	  improvement?
	What qualities wish to develop
	  further?
	What constructive criticism
	  from others?
	How might you be risk for
	  employer?
	What further training, or
	  experience, might you need?
		PLUS (+) AND
		  MINUS (−)
		Talents, skills
		Knowledge
		Energy
		Motivation
		Interests
		Personal qualities
		Social qualities
		Character
		Situational factors

(continues)

KEEP QUESTIONS OPEN-ENDED *(continued)*

Closing Remarks

Cover:

Comments regarding interview and applicant
Further contacts to be made
Course of action to be taken

Cordial parting _____

Applicant: _____   Date: _____

Position: _____

Interviewer: _____

Comment on the applicant's background and behavior, taking into consideration the elements listed in the right-hand column of each section. Then circle a rating for each section based on the evidence you have cited. Finally, at the end of this report, make one overall rating of the candidate.

Initial Impression

Favorable 1 2 3 4 5 Unfavorable	Manner Self-expression Responsiveness

Work Experience

Favorable 1 2 3 4 5 Unfavorable	Relevance of work Sufficiency of work Skill and competence Adaptability Productivity Motivation Interpersonal relations Leadership Growth and development

Education	

Favorable 1 2 3 4 5 Unfavorable	Relevance of schooling
	Sufficiency of schooling
	Intellectual abilities
	Versatility
	Breadth and depth of
	  knowledge
	Level of
	  accomplishment
	Motivation, interests
	Reaction to authority
	Leadership
	Teamwork

Present Activities and Interests	
Favorable 1 2 3 4 5 Unfavorable	Maturity and judgment Intellectual growth Diversity of interests Social skills Leadership

Summary of Strengths (+)

Summary of Weaknesses (−)

(continues)

Overall Summary Recommendations (Write Three Paragraphs)							
1. In favor of hiring: _____ _____							
2. Against hiring: _____ _____							
3. Final recommendations: _____ _____							
4. Overall Rating: Favorable 1 2 3 4 5 Unfavorable							
Thank you for your feedback. Please forward to Personnel.							

You might also ask, depending on the interviewer's personality, about the interviewer's own experiences and length of service at the company. "How long have you been here, and what do you see as the strengths and weaknesses of the company?" Remember, the word "interview" means "to see one another." Most people think it means one person questioning another, but the original meaning is for two people to see each other. Use the situation to establish a rapport with your interviewer and get a friendly, two-way conversation going. If you think the offices are beautiful, say so; if the building or factory is impressive, say so. Conversation is an art that will certainly help you score well in any interview situation.

Write your questions down in advance, and don't be afraid when the time comes to say, "Yes. I wrote a few down," and then refer to your notes.

One of the "loaded" questions most interviewers will almost certainly ask you is to tell them about your weak points. Nobody's perfect, and your interviewer knows that. You'll appear rather conceited if you say you have none, and you'll show a lack of self-knowledge if you say you don't know what they are. There are two rules for handling the problem. The first is to discuss all weak points that will ultimately surface in a check of your application facts and your references. You're far better off discussing such weaknesses in advance so that they don't come as a surprise later and force the company to reject your application. Often by explaining some weak point at the interview, you can reduce it's importance and make it seem insignificant.

If no weak points will ever turn up in the company's check into your background and references, the way to prepare for an interviewer's question about them is to list them all before the interview at the same time you list all your strong points. Be honest with yourself. No one will see the list but you. Then cross out the worst of the weak points and save the most common, almost humorous ones that will not or cannot in any way affect your job performance. Then discuss them with a smile and show yourself to be human.

An important rule in interview techniques is never to begin or end an interview on a negative note, and, after any discussion of weak points, be certain to show how you've converted a weakness into a strength. Someone weak in high school math, for example, might well have taken a special summer school course to strengthen mathematical skills.

Another "loaded" question many prospective employers will ask is, "What kind of salary do you expect to get on the job?" If you've done your homework, you should know what the pay range is for the type of job you want, and, if you're just starting out, show the boss that you have done your homework by saying, "Well, I understand the company usually pays beginners ___ dollars (an hour, a week, etc.)."

Another important rule at job interviews is to show that you want the job. If an interviewer doesn't think you want it, you won't get it. As in any relationship, clear communication is vital in interviews. *You must tell other people what you need and want or they'll never know.* So, at an appropriate point—usually, toward the end of the interview when you're asked if you have any other questions or if "there's anything else you'd like to discuss"—speak up and say something like, "I just want you to know that I'd really like to work for this company, and I'd really like this job. I think I can do a good job and make a contribution to the company." Or, if the interviewer is the person you'll actually be working for: "I'd really like to work for you. I know I can do a good job and make a contribution to your department." Don't be afraid to say things such as, "I promise you won't be sorry if you hire me" or "This job is exactly what I've been looking for—it ties in perfectly with everything I've ever learned and studied about . . ." Be enthusiastic, however, and say you want the job!

Chances are you won't get a job offer on the spot. Usually, the interviewer will tell you that the company will give your application careful consideration and that they will let you know within a few days. Regardless of how friendly or enthusiastic your interviewer may seem, keep looking for other jobs while awaiting the company's decision.

After your interview, write a thank-you letter that reinforces your interest in and qualifications for the job. Figure 3, on page 141, shows a sample letter.

Don't be disappointed if you don't get the job. Remember, there is no way for you to know the qualifications of other job applicants. Moreover, many companies make mistakes, and there's nothing you can do about it except to keep applying at other companies until you find the job that's right for you at a company that's eager to have you on its team.

FILLING IN APPLICATIONS

As in all other written work in the job application process, your application must be filled in neatly, with no spelling, grammatical or typographical errors. Unlike résumés and letters, however, you probably won't be able to fill in your job application in the serenity of your home. In all likelihood, a personnel department official will give you the application and a pen or pencil and direct you to a small corner table or desk where you'll have to fill it in on the spur of the moment. So, be prepared. Figure 4 is a sample of a typical application. First, practice filling it in carefully and neatly. Make a few copies and see if you can do it error free without having to cross out or erase any entries. Next, use it to make a list of the information and vital statistics *you know* every job application will demand. There is nothing worse than having to tell the personnel office that you don't have or forgot some information about yourself—like your Social Security number—and that you'll telephone them later with the information. That is inefficiency of the worst kind—and usually unforgivable because it demonstrates what you may be like on the job. So make a list of the data required in most job applications and have it with you whenever you visit a prospective employer.

And, once again, good luck!

Eugene Everett Richards
687 Saybrook Court
Yalesville, CT 10101
eerichards@eli.com

June 1, 2005

Ms. Cherie Lorraine
Director
Executive Training Program
Smith's Department Store
Barclay Square
New York, NY 10036

Dear Ms. Lorraine:

It was kind of you to take so much time to see me yesterday. I enjoyed meeting you and learning so much about Smith's and the Executive Training Program. I'm even more excited now about the prospect of a career in merchandising, and there's no place I'd rather work than at Smith's. Obviously, a chance to join the Smith's Executive Training Program would be the opportunity of a lifetime, and I promise that, given that chance, I would not let you or Smith's down.

All my thanks for your consideration.

Sincerely,

Eugene Everett Richards

FIGURE 3.   Sample interview thank-you letter

FIGURE 4.   A standard employment application used by companies across the United States. Make a copy and practice filling it out neatly and *error-free*. Make a list of the data required so you have all the pertinent facts with you when you have to fill applications in actual situations.

APPLICATION FOR EMPLOYMENT

We consider applicants for all positions without regard to race, color, religion, sex, national origin, age, marital or veteran status, the presence of a non-job-related medical condition or handicap, or any other legally protected status.

(PLEASE PRINT)

Positions Applied For   Date of Application

How Did You Learn About Us?

❏ Advertisement   ❏ Friend   ❏ Walk-In

❏ Employment Agency   ❏ Relative   ❏ Other _____

Last Name   First Name   Middle Name

Address   *Number*   *Street*   *City*   *State*   *Zip Code*

Telephone   e-mail   Social Security Number

If you are under 18 years of age, can you provide   ❏ Yes   ❏ No
required proof of your eligibility to work?

Have you ever filed an application with us before?   ❏ Yes   ❏ No

                                                         If Yes, give date _____

Are you currently employed?   ❑ Yes   ❑ No

May we contact your present employer?   ❑ Yes   ❑ No

Are you prevented from lawfully becoming employed in this
country because of Visa or Immigration Status?   ❑ Yes   ❑ No
Proof of citizenship or immigration status will be required upon employment.

On what date would you be available for work?   _____

Are you available to work: ❑ Full Time   ❑ Part Time   ❑ Shift Work   ❑ Temporary

Are you currently on "lay-off" status and subject to recall?   ❑ Yes   ❑ No

Can you travel if a job requires it?   ❑ Yes   ❑ No

Have you been convicted of a felony within the last 7 years?
Conviction will not necessarily disqualify an applicant from employment.   ❑ Yes   ❑ No

If Yes, please explain   _____

_____

_____

_____

_____

_____

_____

_____

_____

WE ARE AN EQUAL OPPORTUNITY EMPLOYER

EDUCATION

	Elementary School					High School				Undergraduate College/University				Graduate/ Professional			
School Name and Location																	
Years Completed	4	5	6	7	8	9	10	11	12	1	2	3	4	1	2	3	4
Diploma/Degree																	
Describe Course of Study																	

Describe any specialized training, apprenticeship, skills and extra-curricular activities	
State any additional information you feel may be helpful to us in considering your application	

Indicate any foreign languages you can speak, read and/or write

	FLUENT	GOOD	FAIR
SPEAK			
READ			
WRITE			

List professional, trade, business or civic activities and office held.

You may exclude memberships which would reveal sex, race, religion, national origin, age, ancestry, or handicap or other protected status.

_____

_____

_____

_____

_____

References

Give name, address and telephone number of three references who are not related to you and are not previous employers.

1. _____

2. _____

3. _____

Have you ever had any job-related training in the United States military?
☐ Yes   ☐ No

If Yes, please describe _____

_____

Are you physically or otherwise unable to perform the duties of the job for which you are applying?

☐ Yes   ☐ No

EMPLOYMENT EXPERIENCE

Start with your present or last job. Include any job-related military service assignments and volunteer activities. You may exclude organizations which indicate race, color, religion, gender, national origin, handicap or other protected status.

	Employer		Dates Employed From / To		Work Performed
1.	Address				
	Telephone Number(s)	e-mail	Hourly Rate/Salary Starting / Final		
	Job Title	Supervisor			
	Reason for Leaving				
2.	Employer		Dates Employed From / To		Work Performed
	Address				
	Telephone Number(s)	e-mail	Hourly Rate/Salary Starting / Final		
	Job Title	Supervisor			
	Reason for Leaving				
3.	Employer		Dates Employed From / To		Work Performed
	Address				
	Telephone Number(s)	e-mail	Hourly Rate/Salary Starting / Final		
	Job Title	Supervisor			
	Reason for Leaving				
4.	Employer		Dates Employed From / To		Work Performed
	Address				
	Telephone Number(s)	e-mail	Hourly Rate/Salary Starting / Final		
	Job Title	Supervisor			
	Reason for Leaving				

If you need additonal space, please continue on a separate sheet of paper.

Special Skills and Qualifications

Summarize special job-related skills and qualifications acquired from employment or other experience.

APPLICANT'S STATEMENT

I certify that answers given herein are true and complete to the best of my knowledge.

I authorize investigation of all statements contained in this application for employment as may be necessary in arriving at an employment decision.

This application for employment shall be considered active for a period of time not to exceed 45 days. Any applicant wishing to be considered for employment beyond this time period should inquire as to whether or not applications are being accepted at that time.

I hereby understand and acknowledge that, unless otherwise defined by applicable law, any employment relationship with this organization is of an "at will" nature, which means that the Employee may resign at any time and the Employer may discharge Employee at any time with or without cause. It is further understood that this "at will" employment relationship may not be changed by any written document or by conduct unless such change is specifically acknowledged in writing by an authorized executive of this organization.

In the event of employment, I understand that false or misleading information given in my application or interview(s) may result in discharge. I understand, also, that I am required to abide by all rules and regulations of the employer.

_____   _____
Signature of Applicant   Date

FOR PERSONNEL DEPARTMENT USE ONLY

Arrange Interview   ❏ Yes   ❏ No

Remarks _____

_____   _____
                                              INTERVIEWER   DATE

Employed   ❏ Yes   ❏ No   Date of Employment _____

                                          Hourly Rate/
Job Title _____   Salary _____   Department _____

          By _____   _____
                              NAME AND TITLE   DATE

NOTES _____

_____

_____

_____

_____

APPENDIX A

NATIONALLY RECOGNIZED ACCREDITING ASSOCIATIONS

The following regional and national accrediting associations are recognized by the U.S. Secretary of Education as reliable authorities on the quality of secondary education, postsecondary education or training offered by educational institutions or programs. Contact any of the appropriate associations to check whether the educational institution you're considering is accredited and approved.

Regional Institutional Accrediting Associations and Commissions for High Schools, Community Colleges, Junior Colleges, Technical Institutes and Four-Year Colleges and Universities

Middle States Association of Colleges and Schools (Delaware, District of Columbia, Maryland, New Jersey, New York, Pennsylvania, Puerto Rico, Virgin Islands), 3624 Market Street, Philadelphia, PA 19104, (215) 662-5606 (http://www.msache.org)

New England Association of Schools and Colleges (Connecticut, Maine, Massachusetts, New Hampshire, Rhode Island, Vermont), 209 Burlington Road, Bedford, MA 01730, (781) 271-0022 (http://www.neasc.org)

North Central Association of Colleges and Schools (Arizona, Arkansas, Colorado, Illinois, Indiana, Iowa, Kansas, Michigan, Minnesota, Missouri, Nebraska, New Mexico, North Dakota, Ohio, Oklahoma, South Dakota, West Virginia, Wisconsin, Wyoming), 30 North LaSalle Street, Chicago, IL 60602, (312) 263-0456 or (800) 621-7440 (http://www.ncacihe.org)

Northwest Association of Schools and Colleges (Alaska, Idaho, Montana, Nevada, Oregon, Utah, Washington), 11130 Northeast 33rd Place, Suite 120, Bellevue, WA 98004, (425) 558-4224 (http://www.cocnasc.org)

Southern Association of Colleges and Schools (Alabama, Florida, Georgia, Kentucky, Louisiana, Mississippi, North Carolina, South Carolina, Tennessee, Texas, Virginia) 1866 Southern Lane, Decatur, GA 30033, (404) 679-4500 (http://www.sacscoc.org)

Western Association of Schools and Colleges (American Samoa, California, Guam, Hawaii, Trust Territory of the Pacific Islands, Commonwealth of the Northern Marianas). For two-year colleges: Accrediting Commission for Community and Junior Colleges, 10 Commercial Boulevard, Novato, CA 94949, (415) 506-0234 (http://www.accjc.org). For four-year colleges: Senior College Commission, 985 Atlantic Avenue, Alameda, CA 94501, (510) 748-9001 (http://www.wascweb.org/senior).

Community Colleges

American Association of Community Colleges, One Dupont Circle NW, Washington, DC 20036 (http://www.aacc.nche.edu)

Correspondence Schools—Degree and Nondegree Programs

Distance Education and Training Council, 1601 18th Street NW, Washington, DC 20009 (http://www.detc.org)

Privately Owned and Operated Trade and Business Schools

Accrediting Commission of Career Schools and Colleges of Technology, 2101 Wilson Boulevard, Arlington, VA 22011 (http://www.accsct.org)

Accrediting Council for Independent Colleges and Schools, 750 First Street NE, Washington, DC 20002 (http://www. acics.org)

National Apprenticeship Program

To check accreditation of apprenticeship programs in the United States, contact the U.S. Department of Labor Bureau of Apprenticeship and Training web site at http://www.doleta.gov/atels_bat. From this central web site, you can access the offices of the Bureau of Apprenticeship and Training in every state and, in turn, the specific apprenticeship programs that interest you to see if the Department of Labor has granted them accreditation.

APPENDIX B

ESSENTIAL GUIDES AND DIRECTORIES

The guides and directories listed below are all available in retail book-stores. Where two directories are listed in the same category, they are of equal quality, and you need only buy one. (Note: Neither the author nor the publisher of *But What If I Don't Want to Go to College?* has any association with the directories listed below.)

Distance Learning

Barron's Guide to Distance Learning (Internet orders: http://www.barronseduc.com)

Peterson's Guide to Distance Learning Programs (Internet orders: http://www.petersons.com)

Both directories describe online learning programs at about 1,000 accredited American colleges, listing courses offered as part of their degree programs and those offered outside their degree programs. Both directories list colleges by geographic location *and* by subject of occupational training.

Internet Employment Sites

Weddle's Guide to Employment Sites on the Internet (Internet orders: http://www.weddles.com)

Lists about 350 sites, with location, number and types of job postings, top salaries offered, and services to job applicants (résumés, etc.). Cross-referenced indexes list sites by career category and by state, region and city.

Four-Year Colleges

Barron's Profiles of American Colleges (Internet orders: http://www.barronseduc.com)

Peterson's Four-Year Colleges (Internet orders: http://www.petersons.com)

Both directories describe more than 1,500 four-year colleges and universities, with admission requirements, academic programs, student-faculty ratios, costs of tuition and room and board, available financial aid, athletic and extracurricular activities, e-mail addresses and web sites.

Two-Year Colleges

Peterson's Two-Year Colleges (Internet orders: http://www.petersons.com)

Describes nearly 2,000 two-year colleges in the United States—community colleges, junior colleges and technical institutes—with admission requirements, academic programs, costs, financial aid, athletic and extracurricular activities, e-mail addresses and web sites. Of great importance is the inclusion of a list of associate degree (one- and two-year) programs at four-year colleges.

Vocational and Technical Schools

Arco Vocational and Technical Schools East/West, 2 vols. (Internet orders: http://www.petersons.com)

An absolutely essential guide to more than 5,200 vocational schools, colleges and training institutes across the United States—half of them east and half of them west of the Mississippi River. In addition to four- and two-year colleges, this directory lists privately owned career colleges, technical training centers and vo-tech schools. Described in detail state-by-state, the schools are also listed by career or occupational category. That allows you to look under any career category—carpenter, cosmetologist, emergency medical technician, etc.—and find all the listings in every state across the nation.

APPENDIX C

ESSENTIAL EMPLOYABILITY SKILLS

Together with employers, community leaders and educators, the Colorado Department of Education developed the following list of "employability skills" that every good career education program should be teaching its students. If your school's vocational education program is not teaching most of these skills, it is not preparing you for the world of work. If you cannot find a high school career education program that teaches these skills, switch to a strong academic program and postpone plans for vocational education until you graduate from high school and can enroll in a community college, technical institute or some other post-high school career training program.

Identification of Essential Employability Skills

DIRECTIONS: Check those skills that are essential for students to acquire so that they will be well prepared to obtain employment and be successful on the job. In making judgments consider your own job experience. Add to part "M. Other" any skills which you consider essential which are not listed.

Name   _____

Date   _____

Please refer to the handout entitled "Identification of Employability Skills" for examples of each skill.

A. JOB SEEKING—CAREER DEVELOPMENT SKILLS

❏ 1. Knows sources of information
❏ 2. Knows own abilities, aptitudes, interests
❏ 3. Knows occupational characteristics
❏ 4. Identifies career/ occupational goals
❏ 5. Develops a career plan
❏ 6. Identifies and researches potential employers
❏ 7. Knows employment position(s) desired
❏ 8. Accurately completes:
   ❏ a. Inquiry letter
   ❏ b. Résumé
   ❏ c. Follow-up letter
❏ 9. Accurately completes job application
❏ 10. Handles interviews without errors
❏ 11. Seeks information about future education/training

B. MATH SKILLS

❏ 1. Understands importance of math in jobs
❏ 2. Performs basic calculations $(+, -, \times, \div)$
❏ 3. Performs calculations in:
   ❏ a. Fractions
   ❏ b. Percentages
   ❏ c. Proportions/ratios
❏ 4. Makes reasonable estimates

❏ 5. Uses values from graphs, maps, tables
❏ 6. Uses English/metric measurement
❏ 7. Compares numerical values
❏ 8. Applies geometric principles
❏ 9. Uses formulas correctly
❏ 10. Constructs diagrams, tables, records
❏ 11. Uses elementary statistics
❏ 12. Uses instruments to solve problems:
   ❏ a. Gauges, meters, scales
   ❏ b. Calculators
   ❏ c. Computers

C. COMPUTER SKILLS

❏ 1. Becomes aware of computer functions
❏ 2. Inputs and accesses data from computer
❏ 3. Has experience with computer programs
   ❏ a. Business applications
   ❏ b. Data management
   ❏ c. Simple programming
   ❏ d. Word processing
❏ 4. Understands issues associated with computer use

D. READING SKILLS

❏ 1. Understands the importance of reading in jobs
❏ 2. Develops vocabulary related to careers and occupations

❏   3. Reads for details and
         special information
❏   4. Interprets pictures, graphs
         and symbols
❏   5. Locates information in
         reference materials
❏   6. Follows intent of written
         directions/instructions
❏   7. Interprets ideas and con-
         cepts (comprehension)
❏   8. Reads accurately at appro-
         priate rate

E. WRITING SKILLS

❏   1. Understands the impor-
         tance of writing in jobs
❏   2. Develops handwriting
         legibility
❏   3. Composes formal letters
❏   4. Fills out forms
❏   5. Records messages
❏   6. Writes memorandums
❏   7. Composes ads/telegrams
❏   8. Writes instructions and
         directions
❏   9. Writes reports
❏ 10. Develops summaries
❏ 11. Takes notes and/or outlines
❏ 12. Corrects written materials

F. COMMUNICATION SKILLS

❏   1. Reports accurately/concisely
❏   2. Follows intent of oral
         directions/instructions

❏   3. Speaks distinctly
❏   4. Formulates questions
❏   5. Answers questions
         accurately
❏   6. Explains activities and
         ideas clearly
❏   7. Uses appropriate vocabulary/
         grammar
❏   8. Gives clear instructions
         and directions
❏   9. Stays on topic
❏ 10. Uses nonverbal signs
         appropriately
❏ 11. Develops oral presentations
❏ 12. Presents information
         effectively to groups

G. INTERPERSONAL SKILLS

❏   1. Functions cooperatively
         with fellow students
❏   2. Functions cooperatively in
         team efforts
❏   3. Functions cooperatively
         with adults outside school
❏   4. Exhibits openness and
         flexibility
❏   5. Seeks clarification of in-
         structions
❏   6. Exercises patience and
         tolerance
❏   7. Utilizes suggestions about
         improving skills
❏   8. Uses initiative in getting
         work done
❏   9. Expresses opinions with
         tact

❏ 10. Demonstrates ability to negotiate differences with others

H. BUSINESS ECONOMIC SKILLS

❏ 1. Understands business organization
❏ 2. Understands business competition
❏ 3. Knows about processes of marketing
❏ 4. Knows about processes of production
❏ 5. Understands business costs
❏ 6. Understands factors affecting profits

I. PERSONAL ECONOMIC SKILLS

❏ 1. Knows how to evaluate products and services
❏ 2. Knows how to access community resources/services
❏ 3. Can compute working hours/wages
❏ 4. Knows how to handle financial affairs
❏ 5. Can handle records of income and expenses
❏ 6. Knows how to make price-quality comparisons
❏ 7. Knows how to prepare state/federal tax forms

❏ 8. Can evaluate insurance programs
❏ 9. Knows how to determine credit costs
❏ 10. Understands legal rights in agreements
❏ 11. Maintains and utilizes various forms of transportation

J. MANUAL PERCEPTUAL SKILLS

❏ 1. Constructs/assembles materials
❏ 2. Uses specific hand tools and instruments
❏ 3. Develops visual presentations
❏ 4. Masters keyboard skills
❏ 5. Operates power equipment

K. WORK ACTIVITY SKILLS

❏ 1. Produces type/amount of work required
❏ 2. Maintains punctuality
❏ 3. Meets attendance requirements
❏ 4. Accepts assignments/responsibilities
❏ 5. Takes responsibility for own actions
❏ 6. Maintains consistent effort
❏ 7. Works independently
❏ 8. Manages time effectively

❏ 9. Respects rights and
       property of others
❏ 10. Adheres to policies and
       regulations
   ❏ a. Health
   ❏ b. Honesty
   ❏ c. Safety
❏ 11. Presents a neat appearance
❏ 12. Keeps work area in good/
       safe condition
❏ 13. Exhibits interest in future
       career
❏ 14. Suggests or makes work-
       place improvements
❏ 15. Knows sources of continu-
       ing education
❏ 16. Knows about basic
       employee/student rights
❏ 17. Knows about basic employee/
       student responsibilities
❏ 18. Knows about basic steps in
       getting a raise or promotion
❏ 19. Knows how to terminate
       employment

L. PROBLEM-SOLVING/
REASONING SKILLS

❏ 1. Recognizes problems that
       need solution
❏ 2. Identifies procedures

❏ 3. Obtains resources
❏ 4. Prepares or sets up materials/
       equipment
❏ 5. Collects information
❏ 6. Organizes information
❏ 7. Interprets information
❏ 8. Formulates alternative
       approaches
❏ 9. Selects efficient approaches
❏ 10. Reviews progress
❏ 11. Evaluates activities
❏ 12. Corrects errors
❏ 13. Makes conclusions
❏ 14. Summarizes and
       communicates results
❏ 15. Uses results to develop new
       ideas

M. OTHER

1. _____
2. _____
3. _____
4. _____
5. _____
6. _____
7. _____
8. _____
9. _____

Source: Colorado Department of Education

APPENDIX D

Jobs, Education and Pay

Educational Requirements and Earnings for More Than 700 Jobs; Number of Workers in Each Job and Projections for 2012

The table on the following pages lists more than 700 occupations, with the "most significant source of education and training" and the average annual wage for each job. The table also shows the number of workers in each job, the probable number expected by 2012 and the percentage of expected change.

Occupation	Most Significant Source of Postsecondary Education or Training	Percent of Workers Aged 25 to 44, by Educational Attainment			2002 Median Annual Earnings	Employment (in Thousands)		Employment Change, 2002–12	
		High School or Less	Some College	College or Higher	Dollars	2002	2012	Numeric	Percent
Brickmasons and block-masons	Long-term on-the-job training	83.2	13.3	3.5	$41,840	148	169	21	14.2
Pile-driver operators	Moderate-term on-the-job training	80.5	17.1	2.4	45,420	5	6	0	8.2
Captains, mates, and pilots of water vessels	Work experience in a related occupation	72.4	13.6	13.9	49,850	25	26	1	2.4
Hazardous materials removal workers	Moderate-term on-the-job training	74.3	18.0	7.7	32,460	38	54	16	43.1
Tile and marble setters	Long-term on-the-job training	77.6	18.4	3.9	35,770	33	42	9	26.5
Cement masons and concrete finishers	Moderate-term on-the-job training	85.4	12.7	2.0	30,660	182	229	47	26.1
Drywall and ceiling tile installers	Moderate-term on-the-job training	83.8	13.8	2.3	33,710	135	164	29	21.4
Tapers	Moderate-term on-the-job training	83.8	13.8	2.3	39,000	41	49	8	20.8
Roofers	Moderate-term on-the-job training	84.6	12.1	3.2	30,180	166	197	31	18.6
Carpet installers	Moderate-term on-the-job training	77.6	18.4	3.9	32,590	82	96	14	16.8
Reinforcing iron and rebar workers	Long-term on-the-job training	83.8	10.7	5.6	36,740	29	33	5	16.7
Terrazzo workers and finishers	Long-term on-the-job training	85.4	12.7	2.0	27,910	6	7	1	15.2

Table caption: Educational attainment cluster, most significant source of postsecondary education or training, and educational attainment distribution, by occupation

Occupation	Training								
Stonemasons	Long-term on-the-job training	83.2	13.3	3.5	34,040	17	19	2	14.1
Plasterers and stucco masons	Long-term on-the-job training	86.7	10.6	2.7	33,100	59	67	8	13.5
Floor layers, except carpet, wood, and hard tiles	Moderate-term on-the-job training	77.6	18.4	3.9	33,590	31	35	4	13.4
Hoist and winch operators	Moderate-term on-the-job training	78.1	19.4	2.5	31,400	9	10	1	13.0
Paving, surfacing, and tamping equipment operators	Moderate-term on-the-job training	88.4	11.4	.2	28,860	58	65	7	12.6
Patternmakers, wood	Long-term on-the-job training	70.2	19.4	10.4	29,780	4	5	0	11.8
Painters, construction and maintenance	Moderate-term on-the-job training	77.2	16.9	5.9	29,070	448	500	52	11.6
Supervisors, farming, fishing, and forestry workers	Work experience in a related occupation	77.6	12.1	10.4	31,140	52	58	6	11.4
Crane and tower operators	Moderate-term on-the-job training	87.4	10.9	1.7	36,330	50	55	5	10.8
Operating engineers and other construction equipment operators	Moderate-term on-the-job training	78.5	19.1	2.4	35,240	353	389	37	10.4
Excavating and loading machine and dragline operators	Moderate-term on-the-job training	83.9	15.5	.7	32,410	80	87	7	8.9
Hunters and trappers	Moderate-term on-the-job training	74.0	18.0	8.0	30,660	1	2	0	6.4
Floor sanders and finishers	Moderate-term on-the-job training	77.6	18.4	3.9	27,500	17	18	1	4.2
Explosives workers, ordnance handling experts, and blasters	Moderate-term on-the-job training	76.6	19.5	3.8	35,110	5	5	0	2.0

Educational attainment cluster, most significant source of postsecondary education or training, and educational attainment distribution, by occupation *(continued)*

Occupation	Most Significant Source of Postsecondary Education or Training	Percent of Workers Aged 25 to 44, by Educational Attainment			2002 Median Annual Earnings	Employment (in Thousands)		Employment Change, 2002–12	
		High School or Less	Some College	College or Higher	Dollars	2002	2012	Numeric	Percent
Rolling machine setters, operators, and tenders, metal and plastic	Moderate-term on-the-job training	75.7	18.1	6.2	28,330	44	45	1	2.0
Rotary drill operators, oil and gas	Moderate-term on-the-job training	69.5	18.1	12.4	33,750	14	14	0	1.5
Milling and planing machine setters, operators, and tenders, metal and plastic	Moderate-term on-the-job training	78.4	19.0	2.6	29,210	31	31	0	.8
Derrick operators, oil and gas	Moderate-term on-the-job training	69.5	18.1	12.4	29,820	15	15	0	.8
Dredge operators	Moderate-term on-the-job training	83.9	15.5	.7	27,730	3	3	0	.3
Heat treating equipment setters, operators, and tenders, metal and plastic	Moderate-term on-the-job training	78.6	18.5	2.9	28,200	29	29	0	-.6
Service unit operators, oil, gas, and mining	Moderate-term on-the-job training	69.5	18.1	12.4	28,670	13	13	0	-.8
Extraction workers, all other	Moderate-term on-the-job training	83.2	14.4	2.4	29,210	12	12	0	-.8
Metal-refining furnace operators and tenders	Moderate-term on-the-job training	77.9	18.2	3.9	30,770	18	17	0	-.8

Occupation	Training								
Pourers and casters, metal	Moderate-term on-the-job training	78.5	15.5	6.0	27,880	13	13	0	-2.0
Tank car, truck, and ship loaders	Moderate-term on-the-job training	77.0	19.5	3.5	32,500	17	17	0	-2.1
Fallers	Moderate-term on-the-job training	85.1	10.8	4.1	28,160	14	14	0	-3.4
Extruding and forming machine setters, operators, and tenders, synthetic and glass fibers	Moderate-term on-the-job training	80.3	14.5	5.2	27,500	27	24	-4	-13.1
Loading machine operators, underground mining	Moderate-term on-the-job training	83.9	15.5	.7	31,930	4	3	-1	-14.1
Roof bolters, mining	Moderate-term on-the-job training	76.6	19.5	3.8	38,430	4	3	-1	-27.7
Shuttle car operators	Short-term on-the-job training	77.0	19.5	3.5	38,360	3	2	-1	-31.3
All other construction trades and related workers	Moderate-term on-the-job training	81.0	11.4	7.6	22,900	110	146	35	32.0
Manufactured building and mobile home installers	Moderate-term on-the-job training	73.7	18.5	7.8	23,170	18	22	4	23.4
Landscaping and groundskeeping workers	Short-term on-the-job training	76.5	17.7	5.8	19,770	1,074	1,311	237	22.0
Recreational vehicle service technicians	Long-term on-the-job training	87.9	9.8	2.3	27,080	13	15	3	21.8
Packaging and filling machine operators and tenders	Short-term on-the-job training	81.7	15.5	2.8	21,210	387	468	82	21.2

Occupation	Most Significant Source of Postsecondary Education or Training	Percent of Workers Aged 25 to 44, by Educational Attainment			2002 Median Annual Earnings	Employment (in Thousands)		Employment Change, 2002–12	
		High School or Less	Some College	College or Higher	Dollars	2002	2012	Numeric	Percent
Helpers—installation, maintenance, and repair workers	Short-term on-the-job training	83.6	15.5	.9	21,440	150	181	30	20.3
All other helpers, construction trades	Short-term on-the-job training	82.3	14.0	3.7	20,230	44	53	9	19.4
Helpers—roofers	Short-term on-the-job training	81.2	12.8	6.1	20,480	21	25	4	19.3
Tree trimmers and pruners	Short-term on-the-job training	76.5	17.7	5.8	25,110	59	69	11	18.6
Slaughterers and meat packers	Moderate-term on-the-job training	81.2	16.2	2.6	20,370	128	151	23	18.2
Helpers—electricians	Short-term on-the-job training	81.2	12.8	6.1	23,090	99	117	18	18.0
Refuse and recyclable material collectors	Short-term on-the-job training	79.0	14.6	6.4	24,130	134	158	24	17.6
Segmental pavers	Moderate-term on-the-job training	81.0	11.4	7.6	26,940	2	3	0	16.5
All other building and grounds cleaning and maintenance workers	Short-term on-the-job training	79.2	17.3	3.5	20,990	125	145	20	16.1
Helpers—painters, paperhangers, plasterers, and stucco masons	Short-term on-the-job training	81.2	12.8	6.1	20,100	31	36	5	15.9
Rock splitters, quarry	Moderate-term on-the-job training	84.0	12.8	3.3	26,170	3	3	0	14.3

Educational attainment cluster, most significant source of postsecondary education or training, and educational attainment distribution, by occupation *(continued)*

Occupation	Training							
Construction laborers	Moderate-term on-the-job training	79.5	15.6	4.8	24,740	938	1,070	133	14.2
Helpers—carpenters	Short-term on-the-job training	81.2	12.8	6.1	21,510	97	111	14	14.0
Fence erectors	Moderate-term on-the-job training	75.5	17.5	7.0	22,160	27	31	4	13.4
Conveyor operators and tenders	Short-term on-the-job training	77.0	19.5	3.5	24,250	58	65	7	12.4
Industrial truck and tractor operators	Short-term on-the-job training	78.8	17.9	3.3	26,070	594	659	66	11.1
Helpers—pipelayers, plumbers, pipefitters, and steamfitters	Short-term on-the-job training	80.8	13.8	5.4	22,230	79	88	9	10.9
Automotive glass installers and repairers	Long-term on-the-job training	77.6	12.7	9.7	26,890	22	24	2	10.7
Model makers, wood	Long-term on-the-job training	70.2	19.4	10.4	24,740	4	5	0	10.3
Pesticide handlers, sprayers, and applicators, vegetation	Moderate-term on-the-job training	76.5	17.7	5.8	24,830	27	30	3	9.7
Food cooking machine operators and tenders	Short-term on-the-job training	81.7	14.0	4.4	21,860	34	37	3	8.8
Tire repairers and changers	Short-term on-the-job training	87.9	9.8	2.3	20,160	83	89	7	8.0
Cutters and trimmers, hand	Short-term on-the-job training	81.1	17.0	1.9	22,020	31	33	2	7.6
Food batchmakers	Short-term on-the-job training	77.1	18.4	4.5	21,920	74	79	5	7.2
Cooling and freezing equipment operators and tenders	Moderate-term on-the-job training	75.3	19.9	4.8	21,240	7	8	1	7.1
Cleaning, washing, and metal pickling equipment operators and tenders	Moderate-term on-the-job training	88.0	8.9	3.1	22,850	18	19	1	6.9

Educational attainment cluster, most significant source of postsecondary education or training, and educational attainment distribution, by occupation *(continued)*

Occupation	Most Significant Source of Postsecondary Education or Training	Percent of Workers Aged 25 to 44, by Educational Attainment			2002 Median Annual Earnings	Employment (in Thousands)		Employment Change, 2002–12	
		High School or Less	Some College	College or Higher	Dollars	2002	2012	Numeric	Percent
Cutting and slicing machine setters, operators, and tenders	Moderate-term on-the-job training	81.1	17.0	1.9	25,690	77	83	5	6.6
Roustabouts, oil and gas	Moderate-term on-the-job training	76.6	19.5	3.8	22,280	32	34	2	6.4
Molders, shapers, and casters, except metal and plastic	Moderate-term on-the-job training	64.6	17.3	18.1	24,700	46	49	3	6.4
Animal breeders	Moderate-term on-the-job training	81.8	12.9	5.3	25,090	9	10	1	6.1
All other farming, fishing, and forestry workers	Moderate-term on-the-job training	83.6	11.8	4.6	21,450	96	101	4	4.5
Food and tobacco roasting, baking, and drying machine operators and tenders	Short-term on-the-job training	76.9	18.9	4.2	23,260	19	20	1	4.2
Helpers—extraction workers	Short-term on-the-job training	76.6	19.5	3.8	25,200	29	30	1	3.9
Furniture finishers	Long-term on-the-job training	76.3	17.2	6.5	22,710	39	41	1	3.3
Motorboat operators	Moderate-term on-the-job training	72.4	13.6	13.9	26,440	4	4	0	2.7

Occupation	Training								
Grinding, lapping, polishing, and buffing machine tool setters, operators, and tenders, metal and plastic	Moderate-term on-the-job training	82.5	13.8	3.6	26,120	104	106	3	2.4
Helpers—brickmasons, blockmasons, stonemasons, and tile and marble setters	Short-term on-the-job training	82.3	14.0	3.7	24,390	59	61	1	2.2
Cementing and gluing machine operators and tenders	Moderate-term on-the-job training	82.7	17.3	.0	23,190	27	28	0	1.0
Sawing machine setters, operators, and tenders, wood	Moderate-term on-the-job training	86.1	13.5	.4	22,080	56	56	0	-.2
Log graders and scalers	Moderate-term on-the-job training	85.1	10.8	4.1	27,200	10	10	0	-1.2
Machine feeders and offbearers	Short-term on-the-job training	81.0	15.7	3.3	21,840	164	162	-2	-1.4
Butchers and meat cutters	Long-term on-the-job training	81.2	16.2	2.6	25,500	132	129	-3	-2.5
Plating and coating machine setters, operators, and tenders, metal and plastic	Moderate-term on-the-job training	86.4	7.4	6.3	25,420	44	42	-1	-2.6
Logging equipment operators	Moderate-term on-the-job training	83.3	12.5	4.2	26,790	43	41	-2	-3.6
Upholsterers	Long-term on-the-job training	80.1	19.9	.0	24,670	56	51	-5	-8.7
Textile cutting machine setters, operators, and tenders	Moderate-term on-the-job training	90.7	8.5	.8	20,320	34	26	-8	-22.6
Fabric and apparel patternmakers	Long-term on-the-job training	80.3	14.5	5.2	26,360	11	8	-3	-24.6

169

Educational attainment cluster, most significant source of postsecondary education or training, and educational attainment distribution, by occupation *(continued)*

Occupation	Most Significant Source of Postsecondary Education or Training	Percent of Workers Aged 25 to 44, by Educational Attainment			2002 Median Annual Earnings	Employment (in Thousands)		Employment Change, 2002–12	
		High School or Less	Some College	College or Higher	Dollars	2002	2012	Numeric	Percent
Shoe machine operators and tenders	Moderate-term on-the-job training	83.7	10.4	6.0	20,600	7	5	–2	–26.1
Fishers and related fishing workers	Moderate-term on-the-job training	75.4	16.2	8.4	20,710	36	27	–10	–26.8
Textile bleaching and dyeing machine operators and tenders	Moderate-term on-the-job training	88.5	9.8	1.7	20,800	27	19	–8	–28.7
Textile winding, twisting, and drawing out machine setters, operators, and tenders	Moderate-term on-the-job training	87.9	11.7	.4	21,920	66	46	–20	–30.3
Textile knitting and weaving machine setters, operators, and tenders	Long-term on-the-job training	89.3	7.9	2.8	22,970	53	33	–20	–38.6
All other motor vehicle operators	Short-term on-the-job training	73.0	16.8	10.2	18,820	111	139	28	25.2
Combined food preparation and serving workers, including fast food	Short-term on-the-job training	76.7	18.1	5.3	14,500	1,990	2,444	454	22.8
Food preparation workers	Short-term on-the-job training	76.9	17.7	5.4	16,330	850	1,022	172	20.2

Occupation	Training							
Parking lot attendants	Short-term on-the-job training	70.3	19.4	10.3	16,320	107	128	21	19.2
Bicycle repairers	Moderate-term on-the-job training	87.9	9.8	2.3	19,230	7	8	1	18.8
Janitors and cleaners, except maids and housekeeping cleaners	Short-term on-the-job training	79.2	17.3	3.5	18,250	2,267	2,681	414	18.3
Meat, poultry, and fish cutters and trimmers	Short-term on-the-job training	81.2	16.2	2.6	17,820	154	179	25	16.4
Cooks, restaurant	Long-term on-the-job training	78.3	16.4	5.3	19,050	727	843	116	15.9
All other food preparation and serving related workers	Short-term on-the-job training	78.3	16.4	5.3	16,320	117	134	18	15.2
Dining room and cafeteria attendants and bartender helpers	Short-term on-the-job training	78.4	14.6	7.0	14,530	409	470	61	14.9
Packers and packagers, hand	Short-term on-the-job training	83.3	12.6	4.1	16,700	920	1,052	132	14.4
All other food processing workers	Short-term on-the-job training	81.2	16.2	2.6	19,410	42	48	6	13.4
Laundry and dry-cleaning workers	Moderate-term on-the-job training	82.4	13.6	4.0	16,780	231	260	29	12.3
Maid and housekeeping cleaners	Short-term on-the-job training	81.5	13.9	4.6	16,440	1,492	1,629	137	9.2
Dishwashers	Short-term on-the-job training	89.6	7.4	3.0	14,860	505	551	46	9.0
Cooks, short order	Short-term on-the-job training	78.3	16.4	5.3	16,270	227	247	20	9.0
Cleaners of vehicles and equipment	Short-term on-the-job training	78.1	17.4	4.5	17,060	344	374	30	8.7
Helpers—production workers	Short-term on-the-job training	77.3	17.3	5.4	19,240	467	503	36	7.7

Occupation	Most Significant Source of Postsecondary Education or Training	Percent of Workers Aged 25 to 44, by Educational Attainment			2002 Median Annual Earnings	Employment (in Thousands)		Employment Change, 2002–12	
		High School or Less	Some College	College or Higher	Dollars	2002	2012	Numeric	Percent
Agricultural equipment operators	Moderate-term on-the-job training	83.6	11.8	4.6	17,290	61	65	4	7.3
Graders and sorters, agricultural products	Work experience in a related occupation	80.9	12.0	7.1	15,940	49	52	3	6.7
Cooks, fast food	Short-term on-the-job training	78.3	16.4	5.3	14,350	588	617	29	5.0
Forest and conservation workers	Moderate-term on-the-job training	73.2	16.3	10.6	18,960	14	15	1	4.5
Farmworkers, farm and ranch animals	Short-term on-the-job training	83.6	11.8	4.6	17,090	53	56	2	4.4
Farmworkers and laborers, crop, nursery, and greenhouse	Short-term on-the-job training	83.6	11.8	4.6	15,070	617	641	24	4.0
All other textile, apparel, and furnishings workers	Short-term on-the-job training	86.2	10.5	3.4	18,740	61	63	2	3.3
Cooks, institution and cafeteria	Moderate-term on-the-job training	78.3	16.4	5.3	18,140	436	445	9	2.1
Pressers, textile, garment, and related materials	Short-term on-the-job training	89.8	8.4	1.8	17,070	91	91	0	-.2
Cooks, private household	Long-term on-the-job training	78.3	16.4	5.3	16,692	8	8	0	-5.4

Educational attainment cluster, most significant source of postsecondary education or training, and educational attainment distribution, by occupation *(continued)*

172

Occupation	Training							
Sewing machine operators	Moderate-term on-the-job training	86.7	10.2	3.1	17,440	315	216	-99	-31.5
Elevator installers and repairers	Long-term on-the-job training	68.4	31.3	.3	54,070	21	25	4	17.1
First-line supervisors/managers of mechanics, installers, and repairers	Work experience in a related occupation	47.7	40.2	12.1	47,580	444	512	68	15.4
First-line supervisors/managers of construction trades and extraction workers	Work experience in a related occupation	63.0	26.9	10.1	47,670	633	722	89	14.1
Subway, streetcar operators and all other rail transportation workers	Work experience in a related occupation	50.9	37.6	11.6	44,680	15	17	2	13.2
Gaming managers	Work experience in a related occupation	38.0	45.8	16.2	54,330	6	7	1	12.4
First-line supervisors of transportation and material-moving machine and vehicle operators	Work experience in a related occupation	50.0	36.5	13.5	42,910	207	232	25	12.0
Control and valve installers and repairers, except mechanical door	Moderate-term on-the-job training	55.9	34.2	9.9	43,460	38	42	5	12.0
Fire inspectors	Work experience in a related occupation	44.7	38.9	16.4	44,250	14	16	2	11.6
Aircraft mechanics and service technicians	Postsecondary vocational award	36.1	52.7	11.2	43,070	131	145	14	11.0
Electrical and electronic engineering technicians	Associate degree	28.8	54.5	16.7	42,950	204	224	20	10.0
First-line supervisors/managers of production and operating workers	Work experience in a related occupation	58.7	28.8	12.5	42,930	733	803	70	9.5

Occupation	Most Significant Source of Postsecondary Education or Training	Percent of Workers Aged 25 to 44, by Educational Attainment			2002 Median Annual Earnings	Employment (in Thousands)		Employment Change, 2002–12	
		High School or Less	Some College	College or Higher	Dollars	2002	2012	Numeric	Percent
Industrial engineering technicians	Associate degree	28.8	54.5	16.7	41,910	62	67	5	8.7
Transportation inspectors	Work experience in a related occupation	39.7	45.9	14.4	48,450	29	32	2	7.7
All other precision instrument and equipment repairers	Long-term on-the-job training	38.6	43.4	18.0	44,090	17	18	1	7.0
Gas plant operators	Long-term on-the-job training	54.6	39.0	6.4	48,340	12	13	1	6.7
Millwrights	Long-term on-the-job training	60.2	39.3	.5	41,990	69	73	4	5.3
Ship engineers	Postsecondary vocational award	59.5	26.6	13.9	51,190	8	9	0	4.5
Avionics technicians	Postsecondary vocational award	49.4	44.1	6.5	42,030	23	24	1	3.4
Boilermakers	Long-term on-the-job training	66.0	31.2	2.8	41,960	25	25	0	1.7
Electrical power-line installers and repairers	Long-term on-the-job training	61.1	34.6	4.3	48,530	101	103	2	1.6
Aerospace engineering and operations technicians	Associate degree	29.9	53.8	16.2	51,650	15	15	0	1.5
Gas compressor and gas pumping station operators	Moderate-term on-the-job training	52.2	38.8	9.0	42,510	7	7	0	1.0

Educational attainment cluster, most significant source of postsecondary education or training, and educational attainment distribution, by occupation *(continued)*

Occupation	Training							
Tool and die makers	Long-term on-the-job training	47.5	47.3	5.2	42,730	109	110	0	.4
Power plant operators	Long-term on-the-job training	49.8	38.0	12.2	49,920	35	36	0	.3
Stationary engineers and boiler operators	Long-term on-the-job training	53.7	35.4	11.0	43,240	55	56	0	.3
Electrical and electronics repairers, power-house, substation, and relay	Postsecondary vocational award	31.5	63.4	5.1	51,690	21	21	0	-.6
Telecommunications equipment installers and repairers, except line installers	Long-term on-the-job training	40.8	48.2	11.0	47,380	219	217	-1	-.6
Power distributors and dispatchers	Long-term on-the-job training	47.1	40.5	12.4	54,120	12	12	0	-3.0
Signal and track switch repairers	Moderate-term on-the-job training	63.2	28.2	8.6	43,370	8	8	0	-3.0
Nuclear power reactor operators	Long-term on-the-job training	49.8	38.0	12.2	61,060	3	3	0	-3.2
Railroad conductors and yardmasters	Work experience in a related occupation	46.8	42.4	10.9	44,490	38	36	-2	-4.2
Locomotive engineers and firers	Work experience in a related occupation	46.8	47.3	5.9	45,450	33	31	-2	-7.2
Petroleum pump system operators, refinery operators, and gaugers	Long-term on-the-job training	57.6	37.5	4.9	49,280	39	35	-4	-11.0
Chemical plant and system operators	Long-term on-the-job training	54.6	39.0	6.4	43,940	58	51	-7	-12.3
Railroad brake, signal, and switch operators	Work experience in a related occupation	50.9	37.6	11.6	43,520	15	12	-3	-22.8
Respiratory therapy technicians	Postsecondary vocational award	33.7	54.0	12.3	34,130	26	35	9	34.2

175

Educational attainment cluster, most significant source of postsecondary education or training, and educational attainment distribution, by occupation *(continued)*

Occupation	Most Significant Source of Postsecondary Education or Training	Percent of Workers Aged 25 to 44, by Educational Attainment			2002 Median Annual Earnings	Employment (in Thousands)		Employment Change, 2002–12	
		High School or Less	Some College	College or Higher	Dollars	2002	2012	Numeric	Percent
Heating, air conditioning, and refrigeration mechanics and installers	Long-term on-the-job training	59.6	36.8	3.6	34,900	249	328	79	31.8
Security and fire alarm systems installers	Postsecondary vocational award	49.0	44.8	6.2	32,370	46	60	14	30.2
Desktop publishers	Postsecondary vocational award	42.6	41.1	16.3	31,620	35	45	10	29.2
Environmental engineering technicians	Associate degree	29.9	53.8	16.2	36,850	19	24	5	28.4
Surgical technologists	Postsecondary vocational award	33.7	54.0	12.3	31,210	72	92	20	27.9
Correctional officers and jailers	Moderate-term on-the-job training	43.1	46.9	10.0	32,670	427	531	103	24.2
Electricians	Long-term on-the-job training	49.8	44.1	6.1	41,390	659	814	154	23.4
Surveying and mapping technicians	Moderate-term on-the-job training	47.5	45.4	7.2	29,230	60	74	14	23.2
Mechanical door repairers	Moderate-term on-the-job training	59.2	30.0	10.8	29,190	11	13	2	21.8
First-line supervisors/managers of landscaping, lawn service, and groundskeeping workers	Work experience in a related occupation	50.7	29.5	19.8	33,050	150	182	32	21.6

Occupation	Training							
Septic tank servicers and sewer pipe cleaners	Moderate-term on-the-job training	66.2	28.5	5.3	27,940	18	22	4	21.2
Locksmiths and safe repairers	Moderate-term on-the-job training	70.7	25.2	4.1	28,430	23	28	5	21.0
Fire fighters	Long-term on-the-job training	25.9	57.8	16.3	36,230	282	340	58	20.7
Licensed practical and licensed vocational nurses	Postsecondary vocational award	23.2	71.7	5.1	31,440	702	844	142	20.2
Sheet metal workers	Moderate-term on-the-job training	68.7	29.5	1.8	34,560	205	246	41	19.8
All other electrical and electronic equipment mechanics, installers, and repairers	Postsecondary vocational award	40.8	48.2	11.0	35,160	22	26	4	19.6
Truck drivers, heavy and tractor-trailer	Moderate-term on-the-job training	70.9	24.2	4.9	33,210	1,767	2,104	337	19.0
Legal secretaries	Postsecondary vocational award	37.2	47.0	15.9	35,020	264	313	50	18.8
Telecommunications line installers and repairers	Long-term on-the-job training	48.1	46.5	5.3	39,640	167	199	31	18.8
Plumbers, pipefitters, and steamfitters	Long-term on-the-job training	67.0	28.8	4.2	40,170	492	584	92	18.7
Motorboat mechanics	Long-term on-the-job training	62.9	34.7	2.4	29,050	22	26	4	18.3
Painters, transportation equipment	Moderate-term on-the-job training	76.7	20.8	2.5	33,550	50	59	9	17.5
Glaziers	Long-term on-the-job training	61.3	33.9	4.8	31,620	49	57	8	17.2
Welders, cutters, solderers, and brazers	Long-term on-the-job training	74.6	23.2	2.2	29,160	391	457	66	17.0
Maintenance and repair workers, general	Moderate-term on-the-job training	56.7	34.8	8.5	29,370	1,266	1,472	207	16.3

Educational attainment cluster, most significant source of postsecondary education or training, and educational attainment distribution, by occupation *(continued)*

Occupation	Most Significant Source of Postsecondary Education or Training	Percent of Workers Aged 25 to 44, by Educational Attainment			2002 Median Annual Earnings	Employment (in Thousands)		Employment Change, 2002–12	
		High School or Less	Some College	College or Higher	Dollars	2002	2012	Numeric	Percent
First-line supervisors/managers of housekeeping and janitorial workers	Work experience in a related occupation	61.7	29.6	8.6	28,140	230	267	37	16.2
Medical appliance technicians	Long-term on-the-job training	50.4	34.2	15.4	27,680	14	16	2	16.1
Water and liquid waste treatment plant and system operators	Long-term on-the-job training	48.7	43.8	7.5	33,390	99	115	16	16.0
Structural iron and steel workers	Long-term on-the-job training	70.9	27.8	1.3	40,660	78	90	12	15.9
Choreographers	Work experience in a related occupation	57.5	33.5	9.0	29,470	17	20	3	15.8
Chefs and head cooks	Work experience in a related occupation	47.7	38.0	14.3	27,940	132	153	21	15.8
Insulation workers	Moderate-term on-the-job training	66.1	30.6	3.4	28,930	53	62	8	15.8
Aircraft cargo handling supervisors	Work experience in a related occupation	50.0	36.5	13.5	37,220	9	10	1	15.6
Lay-out workers, metal and plastic	Moderate-term on-the-job training	76.3	20.0	3.7	30,760	13	15	2	15.6
Cargo and freight agents	Moderate-term on-the-job training	50.1	36.7	13.2	31,410	59	68	9	15.5

Occupation	Training							
All other vehicle and mobile equipment mechanics, installers, and repairers	Moderate-term on-the-job training	66.8	30.0	3.2	35,840	36	41	6	15.4
Bus drivers, transit and intercity	Moderate-term on-the-job training	63.9	29.2	7.0	29,580	202	233	31	15.2
Medical equipment repairers	Associate degree	36.0	49.0	15.0	36,380	29	33	4	14.8
Model makers, metal and plastic	Moderate-term on-the-job training	59.0	38.5	2.4	38,000	9	10	1	14.6
Dispatchers, except police, fire, and ambulance	Moderate-term on-the-job training	44.1	43.7	12.2	30,280	170	194	24	14.4
Riggers	Short-term on-the-job training	63.2	28.2	8.6	33,790	14	16	2	14.3
Bus and truck mechanics and diesel engine specialists	Postsecondary vocational award	66.0	30.6	3.4	34,380	267	305	38	14.2
First-line supervisors/managers of helpers, laborers, and material movers, hand	Work experience in a related occupation	50.0	36.5	13.5	37,180	147	168	21	14.0
Automotive body and related repairers	Long-term on-the-job training	73.7	21.8	4.5	32,680	198	225	26	13.2
Numerical tool and process control programmers	Long-term on-the-job training	58.5	36.5	5.0	37,520	19	22	3	13.0
Police, fire, and ambulance dispatchers	Moderate-term on-the-job training	44.1	43.7	12.2	27,660	92	104	12	12.7
Automotive service technicians and mechanics	Postsecondary vocational award	66.8	30.0	3.2	30,590	818	919	101	12.4

Educational attainment cluster, most significant source of postsecondary education or training, and educational attainment distribution, by occupation (continued)

Occupation	Most Significant Source of Postsecondary Education or Training	Percent of Workers Aged 25 to 44, by Educational Attainment			2002 Median Annual Earnings	Employment (in Thousands)		Employment Change, 2002–12	
		High School or Less	Some College	College or Higher	Dollars	2002	2012	Numeric	Percent
Installation, maintenance, and repair workers, all other	Moderate-term on-the-job training	62.3	25.6	12.1	33,010	185	207	23	12.2
Pipelayers	Moderate-term on-the-job training	67.0	28.8	4.2	28,500	58	65	7	11.8
Electro-mechanical technicians	Associate degree	28.8	54.5	16.7	38,120	31	35	4	11.5
Mechanical engineering technicians	Associate degree	28.8	54.5	16.7	41,280	55	61	6	11.0
Commercial divers	Moderate-term on-the-job training	63.2	28.2	8.6	34,710	4	5	0	10.6
Highway maintenance workers	Moderate-term on-the-job training	74.9	23.2	1.9	28,390	154	170	16	10.4
Electrical and electronics repairers, commercial and industrial equipment	Postsecondary vocational award	31.5	63.4	5.1	41,110	85	94	9	10.4
Carpenters	Long-term on-the-job training	72.7	22.2	5.1	34,190	1,209	1,331	122	10.1
Mobile heavy equipment mechanics, except engines	Postsecondary vocational award	63.2	31.1	5.7	35,970	126	138	12	9.6
Bailiffs	Moderate-term on-the-job training	44.8	43.9	11.3	32,710	15	16	1	9.5
First-line supervisors/managers of personal service workers	Work experience in a related occupation	45.6	39.7	14.8	28,960	216	236	20	9.4

Occupation	Training								
Computer-controlled machine tool operators, metal and plastic	Moderate-term on-the-job training	58.5	36.5	5.0	29,050	132	144	12	9.3
Traffic technicians	Short-term on-the-job training	36.7	54.9	8.4	31,650	6	6	1	9.3
Job printers	Long-term on-the-job training	66.5	27.0	6.5	30,100	56	61	5	9.2
Executive secretaries and administrative assistants	Moderate-term on-the-job training	37.2	47.0	15.9	33,410	1,526	1,658	132	8.7
Multiple machine tool setters, operators, and tenders, metal and plastic	Moderate-term on-the-job training	72.3	24.3	3.3	28,690	99	107	8	8.3
Machinists	Long-term on-the-job training	63.9	32.4	3.7	32,570	387	419	32	8.2
Earth drillers, except oil and gas	Moderate-term on-the-job training	78.4	20.5	1.2	32,490	23	25	2	7.7
Civil engineering technicians	Associate degree	28.8	54.5	16.7	37,720	92	99	7	7.6
Electrical and electronics installers and repairers, transportation equipment	Postsecondary vocational award	49.4	44.1	6.5	38,610	18	19	1	7.1
Tire builders	Moderate-term on-the-job training	49.9	44.2	6.0	38,840	14	15	1	6.6
All other metal workers and plastic workers	Moderate-term on-the-job training	75.7	21.5	2.7	28,400	104	111	7	6.6
Payroll and timekeeping clerks	Moderate-term on-the-job training	37.9	46.8	15.2	29,000	198	211	13	6.5
Musical instrument repairers and tuners	Long-term on-the-job training	36.0	49.0	15.0	29,440	6	7	0	6.3
Structural metal fabricators and fitters	Moderate-term on-the-job training	79.3	20.7	.0	28,620	89	94	6	6.2
Paperhangers	Moderate-term on-the-job training	57.9	34.9	7.2	31,650	20	21	1	5.9

Educational attainment cluster, most significant source of postsecondary education or training, and educational attainment distribution, by occupation *(continued)*

Occupation	Most Significant Source of Postsecondary Education or Training	Percent of Workers Aged 25 to 44, by Educational Attainment			2002 Median Annual Earnings	Employment (in Thousands)		Employment Change, 2002–12	
		High School or Less	Some College	College or Higher	Dollars	2002	2012	Numeric	Percent
Maintenance workers, machinery	Short-term on-the-job training	72.6	25.3	2.2	32,520	92	97	5	5.9
Refractory materials repairers, except brick-masons	Moderate-term on-the-job training	60.4	34.3	5.3	35,100	4	4	0	5.6
All other plant and system operators	Long-term on-the-job training	57.6	37.5	4.9	36,660	32	33	2	5.6
All other water trans-portation workers	Short-term on-the-job training	50.0	36.5	13.5	30,520	4	4	0	5.6
Industrial machinery mechanics	Long-term on-the-job training	60.4	34.3	5.3	37,980	197	208	11	5.5
Home appliance repairers	Long-term on-the-job training	69.9	25.4	4.7	30,390	42	44	2	5.5
Electric motor, power tool, and related repairers	Postsecondary vocational award	49.4	43.7	6.9	32,210	31	33	2	5.3
Printing machine operators	Moderate-term on-the-job training	70.6	25.3	4.1	29,010	199	208	9	4.6
Rail car repairers	Long-term on-the-job training	65.8	29.5	4.7	39,060	15	15	1	4.5
Sailors and marine oilers	Short-term on-the-job training	69.8	24.8	5.4	28,370	27	28	1	4.0

Occupation	Training							
Insurance claims and policy processing clerks	Moderate-term on-the-job training	39.4	44.4	16.2	28,870	266	276	10	3.6
Dental laboratory technicians	Long-term on-the-job training	51.8	34.6	13.6	28,500	47	49	2	3.6
Patternmakers, metal and plastic	Moderate-term on-the-job training	59.0	38.5	2.4	33,470	6	7	0	3.6
Bookkeeping, accounting, and auditing clerks	Moderate-term on-the-job training	40.4	43.8	15.8	27,380	1,983	2,042	59	3.0
Drilling and boring machine tool setters, operators, and tenders, metal and plastic	Moderate-term on-the-job training	72.9	23.1	4.0	27,530	53	54	1	2.1
Bookbinders	Moderate-term on-the-job training	70.4	21.5	8.1	27,680	7	7	0	1.3
Welding, soldering, and brazing machine setters, operators, and tenders	Moderate-term on-the-job training	74.6	23.2	2.2	28,900	61	62	1	.9
Separating, filtering, clarifying, precipitating, and still machine setters, operators, and tenders	Moderate-term on-the-job training	46.2	36.4	17.5	30,340	36	36	0	.8
Lathe and turning machine tool setters, operators, and tenders, metal and plastic	Moderate-term on-the-job training	77.4	20.9	1.7	30,270	75	75	1	.8
Postal service clerks	Short-term on-the-job training	43.8	41.5	14.7	39,700	77	77	0	-.5
Postal service mail carriers	Short-term on-the-job training	52.0	40.2	7.8	39,530	334	333	-2	-.5
Engine and other machine assemblers	Short-term on-the-job training	70.5	26.0	3.5	29,170	50	49	-1	-1.9

Educational attainment cluster, most significant source of postsecondary education or training, and educational attainment distribution, by occupation *(continued)*

Occupation	Most Significant Source of Postsecondary Education or Training	Percent of Workers Aged 25 to 44, by Educational Attainment			2002 Median Annual Earnings	Employment (in Thousands)		Employment Change, 2002–12	
		High School or Less	Some College	College or Higher	Dollars	2002	2012	Numeric	Percent
Paper goods machine setters, operators, and tenders	Moderate-term on-the-job training	75.0	22.8	2.2	28,280	117	114	–3	–2.8
Chemical equipment operators and tenders	Moderate-term on-the-job training	46.2	36.4	17.5	37,430	58	56	–2	–3.8
Furnace, kiln, oven, drier, and kettle operators and tenders	Moderate-term on-the-job training	71.2	23.0	5.7	28,210	31	29	–2	–4.9
Pump operators, except wellhead pumpers	Moderate-term on-the-job training	52.2	38.8	9.0	36,470	13	13	–1	–5.0
Mixing and blending machine setters, operators, and tenders	Moderate-term on-the-job training	67.9	28.6	3.6	27,530	106	99	–7	–6.5
Procurement clerks	Short-term on-the-job training	55.7	30.9	13.4	29,600	77	72	–5	–6.7
Mine cutting and channeling machine operators	Moderate-term on-the-job training	72.4	24.3	3.3	37,590	5	5	0	–7.1
Camera and photographic equipment repairers	Moderate-term on-the-job training	36.0	49.0	15.0	31,390	7	6	0	–7.2
Tool grinders, filers, and sharpeners	Moderate-term on-the-job training	68.4	22.5	9.1	29,400	26	24	–2	–7.7

Occupation	Training							
Aircraft structure, surfaces, rigging, and systems assemblers	Long-term on-the-job training	74.7	20.4	4.9	38,910	27	24	-2	-9.4
Postal service mail sorters, processors, and processing machine operators	Short-term on-the-job training	44.5	40.7	14.7	38,150	253	226	-26	-10.5
All other mining machine operators	Moderate-term on-the-job training	71.0	24.8	4.2	38,780	4	4	0	-10.8
Prepress technicians and workers	Long-term on-the-job training	57.1	30.0	12.9	31,150	91	81	-10	-11.2
Rail-track laying and maintenance equipment operators	Moderate-term on-the-job training	61.5	28.9	9.6	35,160	11	9	-1	-11.5
Wellhead pumpers	Moderate-term on-the-job training	52.2	38.8	9.0	33,770	11	10	-1	-11.7
Meter readers, utilities	Short-term on-the-job training	57.2	38.8	4.1	28,830	54	46	-8	-14.1
Bridge and lock tenders	Short-term on-the-job training	62.8	30.3	6.9	35,310	4	3	-1	-17.4
Continuous mining machine operators	Moderate-term on-the-job training	70.7	25.7	3.5	34,850	8	7	-2	-18.5
All other communications equipment operators	Short-term on-the-job training	53.5	38.5	8.0	31,640	18	14	-5	-24.6
Radio mechanics	Postsecondary vocational award	40.8	48.2	11.0	36,230	7	5	-2	-29.3
Telephone operators	Short-term on-the-job training	42.3	48.0	9.7	28,600	50	22	-28	-56.3
Medical assistants	Moderate-term on-the-job training	36.6	49.8	13.5	23,940	365	579	215	58.9
Medical records and health information technicians	Associate degree	35.5	48.1	16.4	23,890	147	216	69	46.8
Veterinary technologists and technicians	Associate degree	33.7	54.0	12.3	22,950	53	76	23	44.1

Educational attainment cluster, most significant source of postsecondary education or training, and educational attainment distribution, by occupation *(continued)*

Occupation	Most Significant Source of Postsecondary Education or Training	Percent of Workers Aged 25 to 44, by Educational Attainment			2002 Median Annual Earnings	Employment (in Thousands)		Employment Change, 2002–12	
		High School or Less	Some College	College or Higher	Dollars	2002	2012	Numeric	Percent
Dental assistants	Moderate-term on-the-job training	34.2	57.4	8.4	27,240	266	379	113	42.5
Emergency medical technicians and paramedics	Postsecondary vocational award	24.4	62.9	12.7	24,030	179	238	59	33.1
Receptionists and information clerks	Short-term on-the-job training	49.7	38.6	11.8	21,150	1,100	1,425	325	29.5
Pharmacy technicians	Moderate-term on-the-job training	33.7	54.0	12.3	22,250	211	271	61	28.8
Interviewers, except eligibility and loan	Short-term on-the-job training	30.1	50.3	19.6	21,690	193	247	54	28.0
All other healthcare support workers	Short-term on-the-job training	36.6	49.8	13.5	23,690	198	251	53	26.6
Costume attendants	Short-term on-the-job training	45.8	40.5	13.7	24,160	4	5	1	25.1
Nursing aides, orderlies, and attendants	Short-term on-the-job training	62.7	31.4	5.9	19,960	1,375	1,718	343	24.9
Gaming surveillance officers and gaming investigators	Moderate-term on-the-job training	52.5	34.7	12.8	23,110	9	11	2	24.6
Bill and account collectors	Short-term on-the-job training	45.6	35.7	18.7	26,780	413	514	101	24.4
Truck drivers, light or delivery services	Short-term on-the-job training	60.9	25.9	13.2	23,870	1,022	1,259	237	23.2

Occupation	Training							
Medical transcriptionists	Postsecondary vocational award	36.6	49.8	13.5	27,140	101	124	23	22.6
Dietetic technicians	Moderate-term on-the-job training	33.7	54.0	12.3	22,490	29	35	6	20.2
Skin care specialists	Postsecondary vocational award	58.6	32.8	8.7	22,450	25	30	5	19.4
All other air transportation workers	Moderate-term on-the-job training	50.0	36.5	13.5	23,330	12	14	2	19.4
Outdoor power equipment and other small engine mechanics	Moderate-term on-the-job training	59.6	39.6	.7	24,820	30	36	6	18.9
Motorcycle mechanics	Long-term on-the-job training	63.9	34.0	2.1	27,100	15	18	3	18.7
Makeup artists, theatrical and performance	Postsecondary vocational award	58.6	32.8	8.7	24,730	2	2	0	18.2
Opticians, dispensing	Long-term on-the-job training	22.2	60.1	17.7	25,600	63	75	11	18.2
Medical equipment preparers	Short-term on-the-job training	36.6	49.8	13.5	22,960	36	43	7	18.1
Painting, coating, and decorating workers	Short-term on-the-job training	76.7	20.8	2.5	21,200	34	40	6	17.6
Medical secretaries	Postsecondary vocational award	37.2	47.0	15.9	25,430	339	398	58	17.2
Pest control workers	Moderate-term on-the-job training	60.2	34.4	5.4	24,760	62	72	10	17.0
Bus drivers, school	Short-term on-the-job training	63.9	29.2	7.0	22,390	453	528	76	16.7
First-line supervisors/managers of food preparation and serving workers	Work experience in a related occupation	56.2	30.3	13.5	24,390	692	800	107	15.5
Concierges	Moderate-term on-the-job training	51.9	36.1	12.0	21,720	17	20	3	15.3
Coin, vending, and amusement machine servicers and repairers	Moderate-term on-the-job training	62.6	32.3	5.1	27,380	43	49	6	15.2

Educational attainment cluster, most significant source of postsecondary education or training, and educational attainment distribution, by occupation *(continued)*

Occupation	Most Significant Source of Postsecondary Education or Training	Percent of Workers Aged 25 to 44, by Educational Attainment			2002 Median Annual Earnings	Employment (in Thousands)		Employment Change, 2002–12	
		High School or Less	Some College	College or Higher	Dollars	2002	2012	Numeric	Percent
All other related transportation workers	Short-term on-the-job training	44.5	49.2	6.3	26,600	40	47	6	15.2
Electronic equipment installers and repairers, motor vehicles	Postsecondary vocational award	37.9	59.6	2.5	26,010	18	21	3	14.8
Weighers, measurers, checkers, and samplers, recordkeeping	Short-term on-the-job training	56.4	30.6	13.0	24,170	81	93	12	14.6
Gaming cage workers	Short-term on-the-job training	43.6	42.5	13.9	21,780	18	21	3	14.5
Psychiatric aides	Short-term on-the-job training	62.7	31.4	5.9	22,970	59	68	9	14.5
Animal control workers	Moderate-term on-the-job training	53.7	32.6	13.6	24,780	11	12	1	12.6
Court, municipal, and license clerks	Short-term on-the-job training	39.9	46.1	14.0	27,300	106	119	13	12.3
All other production workers	Moderate-term on-the-job training	74.3	21.0	4.7	22,260	449	500	51	11.3
Bakers	Long-term on-the-job training	73.5	20.5	6.0	20,580	173	192	19	11.2
New accounts clerks	Work experience in a related occupation	41.0	43.0	16.0	25,200	99	110	11	11.2
Dancers	Long-term on-the-job training	57.5	33.5	9.0	21,100	20	22	2	11.1
Office clerks, general	Short-term on-the-job training	40.9	42.4	16.7	22,280	2,991	3,301	310	10.4

Occupation	Training							
Material moving workers, all other	Moderate-term on-the-job training	73.7	22.3	4.1	25,070	78	86	8	10.0
Tellers	Short-term on-the-job training	44.3	42.9	12.7	20,400	530	580	50	9.4
Cabinetmakers and bench carpenters	Long-term on-the-job training	69.0	23.3	7.7	24,000	147	160	14	9.4
Coating, painting, and spraying machine setters, operators, and tenders	Moderate-term on-the-job training	76.7	20.8	2.5	25,290	103	112	10	9.4
All other printing workers	Moderate-term on-the-job training	70.6	25.3	4.1	23,330	21	23	2	9.3
Ophthalmic laboratory technicians	Moderate-term on-the-job training	51.8	34.6	13.6	21,760	33	36	3	9.2
Grinding and polishing workers, hand	Moderate-term on-the-job training	67.9	28.6	3.6	22,970	45	49	4	9.0
Molding, coremaking, and casting machine setters, operators, and tenders, metal and plastic	Moderate-term on-the-job training	71.4	25.7	2.9	23,230	151	165	14	8.9
Electronic home entertainment equipment installers and repairers	Postsecondary vocational award	59.4	33.4	7.1	27,200	43	46	4	8.6
Billing and posting clerks and machine operators	Moderate-term on-the-job training	39.3	43.9	16.8	26,110	507	547	40	7.9
Farm equipment mechanics	Postsecondary vocational award	63.2	31.1	5.7	27,100	35	38	3	7.7
Extruding and drawing machine setters, operators, and tenders, metal and plastic	Moderate-term on-the-job training	76.3	23.6	.1	25,870	98	105	7	7.1

189

Educational attainment cluster, most significant source of postsecondary education or training, and educational attainment distribution, by occupation *(continued)*

Occupation	Most Significant Source of Postsecondary Education or Training	Percent of Workers Aged 25 to 44, by Educational Attainment			2002 Median Annual Earnings	Employment (in Thousands)		Employment Change, 2002–12	
		High School or Less	Some College	College or Higher	Dollars	2002	2012	Numeric	Percent
Cutting, punching, and press machine setters, operators, and tenders, metal and plastic	Moderate-term on-the-job training	72.4	26.1	1.5	24,570	283	302	19	6.8
Laborers and freight, stock, and material movers, hand	Short-term on-the-job training	73.8	21.7	4.5	19,710	2,231	2,378	147	6.6
Etchers and engravers	Long-term on-the-job training	63.1	25.3	11.6	22,450	10	10	1	6.2
Forging machine setters, operators, and tenders, metal and plastic	Moderate-term on-the-job training	76.6	23.4	.0	26,300	45	48	3	6.0
Psychiatric technicians	Moderate-term on-the-job training	33.7	54.0	12.3	25,710	60	63	4	5.9
Fiberglass laminators and fabricators	Moderate-term on-the-job training	73.8	21.2	5.0	24,610	37	39	2	5.6
Inspectors, testers, sorters, samplers, and weighers	Moderate-term on-the-job training	52.9	33.7	13.4	27,060	515	539	24	4.7
Jewelers and precious stone and metal workers	Postsecondary vocational award	61.5	24.8	13.7	26,260	40	42	2	4.5
Driver/sales workers	Short-term on-the-job training	70.9	24.2	4.9	20,640	431	450	19	4.3

Occupation	Training								
Foundry mold and coremakers	Moderate-term on-the-job training	74.9	21.5	3.5	26,100	23	24	1	3.6
Watch repairers	Long-term on-the-job training	36.0	49.0	15.0	26,560	5	5	0	3.5
Shipping, receiving, and traffic clerks	Short-term on-the-job training	64.5	28.6	6.9	23,420	803	827	24	3.0
Switchboard operators, including answering service	Short-term on-the-job training	54.6	34.0	11.4	21,190	236	236	1	.2
Extruding, forming, pressing, and compacting machine setters, operators, and tenders	Moderate-term on-the-job training	69.5	26.0	4.5	26,540	73	73	0	-.1
All other assemblers and fabricators	Moderate-term on-the-job training	73.8	21.2	5.0	22,890	361	360	-1	-.2
File clerks	Short-term on-the-job training	44.7	40.5	14.8	20,020	265	264	-1	-.3
Correspondence clerks	Short-term on-the-job training	44.3	41.0	14.7	25,960	33	33	0	-1.4
Team assemblers	Moderate-term on-the-job training	73.8	21.2	5.0	22,680	1,174	1,155	-19	-1.6
Parts salespersons	Moderate-term on-the-job training	67.3	27.8	4.9	23,950	248	243	-5	-2.0
Fabric menders, except garment	Moderate-term on-the-job training	62.3	25.6	12.1	25,690	2	2	0	-2.2
Crushing, grinding, and polishing machine setters, operators, and tenders	Moderate-term on-the-job training	67.9	28.6	3.6	26,690	45	44	-1	-2.8
Secretaries, except legal, medical, and executive	Moderate-term on-the-job training	37.2	47.0	15.9	25,290	1,975	1,918	-57	-2.9
Mail clerks and mail machine operators, except postal service	Short-term on-the-job training	56.9	36.0	7.1	21,190	170	165	-5	-2.9

Educational attainment cluster, most significant source of postsecondary education or training, and educational attainment distribution, by occupation *(continued)*

Occupation	Most Significant Source of Postsecondary Education or Training	Percent of Workers Aged 25 to 44, by Educational Attainment			2002 Median Annual Earnings	Employment (in Thousands)		Employment Change, 2002–12	
		High School or Less	Some College	College or Higher	Dollars	2002	2012	Numeric	Percent
Timing device assemblers, adjusters, and calibrators	Moderate-term on-the-job training	73.8	21.2	5.0	24,190	7	6	0	-3.0
Office machine operators, except computer	Short-term on-the-job training	58.3	31.9	9.9	21,770	96	91	-4	-4.6
Bindery workers	Short-term on-the-job training	70.4	21.5	8.1	21,860	91	86	-5	-5.2
Data entry keyers	Moderate-term on-the-job training	45.1	41.0	13.9	22,390	392	371	-21	-5.4
Order clerks	Short-term on-the-job training	51.6	36.5	11.8	24,810	330	311	-19	-5.7
Credit authorizers, checkers, and clerks	Short-term on-the-job training	33.0	48.9	18.1	26,690	80	74	-5	-6.7
All other material recording, scheduling, dispatching, and distributing workers	Short-term on-the-job training	65.4	26.0	8.6	25,890	34	32	-2	-6.9
Electromechanical equipment assemblers	Short-term on-the-job training	72.6	21.6	5.8	25,260	60	55	-5	-8.3
Tailors, dressmakers, and custom sewers	Long-term on-the-job training	63.1	24.2	12.7	22,220	53	48	-5	-9.1
Semiconductor processors	Associate degree	68.7	23.9	7.5	27,340	46	42	-5	-10.6

Occupation	Training								
Coil winders, tapers, and finishers	Short-term on-the-job training	72.6	21.6	5.8	23,020	36	31	-5	-13.9
Electrical and electronic equipment assemblers	Short-term on-the-job training	72.6	21.6	5.8	22,940	281	230	-51	-18.3
Farmers and ranchers	Long-term on-the-job training	54.7	28.7	16.6	24,076	1,158	920	-238	-20.6
Word processors and typists	Moderate-term on-the-job training	37.6	48.2	14.2	26,730	241	148	-93	-38.6
Home health aides	Short-term on-the-job training	62.7	31.4	5.9	18,090	580	859	279	48.1
Personal and home care aides	Short-term on-the-job training	59.6	32.1	8.2	16,250	608	854	246	40.5
Security guards	Short-term on-the-job training	52.5	34.7	12.8	19,140	995	1,313	317	31.8
Amusement and recreation attendants	Short-term on-the-job training	45.8	40.5	13.7	14,920	234	299	65	27.8
Ambulance drivers and attendants, except emergency medical technicians	Moderate-term on-the-job training	69.5	24.9	5.6	19,100	17	22	5	26.7
Locker room, coat-room, and dressing room attendants	Short-term on-the-job training	56.9	34.0	9.1	16,930	23	29	6	26.5
Veterinary assistants and laboratory animal caretakers	Short-term on-the-job training	36.6	49.8	13.5	17,790	63	79	16	26.2
Gaming dealers	Postsecondary vocational award	51.4	35.3	13.3	14,090	78	97	19	24.7
Gaming and sports book writers and runners	Postsecondary vocational award	51.4	35.3	13.3	18,660	14	18	3	24.4
Gaming change persons and booth cashiers	Short-term on-the-job training	66.7	24.7	8.6	19,600	33	41	8	24.1
Hotel, motel, and resort desk clerks	Short-term on-the-job training	45.3	38.8	16.0	17,370	178	220	42	23.9

Occupation	Most Significant Source of Postsecondary Education or Training	Percent of Workers Aged 25 to 44, by Educational Attainment			2002 Median Annual Earnings	Employment (in Thousands)		Employment Change, 2002–12	
		High School or Less	Some College	College or Higher	Dollars	2002	2012	Numeric	Percent
Teacher assistants	Short-term on-the-job training	43.7	40.0	16.3	18,660	1,277	1,571	294	23.0
Manicurists and pedicurists	Postsecondary vocational award	58.6	32.8	8.7	17,330	51	63	12	22.7
Nonfarm animal caretakers	Short-term on-the-job training	55.6	31.7	12.7	17,080	125	153	28	22.2
Taxi drivers and chauffeurs	Short-term on-the-job training	60.9	25.9	13.2	18,530	132	161	29	21.7
All other gaming service workers	Moderate-term on-the-job training	51.4	35.3	13.3	17,970	40	49	9	21.3
Pharmacy aides	Short-term on-the-job training	36.6	49.8	13.5	18,430	60	71	11	17.6
Waiters and waitresses	Short-term on-the-job training	55.2	32.3	12.5	14,150	2,097	2,464	367	17.5
Counter attendants, cafeteria, food concession, and coffee shop	Short-term on-the-job training	72.0	20.1	7.9	15,230	467	545	78	16.7
Shampooers	Short-term on-the-job training	58.6	32.8	8.7	14,360	25	29	4	16.6
Crossing guards	Short-term on-the-job training	76.0	23.3	.6	18,680	74	86	12	16.5
Hosts and hostesses, restaurant, lounge, and coffee shop	Short-term on-the-job training	48.1	32.3	19.6	15,310	298	347	49	16.4

Table: Educational attainment cluster, most significant source of postsecondary education or training, and educational attainment distribution, by occupation (continued)

Ushers, lobby attendants, and ticket takers	Short-term on-the-job training	49.8	30.9	19.3	14,600	105	121	16	15.5
Hairdressers, hairstylists, and cosmetologists	Postsecondary vocational award	55.7	40.2	4.1	18,960	585	671	86	14.7
Baggage porters and bellhops	Short-term on-the-job training	44.5	45.8	9.6	17,860	58	67	8	14.4
Cashiers, except gaming	Short-term on-the-job training	66.1	25.6	8.3	15,420	3,432	3,886	454	13.2
Child care workers	Short-term on-the-job training	52.9	34.4	12.7	16,350	1,211	1,353	142	11.7
Food servers, nonrestaurant	Short-term on-the-job training	70.2	24.1	5.6	15,640	165	215	20	10.4
Bartenders	Short-term on-the-job training	49.2	37.9	12.9	15,000	463	503	40	8.6
Barbers	Postsecondary vocational award	59.7	38.6	1.7	19,500	66	70	4	6.4
Couriers and messengers	Short-term on-the-job training	53.2	36.6	10.2	19,390	132	138	5	4.0
Service station attendants	Short-term on-the-job training	67.8	26.4	5.9	16,570	107	111	4	3.3
Motion picture projectionists	Short-term on-the-job training	56.4	33.4	10.2	16,580	9	9	0	.4
Stock clerks and order fillers	Short-term on-the-job training	65.4	26.0	8.6	19,270	1,628	1,560	-68	-4.2
Telemarketers	Short-term on-the-job training	54.8	33.6	11.6	19,550	428	406	-21	-4.9
Shoe and leather workers and repairers	Long-term on-the-job training	70.2	20.3	9.5	19,010	16	14	-3	-16.1
Sewers, hand	Short-term on-the-job training	63.1	24.2	12.7	18,070	36	29	-8	-21.2
Occupational therapist assistants	Associate degree	19.9	63.0	17.1	36,660	18	26	7	39.2
Occupational therapist aides	Short-term on-the-job training	19.9	63.0	17.1	22,040	8	12	42.6	42.6

Educational attainment cluster, most significant source of postsecondary education or training, and educational attainment distribution, by occupation (continued)

Occupation	Most Significant Source of Postsecondary Education or Training	Percent of Workers Aged 25 to 44, by Educational Attainment			2002 Median Annual Earnings	Employment (in Thousands)		Employment Change, 2002–12	
		High School or Less	Some College	College or Higher	Dollars	2002	2012	Numeric	Percent
Administrative services managers	Bachelor's plus experience	22.6	36.8	40.6	52,500	321	384	63	19.8
Transportation, storage, and distribution managers	Work experience in a related occupation	49.0	28.8	22.2	59,660	111	133	22	19.7
Sales representatives, wholesale and manufacturing, technical and scientific products	Moderate-term on-the-job training	24.5	27.0	48.5	55,740	398	475	77	19.3
Sales representatives, wholesale and manufacturing, technical and scientific products	Moderate-term on-the-job training	24.5	27.0	48.5	42,730	1,459	1,738	279	19.2
First-line supervisors/ managers of correctional officers	Work experience in a related occupation	27.7	46.6	25.8	44,940	33	40	6	19.0
Orthotists and prosthetists	Bachelor's degree	31.0	47.0	22.0	46,260	5	6	1	18.9
Cost estimators	Work experience in a related occupation	32.8	38.4	28.8	47,550	188	223	35	18.6
General and operations managers	Bachelor's plus experience	21.3	30.4	48.4	68,210	2,049	2,425	376	18.4

196

Occupation	Education/training								
All other financial specialists	Bachelor's degree	25.2	29.6	45.2	44,140	162	190	28	17.6
Flight attendants	Long-term on-the-job training	25.3	37.9	36.7	43,140	104	121	17	16.0
Transit and railroad police	Long-term on-the-job training	21.0	52.1	26.9	43,710	6	7	1	15.9
Claims adjusters, examiners, and investigators	Long-term on-the-job training	24.1	32.2	43.7	43,020	227	260	32	14.2
Construction managers	Bachelor's degree	41.4	30.6	28.0	63,500	389	435	47	12.0
Insurance appraisers, auto damage	Long-term on-the-job training	24.1	32.2	43.7	42,630	14	16	2	11.7
Purchasing agents, except wholesale, retail, and farm products	Work experience in a related occupation	29.4	33.7	36.9	45,090	245	273	27	11.2
Insurance underwriters	Bachelor's degree	21.3	25.8	53.0	45,590	102	112	10	10.0
Agricultural and food scientists	Bachelor's degree	25.7	12.0	62.3	48,670	18	20	2	9.1
Industrial production managers	Bachelor's degree	29.8	29.7	40.5	67,320	182	197	14	7.9
First-line supervisors/managers of nonretail sales workers	Work experience in a related occupation	34.9	28.7	36.4	53,020	597	637	41	6.8
All other managers	Work experience in a related occupation	24.7	27.3	48.0	66,890	1,256	1,325	69	5.5
Farm, ranch, and other agricultural managers	Bachelor's plus experience	48.0	30.6	21.4	43,740	218	229	11	5.1
Real estate brokers	Work experience in a related occupation	22.2	37.0	40.7	50,330	99	101	2	2.4
Nuclear technicians	Associate degree	26.8	39.0	34.2	59,990	6	6	0	1.5

Educational attainment cluster, most significant source of postsecondary education or training, and educational attainment distribution, by occupation *(continued)*

Occupation	Most Significant Source of Postsecondary Education or Training	Percent of Workers Aged 25 to 44, by Educational Attainment			2002 Median Annual Earnings	Employment (in Thousands)		Employment Change, 2002–12	
		High School or Less	Some College	College or Higher	Dollars	2002	2012	Numeric	Percent
Postmasters and mail superintendents	Work experience in a related occupation	21.3	30.4	48.4	48,540	25	25	0	-.5
Environmental science and protection technicians, including health	Associate degree	20.7	33.6	45.7	35,320	28	38	10	36.8
Kindergarten teachers, except special education	Bachelor's degree	21.7	31.0	47.2	39,810	168	214	46	27.2
All other health practitioners and technical workers	Postsecondary vocational award	31.0	47.0	22.0	31,690	190	241	52	27.2
Audio and video equipment technicians	Long-term on-the-job training	22.7	40.9	36.4	31,110	42	53	11	26.8
Sound engineering technicians	Postsecondary vocational award	25.0	41.7	33.3	36,970	13	16	3	25.5
All other sales and related workers	Moderate-term on-the-job training	22.4	30.5	47.1	35,170	577	717	140	24.3
All other first-line supervisors/managers, protective service workers	Work experience in a related occupation	31.1	46.2	22.8	34,320	56	70	13	23.9
Biological technicians	Associate degree	24.6	16.4	59.0	32,710	48	57	9	19.4

198

Occupation	Education/training							
Human resources assistants, except payroll and timekeeping	Short-term on-the-job training	28.8	48.8	22.4	30,410	174	207	33	19.2
Forensic science technicians	Associate degree	20.7	33.6	45.7	41,040	8	10	2	18.9
Dietitians and nutritionists	Bachelor's degree	28.9	13.6	57.5	41,170	49	58	9	17.8
All other life, physical, and social science technicians	Associate degree	20.7	33.6	45.7	34,030	137	162	24	17.5
Musicians and singers	Long-term on-the-job training	21.0	26.1	52.9	36,290	161	189	27	17.1
All other entertainers and performers, sports and related workers	Long-term on-the-job training	34.4	25.4	40.2	33,740	56	65	9	16.4
Gaming supervisors	Work experience in a related occupation	35.4	31.5	33.1	39,290	39	45	6	15.7
Computer, automated teller, and office machine repairers	Postsecondary vocational award	27.6	50.3	22.0	$33,250	156	180	24	15.0
Production, planning, and expediting clerks	Short-term on-the-job training	37.0	35.2	27.8	33,650	288	328	40	14.0
Construction and building inspectors	Work experience in a related occupation	35.6	41.9	22.4	41,620	84	95	12	13.8
Music directors and composers	Bachelor's plus experience	21.0	26.1	52.9	31,310	54	62	7	13.5
Advertising sales agents	Moderate-term on-the-job training	20.6	28.6	50.8	37,670	157	178	21	13.4
Property, real estate, and community association managers	Bachelor's degree	29.1	33.3	37.7	36,880	293	330	37	12.8
Court reporters	Postsecondary vocational award	25.2	41.1	33.6	41,550	18	20	2	12.7

Occupation	Most Significant Source of Postsecondary Education or Training	Percent of Workers Aged 25 to 44, by Educational Attainment			2002 Median Annual Earnings	Employment (in Thousands)		Employment Change, 2002–12	
		High School or Less	Some College	College or Higher	Dollars	2002	2012	Numeric	Percent
Food service managers	Work experience in a related occupation	42.9	32.6	24.4	35,790	386	430	44	11.5
Parking enforcement workers	Short-term on-the-job training	28.7	47.3	24.0	28,110	11	12	1	11.5
Broadcast technicians	Associate degree	22.7	40.9	36.4	27,760	35	39	4	11.3
Purchasing agents and buyers, farm products	Work experience in a related occupation	55.3	20.1	24.6	40,990	19	21	2	10.2
Agricultural and food science technicians	Associate degree	34.4	26.4	39.3	28,580	20	22	2	9.3
First-line supervisors/managers of retail sales workers	Work experience in a related occupation	41.1	34.4	24.5	29,700	1,798	1,962	163	9.1
Insurance sales agents	Bachelor's degree	22.6	34.0	43.4	40,750	381	413	32	8.4
Embalmers	Postsecondary vocational award	37.1	42.3	20.6	34,240	7	7	1	8.3
All other legal and related workers	Bachelor's degree	25.2	41.1	33.6	38,700	101	109	8	7.6
Fish and game wardens	Long-term on-the-job training	28.7	47.3	24.0	41,010	8	8	1	7.1
Agricultural inspectors	Work experience in a related occupation	36.6	31.4	32.0	28,620	16	17	1	6.8

Educational attainment cluster, most significant source of postsecondary education or training, and educational attainment distribution, by occupation *(continued)*

Occupation	Training/Education								
First-line supervisors/managers of office and administrative support workers	Work experience in a related occupation	33.1	39.5	27.3	38,820	1,459	1,555	96	6.6
Lodging managers	Work experience in a related occupation	30.6	21.9	47.5	33,970	69	73	5	6.6
Real estate sales agents	Postsecondary vocational award	22.2	37.0	40.7	30,930	308	325	18	5.7
Chemical technicians	Associate degree	31.7	39.7	28.7	37,430	69	72	3	4.6
Wholesale and retail buyers, except farm products	Work experience in a related occupation	30.4	34.6	35.0	40,780	155	162	7	4.3
Forest and conservation technicians	Associate degree	23.2	36.7	40.1	30,980	19	20	1	4.0
Law clerks	Bachelor's degree	25.2	41.1	33.6	30,460	48	50	2	3.8
Geological and petroleum technicians	Associate degree	29.2	43.5	27.3	39,430	11	11	0	1.3
All other financial, information, and record clerks	Short-term on-the-job training	26.8	50.3	22.9	30,030	304	306	2	.5
Title examiners, abstractors, and searchers	Moderate-term on-the-job training	25.2	41.1	33.6	32,610	55	53	-1	-2.7
Radio operators	Moderate-term on-the-job training	22.7	40.9	36.4	31,530	3	3	0	-6.2
Statistical assistants	Moderate-term on-the-job training	35.6	35.8	28.6	29,470	23	22	-2	-7.2
Eligibility interviewers, government programs	Moderate-term on-the-job training	20.4	50.8	28.8	31,010	94	83	-11	-11.6
Loan interviewers and clerks	Short-term on-the-job training	33.3	42.8	23.9	27,830	170	146	-24	-14.3
Brokerage clerks	Moderate-term on-the-job training	31.7	40.4	27.9	33,210	78	67	-11	-14.7
Computer operators	Moderate-term on-the-job training	39.1	40.5	20.4	29,650	182	151	-30	-16.8

Educational attainment cluster, most significant source of postsecondary education or training, and educational attainment distribution, by occupation *(continued)*

Occupation	Most Significant Source of Postsecondary Education or Training	Percent of Workers Aged 25 to 44, by Educational Attainment			2002 Median Annual Earnings	Employment (in Thousands)		Employment Change, 2002–12	
		High School or Less	Some College	College or Higher	Dollars	2002	2012	Numeric	Percent
Fitness trainers and aerobics instructors	Postsecondary vocational award	22.0	30.6	47.4	23,950	183	264	81	44.4
Residential advisors	Moderate-term on-the-job training	31.8	43.2	24.9	20,700	53	71	18	33.6
Customer service representatives	Moderate-term on-the-job training	38.3	40.3	21.4	26,240	1,894	2,354	460	24.3
Demonstrators and product promoters	Moderate-term on-the-job training	26.5	38.3	35.2	20,380	175	204	30	17.0
Library technicians	Short-term on-the-job training	23.0	34.6	42.3	24,090	119	139	20	16.8
Slot key persons	Postsecondary vocational award	35.4	31.5	33.1	22,870	21	24	3	14.8
Models	Moderate-term on-the-job training	26.5	38.3	35.2	21,400	5	5	1	14.5
All other protective service workers	Short-term on-the-job training	39.9	37.0	23.1	23,410	237	271	34	14.3
Animal trainers	Moderate-term on-the-job training	47.5	28.3	24.2	22,950	26	30	4	14.3
Reservation and transportation ticket agents and travel clerks	Short-term on-the-job training	31.6	45.3	23.1	25,350	177	199	22	12.2
Photographic process workers	Moderate-term on-the-job training	41.6	32.8	25.5	20,220	28	30	2	5.4
Woodworking machine setters, operators, and tenders, except sawing	Moderate-term on-the-job training	66.5	11.5	22.0	22,030	95	98	3	3.0

Occupation	Training							
All other woodworkers	Moderate-term on-the-job training	56.9	22.7	20.4	21,020	29	29	0	1.7
Travel guides	Moderate-term on-the-job training	41.7	23.7	34.7	26,110	6	6	0	-.3
All other secretaries, administrative assistants, and other office support workers	Short-term on-the-job training	29.5	37.8	32.6	25,840	435	431	-4	-.9
Proofreaders and copy markers	Short-term on-the-job training	32.3	33.7	34.0	24,280	27	26	-1	-4.8
Announcers	Long-term on-the-job training	45.3	31.6	23.0	20,620	76	68	-8	-10.1
Door-to-door sales workers, news and street vendors, and related workers	Short-term on-the-job training	46.1	31.3	22.6	25,340	155	137	-18	-11.8
Travel agents	Postsecondary vocational award	27.9	44.1	28.0	26,630	118	102	-16	-13.8
Preschool teachers, except special education	Postsecondary vocational award	21.7	31.0	47.2	19,270	424	577	153	36.2
Counter and rental clerks	Short-term on-the-job training	49.1	28.1	22.8	17,280	436	550	114	26.2
Personal care and service workers, all other	Short-term on-the-job training	40.1	38.9	21.0	17,820	134	168	35	25.9
Library assistants, clerical	Short-term on-the-job training	25.2	44.7	30.0	19,450	120	146	26	21.5
Recreation workers	Bachelor's degree	22.0	30.6	47.4	18,060	302	364	62	20.5
Transportation attendants, except flight attendants and baggage porters	Short-term on-the-job training	25.3	37.9	36.7	18,720	26	31	5	18.9
Funeral attendants	Short-term on-the-job training	37.1	42.3	20.6	18,190	26	31	5	18.9
Retail salespersons	Short-term on-the-job training	42.0	32.9	25.1	17,710	4,076	4,672	596	14.6
Tour guides and escorts	Moderate-term on-the-job training	41.7	23.7	34.7	18,500	36	40	4	11.0

Educational attainment cluster, most significant source of postsecondary education or training, and educational attainment distribution, by occupation *(continued)*

Occupation	Most Significant Source of Postsecondary Education or Training	Percent of Workers Aged 25 to 44, by Educational Attainment			2002 Median Annual Earnings	Employment (in Thousands)		Employment Change, 2002–12	
		High School or Less	Some College	College or Higher	Dollars	2002	2012	Numeric	Percent
Photographic processing machine operators	Short-term on-the-job training	41.6	32.8	25.5	18,820	54	59	5	9.2
Network systems and data communications analysts	Bachelor's degree	11.3	31.2	57.5	58,420	186	292	106	57.0
Physician assistants	Bachelor's degree	5.1	27.5	67.4	64,670	63	94	31	48.8
Database administrators	Bachelor's degree	9.8	23.0	67.1	55,480	110	159	49	44.2
Dental hygienists	Associate degree	5.3	62.6	32.1	55,320	148	212	64	43.1
Computer systems analysts	Bachelor's degree	10.4	27.2	62.4	62,890	468	653	184	39.4
Network and computer systems administrators	Bachelor's degree	11.1	38.8	50.2	54,810	251	345	94	37.4
All other computer specialists	Associate degree	10.4	27.2	62.4	54,070	192	262	70	36.5
Computer and information systems managers	Bachelor's plus experience	7.3	22.4	70.4	85,240	284	387	103	36.1
Radiation therapists	Associate degree	1.8	57.3	41.0	50,640	14	18	4	31.6
Sales managers	Bachelor's plus experience	9.7	23.2	67.2	75,040	343	448	105	30.5
Computer and information scientists, research	Doctoral degree	10.4	27.2	62.4	77,760	23	30	7	30.0

Occupation	Education/Training							
Medical and health services managers	Bachelor's plus experience	9.4	29.6	61.0	61,370	244	315	71	29.3
Emergency management specialists	Work experience in a related occupation	19.9	30.8	49.3	43,560	11	14	3	28.2
Compensation, benefits, and job analysis specialists	Bachelor's degree	15.8	28.5	55.7	45,100	91	116	25	28.0
Training and development specialists	Bachelor's degree	15.8	28.5	55.7	42,800	209	267	58	27.9
All other business operations specialists	Bachelor's degree	15.8	28.5	55.7	50,680	1,056	1,346	290	27.5
Registered nurses	Associate degree	1.8	40.1	58.1	48,090	2,284	2,908	623	27.3
Technical writers	Bachelor's degree	5.3	25.3	69.4	50,580	50	63	13	27.1
Advertising and promotions managers	Bachelor's plus experience	8.5	21.7	69.9	57,130	85	107	21	25.0
Police and sheriff's patrol officers	Long-term on-the-job training	18.8	53.4	27.8	42,270	619	772	153	24.7
Diagnostic medical sonographers	Associate degree	10.6	65.8	23.6	48,660	37	45	9	24.0
Nuclear medicine technologists	Associate degree	12.1	66.6	21.3	48,750	17	21	4	23.6
Detectives and criminal investigators	Work experience in a related occupation	9.4	35.0	55.6	51,410	94	115	21	22.4
Marketing managers	Bachelor's plus experience	9.7	23.2	67.2	78,250	203	246	43	21.4
Human resources managers	Bachelor's plus experience	13.4	25.8	60.8	64,710	202	242	39	19.4
Medical and clinical laboratory technologists	Bachelor's degree	14.8	35.5	49.7	42,910	150	179	29	19.3
Athletes and sports competitors	Long-term on-the-job training	14.8	25.5	59.7	45,320	15	18	3	19.2

Educational attainment cluster, most significant source of postsecondary education or training, and educational attainment distribution, by occupation *(continued)*

Occupation	Most Significant Source of Postsecondary Education or Training	Percent of Workers Aged 25 to 44, by Educational Attainment			2002 Median Annual Earnings	Employment (in Thousands)		Employment Change, 2002–12	
		High School or Less	Some College	College or Higher	Dollars	2002	2012	Numeric	Percent
Loan officers	Bachelor's degree	19.2	30.5	50.3	43,980	223	266	42	18.8
Credit analysts	Bachelor's degree	17.0	26.7	56.3	42,910	66	78	12	18.7
First-line supervisors/managers of fire fighting and prevention workers	Work experience in a related occupation	17.8	57.2	25.0	55,450	63	74	12	18.7
Financial managers	Bachelor's plus experience	14.4	24.3	61.3	73,340	599	709	109	18.3
Producers and directors	Bachelor's plus experience	4.8	21.9	73.3	46,240	76	90	14	18.2
Chief executives	Bachelor's plus experience	16.1	21.1	62.8	126,260	553	645	93	16.8
Multi-media artists and animators	Bachelor's degree	13.7	27.8	58.5	43,980	75	87	12	15.8
First-line supervisors/managers of police and detectives	Work experience in a related occupation	17.2	54.3	28.4	61,010	114	131	17	15.2
Commercial and industrial designers	Bachelor's degree	17.3	29.7	53.1	52,260	52	59	8	14.6
Computer programmers	Bachelor's degree	7.6	22.4	70.1	60,290	499	571	73	14.6
Securities, commodities, and financial services sales agents	Bachelor's degree	11.9	21.0	67.1	60,990	300	339	39	13.0
Air traffic controllers	Long-term on-the-job training	17.3	33.6	49.1	91,600	26	29	3	12.6

Occupation	Education					7	8	1	
Miscellaneous mathematical science occupations	Master's degree	7.5	24.2	68.3	52,060	7	8	1	11.8
Art directors	Bachelor's plus experience	13.7	27.8	58.5	61,850	51	56	6	11.4
All other drafters, engineering, and mapping technicians	Associate degree	15.5	61.0	23.5	44,450	150	167	17	11.3
Industrial engineers	Bachelor's degree	5.1	26.5	68.3	62,150	158	175	17	10.6
Fashion designers	Bachelor's degree	17.3	29.7	53.1	51,290	15	16	2	10.6
Compliance officers, except agriculture, construction, health and safety, and transportation	Long-term on-the-job training	11.9	30.8	57.3	44,800	158	173	15	9.8
Financial examiners	Bachelor's degree	11.3	23.4	65.3	56,220	25	27	2	8.9
Health and safety engineers, except mining safety engineers and inspectors	Bachelor's degree	5.1	26.5	68.3	58,010	36	38	3	7.9
Funeral directors	Associate degree	4.5	56.2	39.2	43,380	24	26	2	6.6
Operations research analysts	Master's degree	11.0	30.7	58.3	56,920	62	66	4	6.2
Computer hardware engineers	Bachelor's degree	5.9	25.5	68.6	72,150	74	78	5	6.1
Tax examiners, collectors, and revenue agents	Bachelor's degree	14.6	32.1	53.3	42,250	75	79	4	5.0
Purchasing managers	Bachelor's plus experience	15.0	31.0	54.0	59,890	108	113	5	4.8
Foresters	Bachelor's degree	9.7	23.2	67.1	46,730	14	14	1	4.7
Conservation scientists	Bachelor's degree	9.7	23.2	67.1	50,340	19	20	1	4.1
Mathematicians	Master's degree	7.5	24.2	68.3	76,470	3	3	0	-1.0

Educational attainment cluster, most significant source of postsecondary education or training, and educational attainment distribution, by occupation (continued)

Occupation	Most Significant Source of Postsecondary Education or Training	Percent of Workers Aged 25 to 44, by Educational Attainment			2002 Median Annual Earnings	Employment (in Thousands)		Employment Change, 2002–12	
		High School or Less	Some College	College or Higher	Dollars	2002	2012	Numeric	Percent
Physical therapist assistants	Associate degree	16.0	61.5	22.5	36,080	50	73	22	44.6
Self-enrichment education teachers	Work experience in a related occupation	14.4	30.4	55.2	29,320	200	281	80	40.1
Respiratory therapists	Associate degree	4.8	67.6	27.6	40,220	86	116	30	34.8
All other teachers, primary, secondary, and adult	Bachelor's degree	14.4	30.4	55.2	29,250	679	908	229	33.7
Cardiovascular technologists and technicians	Associate degree	10.6	65.8	23.6	36,430	43	58	15	33.5
Computer support specialists	Associate degree	15.5	42.7	41.8	39,100	507	660	153	30.3
Paralegals and legal assistants	Associate degree	15.8	41.9	42.2	37,950	200	257	57	28.7
Employment, recruitment, and placement specialists	Bachelor's degree	15.8	28.5	55.7	39,410	175	223	48	27.3
Massage therapists	Postsecondary vocational award	17.7	47.0	35.3	28,610	92	117	25	27.0
Film and video editors	Bachelor's degree	15.0	34.9	50.1	38,270	19	25	5	26.4

Occupation	Most significant source of training							
Private detectives and investigators	Work experience in a related occupation	18.4	35.9	45.8	29,300	48	60	12	25.3
Directors, religious activities and education	Bachelor's degree	11.1	31.9	57.0	28,020	105	131	25	24.1
Radiologic technologists and technicians	Associate degree	10.6	65.8	23.6	38,970	174	214	40	23.0
Interpreters and translators	Long-term on-the-job training	16.4	30.9	52.8	32,590	24	29	5	22.0
Graphic designers	Bachelor's degree	17.3	29.7	53.1	36,680	212	258	46	21.9
Health educators	Master's degree	18.4	23.7	57.9	36,240	45	54	10	21.9
Interior designers	Bachelor's degree	17.3	29.7	53.1	39,180	60	73	13	21.7
Meeting and convention planners	Bachelor's degree	15.4	26.7	57.9	37,420	37	45	8	21.3
Set and exhibit designers	Bachelor's degree	19.8	31.8	48.4	33,870	12	15	3	20.9
Adult literacy, remedial education, and GED teachers and instructors	Bachelor's degree	14.4	30.4	55.2	36,400	80	96	16	20.4
All other media and communication equipment workers	Moderate-term on-the-job training	19.0	31.9	49.1	34,680	24	29	5	20.1
Medical and clinical laboratory technicians	Associate degree	14.8	35.5	49.7	29,040	147	176	29	19.4
Coaches and scouts	Long-term on-the-job training	14.8	25.5	59.7	27,880	130	153	24	18.3
Loan counselors	Bachelor's degree	19.2	30.5	50.3	32,010	31	37	6	17.8
Appraisers and assessors of real estate	Postsecondary vocational award	14.7	29.9	55.4	41,760	88	104	16	17.6
Airfield operators specialists	Long-term on-the-job training	17.3	33.6	49.1	36,010	6	7	1	17.2

Occupation	Most Significant Source of Postsecondary Education or Training	Percent of Workers Aged 25 to 44, by Educational Attainment			2002 Median Annual Earnings	Employment (in Thousands)		Employment Change, 2002–12	
		High School or Less	Some College	College or Higher	Dollars	2002	2012	Numeric	Percent
All other media and communication workers	Long-term on-the-job training	13.8	32.5	53.7	38,680	58	68	10	17.2
Fine artists, including painters, sculptors, and illustrators	Long-term on-the-job training	13.7	27.8	58.5	35,260	23	27	4	16.5
Probation officers and correctional treatment specialists	Bachelor's degree	15.2	24.0	60.8	38,360	84	97	12	14.6
Camera operators, television, video, and motion picture	Moderate-term on-the-job training	14.5	28.2	57.3	32,720	28	32	4	13.4
All other art and design workers	Bachelor's degree	13.7	27.8	58.5	34,060	95	106	11	11.5
Recreational therapists	Bachelor's degree	12.5	22.3	65.2	30,540	27	29	2	9.1
Architectural and civil drafters	Postsecondary vocational award	15.5	61.0	23.5	37,330	106	110	4	4.2
Mechanical drafters	Postsecondary vocational award	15.5	61.0	23.5	40,730	72	74	1	1.9
Electrical and electronics drafters	Postsecondary vocational award	15.5	61.0	23.5	41,090	38	38	0	.7
Social and human service assistants	Moderate-term on-the-job training	15.2	24.0	60.8	23,370	305	454	149	48.7

Occupation	Education/Training								
Physical therapist aides	Short-term on-the-job training	16.0	61.5	22.5	20,670	37	54	17	46.4
Tax preparers	Moderate-term on-the-job training	16.7	29.2	54.0	25,630	79	98	18	23.2
Actors	Long-term on-the-job training	4.0	29.6	66.4	23,470	63	74	11	17.7
Umpires, referees, and other sports officials	Long-term on-the-job training	16.3	22.9	60.8	20,540	14	16	2	16.9
Photographers	Long-term on-the-job training	19.4	27.4	53.1	24,040	130	148	18	13.6
Merchandise displayers and window trimmers	Moderate-term on-the-job training	17.3	29.7	53.1	22,550	77	86	9	11.3
Floral designers	Moderate-term on-the-job training	17.3	29.7	53.1	19,480	104	117	13	12.4
Computer software engineers, applications	Bachelor's degree	4.1	15.2	80.7	70,900	394	573	179	45.5
Computer software engineers, systems software	Bachelor's degree	4.1	15.2	80.7	74,040	281	409	128	45.5
Environmental engineers	Bachelor's degree	7.3	6.9	85.9	61,410	47	65	18	38.2
Postsecondary teachers	Doctoral degree	2.8	7.4	89.8	49,090	1,581	2,184	603	38.1
Physical therapists	Master's degree	2.7	5.8	91.4	57,330	137	185	48	35.3
Occupational therapists	Bachelor's degree	.1	13.8	86.1	51,990	82	110	29	35.2
Personal financial advisors	Bachelor's degree	4.5	13.7	81.8	56,680	126	170	44	34.6
Epidemiologists	Master's degree	.6	1.8	97.7	53,840	4	5	1	32.5
Management analysts	Bachelor's plus experience	7.5	15.7	76.8	60,340	577	753	176	30.4
Pharmacists	First professional degree	1.3	3.8	94.8	77,050	230	299	69	30.1
Special education teachers	Bachelor's degree	3.8	5.9	90.2	43,450	433	563	130	30.0
Audiologists	Master's degree	2.5	.3	97.1	48,400	11	14	3	29.0

Educational attainment cluster, most significant source of postsecondary education or training, and educational attainment distribution, by occupation (continued)

Occupation	Most Significant Source of Postsecondary Education or Training	Percent of Workers Aged 25 to 44, by Educational Attainment			2002 Median Annual Earnings	Employment (in Thousands)		Employment Change, 2002–12	
		High School or Less	Some College	College or Higher	Dollars	2002	2012	Numeric	Percent
Agents and business managers of artists, performers, and athletes	Bachelor's plus experience	17.4	17.0	65.6	55,730	15	19	4	27.8
Social and community service managers	Bachelor's degree	9.7	19.2	71.1	43,080	129	164	36	27.7
Speech-language pathologists	Master's degree	1.7	1.4	97.0	49,450	94	120	26	27.2
Medical scientists, except epidemiologists	Doctoral degree	.6	1.8	97.7	56,980	58	73	16	26.9
Biomedical engineers	Bachelor's degree	5.9	19.2	74.9	60,410	8	10	2	26.1
Education administrators, postsecondary	Bachelor's plus experience	8.6	17.9	73.5	64,640	125	157	32	25.9
Instructional coordinators	Master's degree	8.2	7.1	84.6	47,350	98	123	25	25.4
Veterinarians	First professional degree	.0	1.2	98.8	63,090	58	72	14	25.1
All other health diagnosing and treating practitioners	Bachelor's degree	7.3	9.4	83.3	52,430	107	134	26	24.5
Clinical, counseling, and school psychologists	Doctoral degree	.0	.6	99.4	51,170	137	171	34	24.4

Occupation	Education/Training							
Environmental scientists and specialists, including health	Master's degree	3.3	4.4	92.3	47,600	65	80	15	23.7
Public relations managers	Bachelor's plus experience	9.7	19.8	70.6	60,640	69	85	16	23.4
Market research analysts	Master's degree	7.4	13.6	79.0	53,810	134	166	31	23.4
Chiropractors	First professional degree	2.0	.2	97.9	65,330	49	60	11	23.3
Biochemists and biophysicists	Doctoral degree	.5	3.6	95.9	60,390	17	21	4	22.9
Biological scientists, all other	Bachelor's degree	.5	3.6	95.9	53,300	27	33	6	22.3
Landscape architects	Bachelor's degree	3.0	9.8	87.2	47,400	23	28	5	22.2
Hydrologists	Master's degree	3.3	4.4	92.3	56,530	8	10	2	21.0
Education administrators, elementary and secondary school	Bachelor's plus experience	8.6	17.9	73.5	71,490	217	262	45	20.7
Microbiologists	Doctoral degree	.5	3.6	95.9	51,020	16	20	3	20.0
Sales engineers	Bachelor's degree	4.2	15.9	79.9	63,660	82	98	16	19.9
Geographers	Master's degree	6.5	11.5	81.9	53,420	1	1	0	19.5
Accountants and auditors	Bachelor's degree	6.7	19.7	73.6	47,000	1,055	1,261	205	19.5
Physicians and surgeons	First professional degree	.8	2.3	96.9	145,600	583	697	114	19.5
Education administrators, all other	Bachelor's plus experience	8.6	17.9	73.5	57,840	27	32	5	19.1
Financial analysts	Bachelor's degree	5.9	15.9	78.2	57,100	172	204	32	18.7

Educational attainment cluster, most significant source of postsecondary education or training, and educational attainment distribution, by occupation *(continued)*

Occupation	Most Significant Source of Postsecondary Education or Training	Percent of Workers Aged 25 to 44, by Educational Attainment			2002 Median Annual Earnings	Employment (in Thousands)		Employment Change, 2002–12	
		High School or Less	Some College	College or Higher	Dollars	2002	2012	Numeric	Percent
Airline pilots, copilots, and flight engineers	Bachelor's degree	5.0	18.9	76.1	109,580	79	94	15	18.5
All other life scientists	Bachelor's degree	.6	1.8	97.7	46,140	26	31	5	18.3
Secondary school teachers, except special and vocational education	Bachelor's degree	1.5	3.6	94.9	43,950	988	1,167	180	18.2
Architects, except landscape and naval	Bachelor's degree	3.0	9.8	87.2	56,620	113	133	20	17.2
Optometrists	First professional degree	8.4	8.0	83.6	86,090	32	38	5	17.1
Lawyers	First professional degree	.7	1.5	97.8	90,290	695	813	118	17.0
Atmospheric and space scientists	Bachelor's degree	.4	9.2	90.4	60,200	8	9	1	16.2
Writers and authors	Bachelor's degree	3.0	13.1	83.8	42,790	139	161	22	16.1
Industrial-organizational psychologists	Master's degree	.0	.6	99.4	63,710	2	2	0	16.0
Elementary school teachers, except special education	Bachelor's degree	2.8	5.3	91.8	41,780	1,467	1,690	223	15.2
Cartographers and photogrammetrists	Bachelor's degree	11.3	14.1	74.6	42,870	9	10	1	15.1

214

Occupation	Education/training								
Podiatrists	First professional degree	.6	.7	98.7	94,870	13	15	2	15.0
Educational, vocational, and school counselors	Master's degree	10.6	19.6	69.8	44,100	228	262	34	15.0
Commercial pilots	Postsecondary vocational award	5.0	18.9	76.1	47,970	21	24	3	14.9
Actuaries	Bachelor's plus experience	2.7	9.0	88.4	69,970	15	18	2	14.9
Budget analysts	Bachelor's degree	7.3	17.6	75.1	52,480	62	71	9	14.0
Arbitrators, mediators, and conciliators	Bachelor's plus experience	.7	1.5	97.8	47,320	6	7	1	13.7
Economists	Master's degree	1.0	8.5	90.4	68,550	16	18	2	13.4
Sociologists	Master's degree	3.5	7.1	89.5	53,160	3	3	0	13.4
Occupational health and safely specialists and technicians	Bachelor's degree	9.2	17.5	73.3	46,010	41	47	5	13.2
Chemists	Bachelor's degree	2.9	3.2	94.0	52,890	84	95	11	12.7
Geoscientists, except hydrologists and geographers	Master's degree	3.3	4.4	92.3	67,470	28	31	3	11.5
Natural sciences managers	Bachelor's plus experience	8.8	4.2	87.0	82,250	45	51	5	11.3
All other architects, surveyors, and cartographers	Bachelor's degree	11.3	14.1	74.6	43,210	3	4	0	10.9
Urban and regional planners	Master's degree	4.5	.0	95.5	49,880	32	36	3	10.7
Agricultural engineers	Bachelor's degree	5.9	19.2	74.9	50,700	3	3	0	10.3
Librarians	Master's degree	8.5	15.0	76.5	43,090	167	184	17	10.1
All other social scientists and related workers	Master's degree	.0	.6	99.4	53,940	68	74	7	9.7

Occupation	Most Significant Source of Postsecondary Education or Training	Percent of Workers Aged 25 to 44, by Educational Attainment			2002 Median Annual Earnings	Employment (in Thousands)		Employment Change, 2002–12	
		High School or Less	Some College	College or Higher	Dollars	2002	2012	Numeric	Percent
All other engineers	Bachelor's degree	3.9	19.1	77.0	70,540	243	267	24	9.7
Electronics engineers, except computer	Bachelor's degree	4.9	14.7	80.4	69,930	136	149	13	9.4
Engineering managers	Bachelor's plus experience	7.6	16.9	75.5	90,930	212	231	20	9.2
Vocational education teachers, secondary school	Bachelor's plus experience	1.5	3.6	94.9	44,340	105	115	10	9.0
Vocational education teachers, middle school	Bachelor's plus experience	2.8	5.3	91.8	42,590	18	19	2	9.0
Middle school teachers, except special and vocational education	Bachelor's degree	2.8	5.3	91.8	41,820	585	637	52	9.0
Judges, magistrate judges, and magistrates	Bachelor's plus experience	.7	1.5	97.8	94,070	27	29	2	8.7
Materials scientists	Bachelor's degree	3.2	5.6	91.2	64,590	7	8	1	8.6
Civil engineers	Bachelor's degree	2.7	9.2	88.1	60,070	228	246	18	8.0
Zoologists and wildlife biologists	Bachelor's degree	.5	3.6	95.9	47,740	15	16	1	7.7
Physicists	Doctoral degree	.0	6.5	93.5	85,020	13	14	1	6.9

Educational attainment cluster, most significant source of postsecondary education or training, and educational attainment distribution, by occupation *(continued)*

Occupation	Degree								
Historians	Master's degree	6.5	11.5	81.9	42,030	2	2	0	6.6
All other physical scientists	Bachelor's degree	.7	1.3	98.0	67,890	37	39	2	6.5
Political scientists	Master's degree	6.5	11.5	81.9	80,560	6	6	0	5.9
Administrative law judges, adjudicators, and hearing officers	Bachelor's plus experience	.7	1.5	97.8	64,540	19	20	1	5.8
Astronomers	Doctoral degree	.0	6.5	93.5	81,690	1	1	0	4.9
Mechanical engineers	Bachelor's degree	5.0	17.7	77.3	62,880	215	225	10	4.8
Statisticians	Master's degree	6.7	10.4	82.9	57,080	20	21	1	4.8
Dentists	First professional degree	1.0	3.5	95.5	123,210	153	159	6	4.1
Materials engineers	Bachelor's degree	10.4	20.0	69.6	62,590	24	25	1	4.1
Electrical engineers	Bachelor's degree	4.9	14.7	80.4	68,180	156	160	4	2.5
Chemical engineers	Bachelor's degree	1.7	5.4	92.9	72,490	33	33	0	.4
Nuclear engineers	Bachelor's degree	5.4	5.5	89.1	81,350	16	16	0	-.1
Mining and geological engineers, including mining safety engineers	Bachelor's degree	5.9	19.2	74.9	61,770	5	5	0	-2.7
Marine engineers and naval architects	Bachelor's degree	5.9	19.2	74.9	66,650	5	5	0	-5.0
Aerospace engineers	Bachelor's degree	4.5	13.8	81.8	72,750	78	74	-4	-5.2
Petroleum engineers	Bachelor's degree	7.5	9.6	82.9	83,370	14	12	-1	-9.8
Mental health and substance abuse social workers	Master's degree	7.8	18.4	73.8	32,850	95	128	33	34.5
Public relations specialists	Bachelor's degree	7.8	14.3	77.8	41,710	158	210	52	32.9

Occupation	Most Significant Source of Postsecondary Education or Training	Percent of Workers Aged 25 to 44, by Educational Attainment			2002 Median Annual Earnings	Employment (in Thousands)		Employment Change, 2002–12	
		High School or Less	Some College	College or Higher	Dollars	2002	2012	Numeric	Percent
Education administrators, preschool and child care center/program	Bachelor's plus experience	8.6	17.9	73.5	33,340	58	77	19	32.0
Athletic trainers	Bachelor's degree	9.2	17.5	73.3	33,820	14	19	4	29.9
Medical and public health social workers	Bachelor's degree	7.8	18.4	73.8	37,380	107	138	31	28.6
All other counselors, social, and religious workers	Bachelor's degree	10.6	19.6	69.8	31,150	248	318	70	28.3
Mental health counselors	Master's degree	10.6	19.6	69.8	29,940	85	107	23	26.6
Substance abuse and behavioral disorder counselors	Master's degree	10.6	19.6	69.8	30,180	67	83	16	23.2
Child, family, and school social workers	Bachelor's degree	7.8	18.4	73.8	33,150	274	338	64	23.2
Marriage and family therapists	Master's degree	9.0	16.3	74.6	35,580	23	29	5	22.4
Archivists, curators, and museum technicians	Master's degree	3.5	8.9	87.6	35,270	22	26	4	17.0
Audio-visual collections specialists	Moderate-term on-the-job training	8.2	7.1	84.6	32,360	10	11	2	16.3

Educational attainment cluster, most significant source of postsecondary education or training, and educational attainment distribution, by occupation *(continued)*

218

Clergy	First professional degree	8.2	13.9	77.8	33,110	400	463	62	15.5
Anthropologists and archeologists	Master's degree	6.5	11.5	81.9	38,620	5	5	1	12.8
Editors	Bachelor's degree	5.6	13.1	81.3	41,170	130	145	15	11.8
Farm and home management advisors	Bachelor's degree	8.2	7.1	84.6	39,430	16	17	1	6.9
News analysts, reporters and correspondents	Bachelor's plus experience	6.6	6.5	86.9	30,510	66	70	4	6.2
Surveyors	Bachelor's degree	11.3	14.1	74.6	39,970	56	58	2	4.2
Rehabilitation counselors	Master's degree	10.6	19.6	69.8	25,840	122	164	41	33.8
Survey researchers	Master's degree	7.5	14.8	77.6	22,200	20	27	7	33.6
All other library, museum, training, and other education workers	Bachelor's degree	8.2	7.1	84.6	27,280	93	116	23	24.6
Legislators	Bachelor's plus experience	.7	1.5	97.8	15,220	67	68	1	1.1

Source: Compiled by the U.S. Labor Department Bureau of Labor Statistics. The complete table may be obtained at http://www.bls.gov/emp/optd/optd001.pdf.

APPENDIX E

COOPERATIVE EDUCATION PROGRAMS

Here is a list of several hundred two- and four-year colleges that offer successful, broad-based, cooperative education programs, combining on-campus classroom study with paying, off-campus, on-the-job training. Simply because a college is not listed below, however, does not mean it may not have an excellent cooperative program. If you don't find the college of your choice below, check with the admissions office to see if the college offers cooperative education. Visit the college web sites listed below and then click onto the cooperative education options on their web sites. Where no web site is available, you'll find a telephone number to contact the college.

Alabama

Alabama State University
Montgomery, AL 36101-0271
http://www.alasu.edu

Auburn University at
 Montgomery
Montgomery, AL 36117-3596
http://www.aum.edu.

Auburn University Main
 Campus
Auburn, AL 36849-5123
http://www.auburn.edu

University of Alabama at
 Birmingham
Birmingham, AL
 35294-4480
http://www.uab.edu

University of Alabama at
 Huntsville
Huntsville, AL 35899
http://www.auh.edu

University of South Alabama
Mobile, AL 36688
http://www.usouthal.edu

Wallace State Community
 College
Hanceville, AL 35077-9080
(256) 352-8278
http://www.wallacestate.edu

Arizona

Cochise College
Douglas, AZ 85607
(800) 966-7946
http://www.cochise.cc.az.us

Embry-Riddle Aeronautical
 University
Prescott, AZ 86303
http://www.pr.erau.edu

Northern Arizona University
Flagstaff, AZ 86011
http://www.nau.edu

Scottsdale Community
 College
Scottsdale, AZ 85230
(602) 423-6128
http://www.sc.maricopa.edu

University of Arizona
Tucson, AZ 85721
http://www.arizona.edu

Arkansas

University of Arkansas
Fayetteville, AR 72701
http://www.uark.edu

University of Arkansas at
 Little Rock
Little Rock, AR 72204
http://www.ualr.edu

California

California Polytechnic State
    University
San Luis Obispo, CA 93407
http://www.calpoly.edu

California State Polytechnic
    University
Pomona, CA 91768
http://www.csupomona.edu

California State University,
    Dominguez Hills
Carson, CA 90747
http://www.csudh.edu

California State University,
    Fresno
Fresno, CA 93740-0048
http://www.csufresno.edu

California State University,
    Long Beach
Long Beach, CA 90840-0113
http://www.csulb.edu

California State University,
    Sacramento
Sacramento, CA 95819-6023
http://www.csus.edu

Golden Gate University
San Francisco, CA
    94105-2968
http://www.ggu.edu

MiraCosta College
Oceanside, CA 92056-3899
(888) 201-8480
http://www.miracosta.cc.ca.us

Santa Clara University
Santa Clara, CA 95053
http://www.scu.edu

Victor Valley Community
    College
Victorville, CA 92392-5849
(760) 245-4271
http://www.vvc.edu

District of Columbia

Gallaudet University
Washington, DC
    20002-3695
(800) 995-0550
http://www.gallaudet.edu

George Washington
    University
Washington, DC 20052
http://www.gwu.edu

Howard University
Washington, DC 20059
http://www.howard.edu

Southeastern University
Washington, DC 20024
(202) 265-5343
http://www.seu.edu

Florida

Central Florida Community
  College
Ocala, FL 34478
(352) 237-2111
http://www.cfcc.cc.fl.us

Florida Agricultural &
  Mechanical University
Tallahassee, FL 32307
http://www.famu.edu

Gulf Coast Community
  College
Panama City, FL 32401
(800) 311-3628
http://www.gc.cc.fl.us

Miami-Dade College
Miami, FL 33176-3393
(303) 237-0633
http://www.mdc.edu

Seminole Community
  College
Sanford, FL 32773-6199
(407) 328-6199
http://www.scc-fl.edu

University of Central Florida
Orlando, FL 32816
http://www.ucf.edu

University of Florida
Gainesville, FL 32611-2042
http://www.ufl.edu

University of West Florida
Pensacola, FL 32514
http://www.uwf.edu

Georgia

Armstrong Atlantic State
  University
Savannah, GA 31419-1997
http://www.armstrong.edu

Atlanta Metropolitan College
Atlanta, GA 30310-4498
(404) 756-4004
http://www.atlm.edu

Clayton College and State
  University
Morrow, GA 30260
http://www.clayton.edu

Darton College
Albany, GA 31707
(229) 430-6740
http://www.darton.edu

Georgia Institute of Technology
Atlanta, GA 30332-0320
http://www.gatech.edu

Georgia Southern University
Statesboro, GA 30460-8033
http://www.georgiasouthern.edu

Mercer University
Macon, GA 31207-0001
http://www.mercer.edu

State University of West Georgia
Carrollton, GA 30118-0001
http://www.westga.edu

University of Georgia
Athens, GA 30602-3332
http://www.uga.edu

Valdosta State University
Valdosta, GA 31698
http://www.valdosta.edu

Hawaii

Hawaii Pacific University
Honolulu, HI 96813
http://www.hpu.edu

University of Hawaii at Manoa
Honolulu, HI 96822
http://www.uhm.hawaii.edu

Idaho

University of Idaho
Moscow, ID 83844-3088
http://www.uidaho.edu

Illinois

Bradley University
Peoria, IL 61625
http://www.bradley.edu

College of DuPage
Glen Ellyn, IL 60137
(630) 942-2442
http://www.cod.edu

East-West University
Chicago, IL 60605
http://www.eastwest.edu

Elmhurst College
Elmhurst, IL 60126
http://www.elmhurst.edu

Lewis & Clark Community College
Godfrey, IL 62035-2466
(800) 500-5222
http://www.lc.edu

Southern Illinois University at
    Carbondale
Carbondale, IL 62901-6603
http://www.siu.edu/siuc

Southern Illinois University at
    Edwardsville
Edwardsville, IL 62026-1620
http://www.siue.edu

Triton College
River Grove, IL 60171
(708) 456-0300
http://www.triton.edu

University of Illinois at Chicago
Chicago, IL 60680
http://www.uic.edu

Indiana

Indiana State University
Terre Haute, IN 47809
http://www.indstate.edu

Indiana University–Purdue
   University at Fort Wayne
Fort Wayne, IN 46805-1499
http://www.ipfw.edu

University of Evansville
Evansville, IN 47722
http://www.evansville.edu

Iowa

Clarke College
Dubuque, IA 52001-9983
http://www.clarke.edu

University of Northern Iowa
Cedar Falls, IA 50614-0002
http://www.uni.edu

Kansas

Butler County Community College
El Dorado, KS 67042
(316) 321-2222
http://www.butlercc.edu

Kansas State University
Manhattan, KS 66506
http://www.k-state.edu

Wichita State University
Wichita, KS 67260
http://www.wichita.edu

Kentucky

Eastern Kentucky University
Richmond, KY 40475
http://www.eku.edu

Murray State University
Murray, KY 42071
http://www.murraystate.edu

Northern Kentucky University
Highland Heights, KY 41099-
   7205
http://www.nku.edu

University of Kentucky
Lexington, KY 40506-0046
http://www.uky.edu

Western Kentucky University
Bowling Green, KY 42101-3576
http://www.wku.edu

Louisiana

Delgado Community College
New Orleans, LA 70119-4399
(504) 483-4004
http://www.dcc.edu

Southeastern Louisiana University
Hammond, LA 70402
http://www.selu.edu

Southern University/A&M at
   Baton Rouge
Baton Rouge, LA 70813
http://www.subr.edu

Maine

University of Maine at Machias
Machias, ME 04654
http://www.umm.maine.edu

University of Southern Maine
Gorham, ME 04038
http://www.usm.maine.edu

Maryland

Bowie State University
Bowie, MD 20715
http://www.bowiestate.edu

Chesapeake College
Wye Mills, MD 21679
(410) 822-5400
http://www.chesapeake.edu

Morgan State University
Baltimore, MD 21251
http://www.morgan.edu

University of Maryland at
    Baltimore County
Baltimore, MD 21250
http://www.umbc.edu

University of Maryland at
    Eastern Shore
Princess Anne, MD 21833
http://www.umes.edu

University of Maryland
    University College
College Park, MD
    20742-1662
http://www.umuc.edu

Villa Julie College
Stevenson, MD 21153
http://www.vjc.edu

Massachusetts

Boston University
Boston, MA 02215
http://www.bu.edu

Bristol Community College
Fall River, MA 02720
(508) 678-2811
http://www.bristol.mass.edu

Gordon College
Wenham, MA 01984-1899
http://www.gordon.edu

Holyoke Community College
Holyoke, MA 01040
(413) 552-2850
http://www.hcc.mass.edu

Merrimack College
North Andover, MA 01845
http://www.merrimack.edu

Mount Wachusett Community
    College
Gardner, MA 01440
(978) 630-9110
http://www.mwcc.mass.edu

Northeastern University
Boston, MA 02115
http://www.northeastern.edu

Northern Essex Community College
Haverhill, MA 01830
(978) 556-3616
http://www.necc.mass.edu

North Shore Community College
Danvers, MA 01923
(978) 762-4000
http://www.northshore.edu

Suffolk University
Boston, MA 02108
http://www.suffolk.edu

University of Massachusetts at
   Amherst
Amherst, MA 01003
http://www.umass.edu

University of Massachusetts at
   Boston
Boston, MA 02125-3393
http://www.umb.edu

University of Massachusetts at
   Dartmouth
Dartmouth, MA 02747
http://www.umassd.edu

Wentworth Institute of
   Technology
Boston, MA 02115
http://www.wit.edu

Worcester Polytechnic Institute
Worcester, MA 01609
http://www.wpi.edu

Michigan

Aquinas College
Grand Rapids, MI 49506-1799
http://www.aquinas.edu

Kettering University
Flint, MI 48504
http://www.kettering.edu

Macomb Community College
Warren, MI 48088-3896
(866) 622-6624
http://www.macomb.edu

Michigan State University
East Lansing, MI 48824-1046
http://www.msu.edu

Michigan Technological
   University
Houghton, MI 49931
http://www.mtu.edu

Northwestern Michigan College
Traverse City, MI 49686
(231) 995-1034
http://www.nmc.edu

Saginaw Valley State University
University Center, MI 48710
http://www.svsu.edu

University of Detroit at Mercy
Detroit, MI 48219
http://www.udmercy.edu

University of Michigan
Ann Arbor, MI 48109-2126
http://www.umich.edu

Washtenaw Community College
Ann Arbor, MI 48106-0978
(734) 973-3626
http://www.wccnet.edu

Minnesota

University of Minnesota at
  Twin Cities
Minneapolis, MN 55455
http://www.umn.edu

Mississippi

Alcorn State University
Lorman, MS 39096
http://www.alcorn.edu

Mississippi State University
Mississippi State, MS 39762
http://www.msstate.edu

University of Southern
  Mississippi
Hattiesburg, MS 39406-5014
http://www.usm.edu

Missouri

Maryville University of
  St. Louis
St. Louis, MO 63141
http://www.maryville.edu

University of Missouri at
  St. Louis
St. Louis, MO 63121-4499
http://www.umsl.edu

Montana

Montana State University at
  Billings

Billings, MT 59101-0298
http://www.msubillings.edu

Montana State University
  at Northern
Havre, MT 59501
http://www.nmclites.edu

University of Montana
Missoula, MT 59812
http://www.umt.edu

Nebraska

Peru State College
Peru, NE 68421
http://www.peru.edu

University of Nebraska at
  Kearney
Kearney, NE 68849-0601
http://www.unk.edu

University of Nebraska at Lincoln
Lincoln, NE 68588-0495
http://www.unl.edu

New Hampshire

New Hampshire College
Manchester, NH 03106
http://www.nhc.edu

New Hampshire Community
  Technical College
Manchester, NH 03102
(603) 668-6706
http://www.nhctc.edu

New Jersey

Atlantic Cape Community
    College
Mays Landing, NJ 08330
(609) 343-5000
http://www.atlantic.edu

Bergen Community College
Paramus, NJ 07652
(201) 612-5482
http://www.bergen.cc.nj.us

Berkeley College
West Paterson, NJ 07424
(800) 446-5400
http://www.berkeleycollege.edu

Brookdale Community
    College
Lincroft, NJ 07738
(732) 224-2268
http://www.brookdale.cc.nj.us

Caldwell College
Caldwell, NJ 07006-6195
http://www.caldwell.edu

County College of Morris
Randolph, NJ 07869
(888) 226-8001
http://www.ccm.edu

Fairleigh Dickinson
    University
Teaneck, NJ 07666
http://www.fdu.edu

Jersey City State College
Jersey City, NJ 07305
(800) 441-5272

Middlesex County College
Edison, NJ 08818-3050
(732) 906-4243
http://www.middlesexcc.edu

Monmouth University
West Long Branch, NJ 07764
http://www.monmouth.edu

Montclair State University
Upper Montclair, NJ 07043
http://www.montclair.edu

New Jersey Institute of
    Technology
Newark, NJ 07102-1982
(800) 222-6548
http://www.njit.edu

Raritan Valley Community
    College
Somerville, NJ 08876-1265
(908) 526-1200
http://www.raritanval.edu

Rutgers, The State University of
    New Jersey, Cook College
New Brunswick, NJ 08903-0231
http://www.rutgers.edu

Saint Peter's College
Jersey City, NJ 07306
http://www.spc.edu

Seton Hall University
South Orange, NJ 07079
http://www.shu.edu

Stevens Institute of Technology
Hoboken, NJ 07030
http://www.stevens.edu

New Mexico

San Juan College
Farmington, NM 87402
(505) 566-3318
http://www.sjc.cc.nm.us

New York

Alfred University
Alfred, NY 14802
http://www.alfred.edu

Clarkson University
Potsdam, NY 13699
http://www.clarkson.edu

Cornell University
Ithaca, NY 14850
http://www.cornell.edu

LaGuardia Community College
Long Island City, NY 11101
(718) 482-7200
http://www.lagcc.cuny.edu

Daemen College
Amherst, NY 14226
http://www.daemen.edu

Dowling College
Oakdale, NY 11768
http://www.dowling.edu

Laboratory Institute of
    Merchandising
New York, NY 10022-5268
(212) 752-1530
http://www.limcollege.edu

Long Island University
    /Brooklyn Campus
Brooklyn, NY 11201
http://www.liu.edu

Long Island University/
    C. W. Post Campus
Brookville, NY 11548-1300
http://www.liunet.edu

Manhattan College
Riverdale, NY 10471
http://www.manhattan.edu

Marist College
Poughkeepsie, NY
    12601-1387
http://www.marist.edu

U.S. Merchant Marine
    Academy
Kings Point, NY 11024
http://www.usmma.edu

Monroe College
Bronx, NY 10468
http://www.monroecollege.edu

Nassau Community College
Garden City, NY 11530
(516) 572-7345
http://www.sunynassau.edu

Niagara University
Niagara, NY 14109
http://www.niagara.edu

Pace University
New York, NY 10038
http://www.pace.edu

Polytechnic University
Brooklyn, NY 11201-2999
http://www.poly.edu

Rensselaer Polytechnic Institute
Troy, NY 12180
http://www.rpi.edu

Rochester Institute of Technology
Rochester, NY 14623
http://www.rit.edu

Russell Sage College
Troy, NY 12180
http://www.sage.edu

State University of New York at
  Brockport
Brockport, NY 14420-2915
http://www.brockport.edu

Syracuse University
Syracuse, NY 13244
http://www.syr.edu

Utica College
Utica, NY 13502
http://www.utica.edu

North Carolina

Alamance Community
  College
Graham, NC 27252-8000
(336) 578-2002
http://www.alamance.cc.nc.us

Central Piedmont Community
  College
Charlotte, NC 28235-5009
(704) 330-6784
http://www.cpcc.cc.nc.us

East Carolina University
Greenville, NC 27858
http://www.ecu.edu

Elizabeth City State
  University
Elizabeth City, NC 27909
http://www.ecsu.edu

Guilford Technical
  Community College
Jamestown, NC 27282
(336) 334-4822
http://www.gtcc.edu

North Carolina Agricultural
  and Technical University
Greensboro, NC 27411
http://www.ncat.edu

University of North Carolina at
  Charlotte
Charlotte, NC 28223
http://www.uncc.edu

Western Carolina University
Cullowhee, NC 28723
http://www.poweryourmind.com

North Dakota

Mayville State University
Mayville, ND 58257
http://www.masu.nodak.edu

Minot State University
Minot, ND 58707
http://www.minotstateu.edu

North Dakota State University
Fargo, ND 58015
http://www.ndsu.nodak.edu

University of North Dakota
Grand Forks, ND 58202
http://www.und.edu

Ohio

Bowling Green State University
Bowling Green, OH 43403
http://www.bgsu.edu

Cincinnati State Technical and
  Community College
Cincinnati, OH 45223

(513) 569-1550
http://www.cinstate.cc.oh.us

Cleveland State University
Cleveland, OH 44115
http://www.csuohio.edu

College of Mount Saint Joseph
Cincinnati, OH 45223-1672
http://www.msj.edu

John Carroll University
Cleveland, OH 44118
http://www.jcu.edu

Mount Union College
Alliance, OH 44601
http://www.muc.edu

Notre Dame College of Ohio
South Euclid, OH 44121
http://www.notredamecollege.edu

Ohio University
Athens, OH 45701
(614) 593-4100
http://www.ohio.edu

Sinclair Community College
Dayton, OH 45402
(800) 315-3000
http://www.sinclair.edu

University of Akron
Akron, OH 44325
http://www.uakron.edu

University of Cincinnati
Cincinnati, OH 45221-0127
http://www.uc.edu

Wilberforce University
Wilberforce, OH 45384
http://www.wilberforce.edu

Wright State University
Dayton, OH 45434
http://www.wright.edu

Youngstown State University
Youngstown, OH 44555
http://www.ysu.edu

Pennsylvania

Beaver College
Glenside, PA 19038
http://www.beaver.edu

Cabrini College
Radnor, PA 19087
http://www.cabrini.edu

Drexel University
Philadelphia, PA 19104
http://www.drexel.edu

Holy Family College
Philadelphia, PA 19114
http://www.hfc.edu

Indiana University of
   Pennsylvania

Indiana, PA 15705
http://www.iup.edu

Neumann College
Aston, PA 19014
http://www.neumann.edu

Pennsylvania Institute of
   Technology
Media, PA 19063
(800) 422-0025
http://www.pit.edu

Philadelphia College of Textiles
   & Science
Philadelphia, PA 19114
http://www.philau.edu

Wilkes University
Wilkes-Barre, PA 18766
http://www.wilkes.edu

Puerto Rico

University of Puerto Rico at
   Mayaguez
Mayaguez, PR 00680
http://www.uprm.edu

Rhode Island

Community College of Rhode
   Island
Warwick, RI 02886
(401) 335-7121
http://www.ccri.edu

Johnson & Wales University
Providence, RI 18766
http://www.jwu.edu

South Carolina

Clemson University
Clemson, SC 29634-5124
http://www.clemson.edu

Morris College
Sumter, SC 29150
http://www.morris.edu

South Carolina State University
Orangeburg, SC 29117
(800) 260-5956
http://www.scsu.edu

Tennessee

Middle Tennessee State
    University
Murfreesboro, TN 37132
http://www.mtsu.edu

Motlow State Community College
Tullahoma, TN 37388-8100
(800) 654-4877
http://www.mscc.cc.tn.us

Nashville State Technical
    Community College
Nashville, TN 37209
(800) 272-7363
http://www.nscc.edu

Tennessee State University
Nashville, TN 37208
http://www.tnstate.edu

Texas

El Centro College
Dallas, TX 75202-2202
(214) 860-2618
http://www.elcentrocollege.edu

Collin County Community
    College
Plano, TX 75073
(972) 881-5174
http://www.ccccd.edu

Houston Community College
    System
Houston, TX 77266
(713) 718-8500
http://www.hccs.cc.tx.us

Jarvis Christian College
Hawkins, TX 75765
http://www.jarvis.edu

Prairie View A & M
    University
Prairie View, TX 77446
http://www.pvamu.edu

Texas State Technical College
Waco, TX 76705
(800) 792-8784
http://www.tstc.edu

University of Houston
Houston, TX 77204
http://www.uh.edu

University of North Texas
Denton, TX 76203
http://www.unt.edu

University of the Incarnate Word
San Antonio, TX 78209-6397
http://www.uiw.edu

Utah

Brigham Young University
Provo, UT 84602
http://www.byu.edu

Snow College
Ephraim, UT 84627
(435) 283-7151
http://www.snow.edu

University of Utah
Salt Lake City, UT 84112
http://www.utah.edu

Utah Valley State College
Orem, UT 84058-5999
(801) 863-8460
http://www.uvsc.edu

Weber State University
Ogden, UT 84408
http://www.weber.edu

Virginia

Hampton University
Hampton, VA 23668
(800) 624-3328
http://www.hamptonu.edu

Norfolk State University
Norfolk, VA 23504
http://www.nsu.edu

Old Dominion University
Norfolk, VA 23529-0050
http://www.odu.edu

Washington

Olympic College
Bremerton, WA 98337-1699
(360) 475-7126
http://www.olympic.edu

Spokane Falls Community
    College
Spokane, WA 99204-5288
(509) 533-3682
http://www.sfcc.spokane.
    cc.wa.us

West Virginia

West Virginia University
    Institute of Technology
Montgomery, WV 25136
http://www.wvutech.edu

Wisconsin

Marian College of Fond Du Lac
Fond Du Lac, WI 54935
http://www.mariancoll.edu

Milwaukee Area Technical
  College
Milwaukee, WI 53233
(414) 297-6274
http://www.matc.edu

University of Wisconsin, River
  Falls
River Falls, WI 54022
http://www.uwrf.edu

University of Wisconsin, Stout
Menomonie, WI 54751
http://www.uwstout.edu

Wyoming

Central Wyoming College
Riverton, WY 82501
(800) 735-8418
http://www.cwc.cc.wy.us

University of Wyoming
Laramie, WY 82071
http://www.uwyo.edu

Western Wyoming Community
  College
Rock Springs, WY 82902-0428
(800) 226-1181
http://www.wwcc.wy.edu

JOB INDEX

Page numbers in *italic* refer to tables and figures.

(Listings limited to jobs not requiring a four-year college degree. See Appendix D for listing of jobs, education, and pay for more than 700 different occupations.)

INDEX

Page numbers in *italic* refer to tables and figures.